# POTASH

# POTASH

## An Inside Account
## of Saskatchewan's Pink Gold

### JOHN BURTON

University of Regina Press

Printed and bound in Canada at Webcom. The text of this book is printed on 100% post-consumer recycled paper with earth-friendly vegetable-based inks.

EDITOR FOR THE PRESS: David McLennan, University of Regina Press.
COVER AND TEXT DESIGN: Duncan Campbell, University of Regina Press.
COVER PHOTO: Don Hall, University of Regina.

LIBRARY AND ARCHIVES CANADA CATALOGUING IN PUBLICATION
Cataloguing in Publication (CIP) data available at the Library and Archives Canada web site: www.collectionscanada.gc.ca and at http://www.uofrpress.ca/publications/Potash

10   9   8   7   6   5   4   3   2   1

**U OF R PRESS**

University of Regina Press, University of Regina
Regina, Saskatchewan, Canada, S4S 0A2
TEL: (306) 585-4758   FAX: (306) 585-4699
WEB: www.uofrpress.ca

The University of Regina Press acknowledges the support of the Creative Industry Growth and Sustainability program, made possible through funding provided to the Saskatchewan Arts Board by the Government of Saskatchewan through the Ministry of Parks, Culture, and Sport. We also acknowledge the financial support of the Government of Canada through the Canada Book Fund and the support of the Canada Council for the Arts for our publishing program. Additionally, this publication was made possible through a Creative Saskatchewan Production Grant.

This account of potash development in Saskatchewan
is dedicated to the memory of Allan Blakeney,
a visionary, who knew how to make dreams come true.

# CONTENTS

# PREFACE

*"Potash has touched my life many times."*

My first job when I graduated from the University of Saskatchewan in May 1951 was as a research assistant in the Industrial Development Office of the Government of Saskatchewan. This was a small, recently established office consisting of the executive director, an industrial engineer, secretarial staff, and myself. Its purpose was to promote, encourage, and assist economic development in order to diversify the Saskatchewan economy.

The executive director, among his other duties, was a member of an internal government potash committee chaired by the minister of mineral resources, Hon. J. H. Brockelbank. It had already been concluded that the only way to get a potash industry in Saskatchewan was through private enterprise. The executive director was among those actively working with private companies interested in potash development. One of those companies was the first to start sinking a mine shaft near Unity. Progress was slow, and it ultimately failed when it reached the Blairmore sands, the major underground water-bearing formation. I provided assistance to the executive director in his activities. I was fascinated by this ray of hope for the future of Saskatchewan. That was the first in a sequence of events that led me further into the world of potash.

Some years later, in 1957, I was nominated to run as a CCF candidate in a federal election. My constituency included Esterhazy and its surrounding area. By that time, International Minerals and Chemical Corporation (IMC) had decided to build a potash mine in the area, had settled on a location, and was just commencing to sink the mine shaft. These activities caused quite a lot of excitement in the area, in part because employment opportunities helped this relatively depressed economic area. Later, in 1962, after IMC had almost lost the mine due to water flooding, I had an opportunity, during another election campaign, to tour their refinery, then under construction, in company with Hon. Russ Brown, minister of industry. The general manager, Merv Upham, told us that the potash zone had just been reached. He had been down the mine shaft to see the potash and it was as good as expected.

In succeeding years, I had further contact with potash affairs from time to time. In late 1969, when I was a Member of Parliament and the Saskatchewan government had introduced pro-rationing in response to the potash oversupply crisis, I asked questions in the House of Commons on a number of occasions concerning federally related issues arising out of the potash crisis.

In December 1972, after having just lost my parliamentary seat, I joined the Saskatchewan public service again. New Democratic Party Premier Allan Blakeney, who had been in office for just over a year, asked me to study a number of resource policy issues and to give potash policy particular attention. He wanted to see a potash policy that would serve Saskatchewan's best interests on a long-term basis. I became involved in potash affairs as described in the text and later served on the Board of Directors of Potash Corporation of Saskatchewan (PCS) from 1975 to 1982. My life then took me in a different direction for some years, but in late 1991, I was commissioned along with two other people to study the state of affairs following the privatization of PCS and to look at the future.

In 2004, I completed a thesis that examined potash affairs in Saskatchewan from its first discovery in 1942 to the tumultuous events of 1975. It was the final requirement to earn a master of arts degree from the University of Regina. This publication builds on that thesis and brings events forward to the present time. It attempts to provide the reader with a better understanding of the factors that went into the phenomena of a new resource coming on the scene, how it was managed, and the impact it had on the province. It is not simply a narrative that provides a comprehensive history of potash in Saskatchewan. Rather, it focuses on the basic factors and features that determined how potash was developed, what role it played in the economy, what influences were brought to bear on its development, and what external factors

influenced the pattern of development. The overarching question identified is to try and find what is best for Saskatchewan. The recent episode
in which Australian-based mining giant BHP Billiton made an unsuccessful attempt to acquire PCS Inc. is examined as another chapter in
the ongoing saga of potash in Saskatchewan. Readers are encouraged
to think of lessons to be learned from the never-ending series of events
concerning potash and to think about what is best for the future.

For some time after first having had contact with potash affairs and
being influenced by the then state of affairs, I agreed that private development was the only way to go. I had considerable reservations about
public ownership when it was first suggested in 1971. However, the more
I delved into the subject the more my thinking shifted, first to it being
feasible, and then to it having real and distinct advantages, making it
the best option for Saskatchewan. Thus I identify and acknowledge
my own views. I have attempted, however, to present events and issues
addressed in this study objectively, and I apologize to the extent that I
may have failed to do so.

However, I do not apologize for my reaction to some of the actions
of the Progressive Conservative government of Grant Devine in the
1980s. I participated in the growth of the Potash Corporation of Saskatchewan from nothing at all to a tower of strength for the province
within a short period of seven years. It was disheartening and dismay-
ing to see the way in which the new government elected in 1982 sys-
tematically undermined and sabotaged this entity such that it became
a burden on the government and people of Saskatchewan, thus paving
the way for its privatization. The actions of that government not only
cost Saskatchewan residents the many millions of dollars that have been
reported but, even more important, frittered away the opportunity to
make Potash Corporation of Saskatchewan, the publicly owned firm,
a world-class industry leader with the potential of giving the province
some genuine economic strength. While potash is now making a noteworthy contribution to Saskatchewan through employment, revenues,
et cetera, it is essential to recognize there is so much more that might
have been accomplished had we not allowed our resource to become a
pawn in the hands of transnational investors and corporations.

John S. Burton
Regina, Saskatchewan, Canada
February 2014

# ACKNOWLEDGEMENTS

This study had its beginnings through the Canadian Plains Research Center. Dr. David Gauthier, then executive director of the center, approved an interdisciplinary studies program to be carried out by me at the University of Regina leading to a master of arts degree. My thesis, "Public Ownership in Saskatchewan Potash: An Analysis of Factors Leading to the Saskatchewan Government's 1975 Decision," was a major feature of my program. Dr. Gauthier later arranged for assistance by the center to enable me to commence preparation of a manuscript for publication that extended the scope of my thesis. This included some useful assistance by Brett Quiring. I am most grateful for the co-operation and assistance received from other staff at the center.

Dr. Howard Leeson, then head of the Department of Political Science, and Dr. Robert McLaren, then professor of history, both at the University of Regina, were my co-supervisors during the preparation of my thesis. Both of them gave valuable assistance and advice to me. I am very grateful for their efforts and advice as well as the congenial environment they generated. During the preparation of this manuscript, I have continued to draw on the knowledge and wisdom of Dr. Leeson in particular, and I am happy to acknowledge his contribution to the final document.

I have conducted many interviews in the preparation of both my thesis and my manuscript. They have contributed materially to the final product, and I appreciate the co-operation I received from all concerned.

Crown Investments Corporation gave me access to minutes and board agenda papers of Potash Corporation of Saskatchewan from 1982 to its demise in 1989. I had my own copy of those papers for the period prior to summer 1982 as a member of the board of directors at that time. Consent was also given to enable me to draw on a portion of the contents of a report prepared in early 1992 for Crown Investments Corporation in which I participated. Their co-operation was invaluable.

Others contributed to the development of the final product. I must thank George Hoffman, history lecturer in Regina, for his time and effort in reviewing a draft document, giving me his thoughts, and doing it again when a later stage was reached. Gary Tompkins, economics chair, University of Regina, provided his comments on Chapter 14. Henry Kloppenburg provided a ream of useful material during the BHP Billiton episode, along with his distinctive salty comments.

Dave Margoshes edited the draft text and pointed out many improvements that could be made in telling the story. Diane Young, then of James Lorimer and Company, was very helpful in providing guidance on the preparation of an acceptable document.

My wife, Zenny, helped me at various times and tolerated long periods of time when I was engaged in this study, waiting for me to finish. My son James came to my assistance on numerous occasions when I reached the limits of my computer skills.

Regardless of any of the above, all of the contents of this manuscript are my responsibility, and I acknowledge same.

# CHAPTER 1
## Introduction

*"How could an unromantic salt like potash*
*be the cause of so much trouble and yet be the hope of so many?"*

"Potash! What's that?" would have been the likely response of most Saskatchewan residents upon hearing the word any time before 1950. That would certainly not be the case now. Virtually everyone in the province knows what potash is today and recognizes the vital role it plays in the provincial economy as well as in the Canadian economy.

Potash[1] is a naturally occurring mineral created during the evaporation of ancient seabeds. Ninety-five percent of commercial potash production is used for fertilizer, while the remainder is utilized in industrial production. Potash is vital for plant and crop growth, but there is a wide variation in the natural occurrence of potassium in soils throughout the world. For example, an adequate amount of the mineral occurs naturally in most Saskatchewan soils, but in the US Midwest it is very much needed to promote greater yields of corn.

When potash was first found in the province in 1942, there were only a limited number of potash mines in operation around the world. Major producers were in New Mexico, Spain, France, East and West Germany, and Russia. The Europeans had formed a cartel long before 1910, but during and after the war, US influence and control increased and helped to keep prices high. Potash became increasingly important following World War II, as the need to increase world food supply in order to meet the demands of a growing world population was recognized. The effort that was undertaken became known as the "green revolution," and one component of that endeavour was the increased use of fertilizers, including potash. Potash demand is growing steadily, but not continuously, as application does not necessarily have to be made each year as is the case with nitrogen and phosphorus.

Nitrogen and phosphorus along with potash are the key plant nutrients. When I was a boy, world population was two billion people. Today, the population is seven billion, and it is expected to be over nine billion by 2050. World capacity to grow enough food was already strained when there were only three billion people in the 1950s, at the time the "green revolution" was undertaken. World-scale famine was avoided in subsequent years because of continuing increases in capacity to grow food. The need for still more increases is ongoing. A diminishing land base makes fertilizers even more essential.

The 1942 discovery of potash in Saskatchewan, which was kept "hush-hush" for some time, was followed by further finds and finally caught the attention of government circles. By 1946, it was recognized that it was a mineral with real potential. A new government at that time was casting about for economic opportunities. Resources received top attention. Public ownership, complete or partial, was favoured initially, but by 1950, the social democratic government in power had to accept the reality that only the private sector was equipped to develop the resource. In the meantime, existing producers became aware of these potash finds and were anxious to gain "a piece of the action" as well as not wanting to upset existing cartel arrangements.

During the 1950s, three potash companies tried to reach potash deposits in Saskatchewan, the closest of which were 3,000–3,500 feet underground. The first company experienced complete failure, while two US companies that already produced potash in New Mexico struggled in vain to overcome the underground water problem. It was not until 1962 that one of them met with success and went into production.

Potash and Saskatchewan might now be regarded as virtually synonymous terms. While wheat dominated the Saskatchewan scene in the first half of the twentieth century, the role of potash increased steadily in the second half of the twentieth century (1950–2000), so that by the end of the century, it equalled or surpassed the value of wheat production. Since then, potash production has regularly surpassed wheat in value.[2] This is quite astonishing! Potash is now part of the fabric of Saskatchewan.

Saskatchewan has a huge quantity of potash, now estimated at 52% of world reserves. The fact that 80% of the mineral resource rights in Saskatchewan are owned and managed by the province strengthens its authority over mineral affairs. Historically, in Canada, development was undertaken by the private sector. The original private entrepreneurs who successfully developed potash operations were large multinational firms, most of them foreign owned, most of which in turn were American, some already producing potash elsewhere.

My involvement in the story of Saskatchewan's potash industry began in 1951, soon after I started my first job following university graduation. I grew up on a farm, and farm work was a significant part of my activities. That included handling fertilizer bags, and I knew that 11–48–0 on the bag meant it was 11% nitrogen, 48% phosphorus, and the zero was for some other stuff I didn't need to worry about. When I took agronomy classes at university, I learned the zero indicated potash content. In a Saskatchewan setting where it wasn't much needed, it was only ranked along with a number of micronutrients.

The executive director of the Saskatchewan Industrial Development Office, where I had started work, gave special attention to development of these recently found potash deposits. He needed information and data, which I had to supply, to support his efforts to persuade companies to consider potash development in the province. The director, D. H. F. (Don) Black, was a lawyer originally from Montreal who came to Saskatchewan because he believed in the political agenda being pursued by the Tommy Douglas CCF government. One day over coffee, I asked Don if there was any chance potash could be developed by the province; that is, through public ownership. His response was, "I'm afraid not, John. We just don't have the finances or personnel that would be required. Besides, the Blairmore sands underground water formation poses too much of a risk for us to tackle."

Across the hall from where I worked was the Government Finance Office, the holding company for the province's crown corporations. The corporate secretary there was another person who had decided to come to Saskatchewan because of the new and innovative things being done. His name was Allan Blakeney. Finding him very personable, I got to know him quickly and we soon became friends. We were on much the same wavelength, and occasionally we talked about potash, a subject that was becoming of interest in the province. Little did we envisage the events that would unfold in future years and the role that each of us would play in those events.

The two of us went our own ways during succeeding years, sometimes not too far away from each other, while potash development in the province continued to roll along. On one occasion, I went over to the Blakeney home after supper to deal with some matter. My wife, Zenny, was almost due for the birth of our youngest son. I made sure she knew where I was in case of need. While I was at the Blakeneys, she called to say that she felt the first twinges of labour. I told them after the call, I had to go home then. While I was putting on my coat, they inquired, "How is Zenny doing? She must be almost due now!" I startled them by my answer: "That was the call!" "Leave us not detain you!" was their astonished reply.

By this time new mines had opened or were being built, and the future looked promising. But by the end of the decade, the industry found itself in a crisis. The Thatcher Liberals who were then in power had promoted overdevelopment, and it now looked as if the industry was ready to come crashing down. In desperation, a government-managed price pro-rationing plan was put in place and the situation was salvaged. In spite of that, the Liberal government was defeated in a subsequent general election, and the New Democratic Party (successor to the CCF) now led by Allan Blakeney assumed office in 1971.

On October 31, 1972, I went to see Allan Blakeney in the Legislative Building in Regina where he had been premier for just over a year. I had been defeated as a Member of Parliament the night before in spite of having increased my vote substantially. As we sat down, his secretary brought us coffee and expressed her regrets at my loss—we had worked together in previous settings. Allan and I proceeded to chew over the election results and the fact that the Trudeau Liberals were holding on to power by a thread. Then, he changed the subject abruptly:

John, I need more help in the government service. Are you interested in working for us?

Well, I was fired last night and I do need to support my family and pay off some debts.

Well, we could sure use you. There are a lot of things to be done.

Our discussion was relaxed but to the point. Allan did not settle on an immediate course of action, but characteristically wanted to take time to determine the most appropriate thing to do. After we finished our coffee, I left and went to have breakfast with my wife and then attend to post-election business: closing up my office in Ottawa, moving my family back to Regina,[3] and a host of other things.

I got a call from the premier a couple of weeks later. He proposed that I join one of the government's central agencies and wanted me to pursue studies on resource policies, giving particular attention to potash issues. This was an area that needed more attention in his view, and potash was of particular concern. The platform on which he was elected had promised new initiatives, and he felt keenly that the province was not getting an adequate return from its resources. Having already had some contact with and interest in potash affairs, I saw this as an exciting prospect for me and I accepted. By early December, I was on the job.

What a change! For almost ten years, I had viewed matters from an active political perspective, first, as a research officer in Opposition Leader Woodrow Lloyd's office and then as a Member of Parliament. While I was in the Saskatchewan public service previous to that, it was quite dramatic for me to make the transition from active political involvement with a public profile to an internal role within government. Some time later, I encountered Eugene Whelan, whom I had known previously while in Parliament and who was now federal agriculture minister. "Kee-rist, I didn't know you had become a bureaucrat!" he exclaimed. "Eugene, I am just a humble civil servant," was my response. "That will be the fat day when the word 'humble' applies to you!" he growled.

While potash had not been the centre of my attention for some time, I was keenly aware of the mess created by the Thatcher government in its management of potash affairs. Premier Thatcher's action to regulate both the production and price of potash aroused federal government concerns about possible incursions into federal areas of jurisdiction.

I had asked a number of questions in the House of Commons about these issues.

Little did I know where my new activities were going to lead. Allan Blakeney wanted to have a better idea of how to proceed. He wanted more revenue from the industry and wanted the province to participate actively in further expansion, thus giving it a "piece of the action." As I started gathering information and talking to people, I found a complex state of affairs. It was difficult to work through the morass, in particular because of the intransigent position of the department that was in charge. One thing that stands out in my mind is that Premier Blakeney was the driving force who was demanding action and wanted a plan of action mapped out. Officials of the Department of Mineral Resources, of course, had to respond to the new government's outlook, but essentially they wanted to maintain the status quo. The premier was forcing them to address fundamental issues that had never been considered. My meetings with them were often strained and difficult.

The next three years were tumultuous as the government first increased its revenue take modestly but followed up with a major revenue-generating measure and persisted in its desire to be a partner in expansions. Industry resisted the government, but eventually their stance backfired when the government took dramatic action, enabling it to acquire part or all of the potash industry by purchase or expropriation. Such drastic action had not been contemplated until the private industry challenged the government by launching court actions that stymied all initiatives it had undertaken. This move, coupled with the federal government's unprecedented action in grabbing a "big piece of the pie," thus restricting provincial revenues, resulted in Saskatchewan facing a stark choice—cave in or take decisive action. In studying the situation, legal officers determined that constitutional problems eliminated some options, so public ownership became an increasingly attractive choice.

I was part of the task force that made preparations for public ownership in the industry so the government would be ready if it made that choice. We operated in a clandestine manner and were told to tell no one unless authorized. We spent many evenings and weekends at work in room 43 of the Legislative Building in what was dubbed "the bunker room." It was obvious to my wife, Zenny, that I was engaged in serious work, but I couldn't tell her anything. She and the kids did know I had to make a trip to London, England. Later, I learned she said to the kids, "Don't tell anyone at school that Daddy is going to London. He is doing some very important work and nobody should know about it." I have to give her full credit because I had not thought of that potential leak. On my return, the kids of course were excited to find out what I brought them from London. In room 43, I reported on my discussions with British Sulphur Corporation, the world's foremost potash intelligence-gathering organization, about how to manage marketing. On the morning of November 12, 1975, when the government's big announcement was made in the Speech from the Throne in the Saskatchewan Legislature, my wife said to me over the breakfast table, "All right, I have figured out what you have been up to. The government is going to announce a takeover of the potash industry." I said nothing, but I did smile.

The outcome is now history. The roller coaster series of events did not stop with the passage of the necessary legislation, as other major developments continued to follow one after the other, starting with the acquisition of mines. Events before and since 1975 support the conclusion that potash will continue to be an important feature of Saskatchewan affairs long into the future.

* * *

This book is about the difficult birth of the potash industry in Saskatchewan, the first in Canada: its growing pains, its emergence as a mature industry, and the way its development has intertwined with political agendas throughout its history, and what issues should be considered for the future. For the past 70 years, potash was never far off the political agenda in Saskatchewan regardless of what political party was in power. The Thatcher government's decision to introduce potash pro-rationing and price management risked federal government and international retaliation. The Blakeney government's dramatic action in 1975 enabling the province to acquire by purchase or expropriation part or all of the privately owned potash industry posed uncertainties, and possibly serious risks. The privatization of the publicly owned Potash Corporation of Saskatchewan by the Devine government in 1989 was done at great cost to the province and contributed materially to the financial morass that was already overwhelming the province. More recently, the active resistance of current Premier Wall to Anglo-Australian mining giant

BHP Billiton's attempted buyout of the privatized Potash Corporation of Saskatchewan Inc. persuaded the federal government to prevent it from happening. This posed problems for the provincial government as well as difficulties for the federal government.

This story is also about Saskatchewan's struggle to overcome the inherent disadvantages foisted on the province when it was created, and later by circumstances such as the 1930s drought-depression. Saskatchewan is the centre of the three prairie provinces that constitute a distinct geographic and economic region within Canada and was settled later than most other provinces. In a broader setting, Canada struggled constantly to secure its identity in the face of the megagiant to the south, the United States. Settling the prairies stopped American encroachment into the region. The Canadian plan was also to have the prairies as an economic hinterland to the economic heartland, that is, Ontario and southern Quebec. Sir Clifford Sifton, minister of interior prior to 1900, oversaw the process. Dale Eisler in his book *False Expectations* quoted another author quoting Sifton's picture of whom he wanted on the prairies, "a stalwart peasant, in a sheep-skinned coat, born on the soil, whose forefathers have been farmers for 10 generations, with a stout wife and a half a dozen children."[4] The primary focus was on agriculture, and Saskatchewan had the initial lead. In time, oil and natural gas became the driving force in the Alberta economy, and cheap hydroelectric power along with mineral development gave Manitoba its strength. Saskatchewan didn't make out as well and was hardest hit by the 1930s depression and a devastating drought. Recovery was not easy. When the potential of potash became known, it generated much excitement, and hopes that it would do for the province what oil, gas, and hydro power had done for its neighbours.

I had the privilege and opportunity to take part in some of these potash events. Canada's constitution assigned management and control of resources to the provinces as part of the balance in federal and provincial areas of jurisdiction. The provinces have the responsibility to ensure resources are managed to the benefit of their residents. Saskatchewan had a tough time for many years. Finally, potash, an innocuous mineral with real potential, was found, but taking advantage of it proved a difficult task. After a series of tumultuous events, a way was found to better manage it to the advantage of the province and its people. But just like the guy who killed the goose that laid the golden egg, some people couldn't leave well enough alone. We lost what we had gained. Think of it! For a period of time, Canadians, residents of Saskatchewan specifically, actually owned and controlled what is now one of the most important resources in the world through a Saskatchewan crown corporation.

Food is also a critical part of this story. I have never wanted for food. But, in the 1930s, I did see men "riding the rods" on trains. Often they got off the train at a railway siding near our farm home and came to the house asking for something to eat. My mother always prepared some food for them, and we kids would often watch them eat at the kitchen table and talk to them. More recently, I was in Zambia when food protests occurred that could have turned into riots. Famines and food riots are not unusual on the news. They could increase unless more food is produced. Fertilizers, including potash, are one of the means for producing more food. That makes our potash one of the most critical resources in the world. That means we have to manage it in the most effective way. We have a responsibility not only to ourselves or even to Canada; we have a responsibility to the world community to do our best.

There are other issues that must be addressed. In the early 1970s, I took part in debates in the Parliament of Canada about the extent of foreign ownership and control in our economy. Eventually action was taken, but those gains were subsequently lost. Recent events have dwarfed the situation then, as giant international corporations have gobbled up numerous pillars of the Canadian economy. Shareholders, whoever they are—Canadian or American—eagerly grasped at the chance to "make some quick bucks" and sold out. Some of the new owners had no hesitation in backing out of commitments, as they thought only of their corporate interests.

Canada is a country that is rich in natural resources. As Canadians, we own these resources, so we have the right to determine how they should be developed and managed and then who should benefit from their development and exploitation. These issues have been on our agenda for a long time. We keep losing the gains made. It is urgent that Canadians focus on these issues—if we want to fulfill our responsibilities. If we want to have a strong nation, we must recognize it is necessary to have control of our resources as well as receiving an adequate return from those resources rather than settling for crumbs, even if some of those crumbs may be substantial.

The Saskatchewan experience is a case in point. There are lessons to be learned from it.

# CHAPTER 2
## Beginnings and Development

Tommy Douglas, political leader of the CCF (Co-operative Commonwealth Federation), led the party to a massive election win on June 15, 1944. He had a strong complement of competent and dedicated people to choose from in selecting a Cabinet for his government. One of those people was Joe Phelps, a dynamic, aggressive, action-oriented man. He was a fiery speaker known for his excitability, verbosity, and temper. Douglas appointed him minister of natural resources but with some misgivings. His mandate was to diversify the economy, and Phelps produced results with a wide variety of initiatives, some of which got the government into trouble. He and his officials constantly looked for new opportunities. One official picked up a report supposed to be kept hush-hush that some stuff called "potash" had been found near Radville by one of the companies drilling for oil in 1942. The informant had to emphasize that the "stuff" was much more important than any of several salts found on the surface. This information was of interest since there was no knowledge of the find until then. Other indications of potash came to light subsequently, and by 1946–47, potash was identified as a resource with significant potential for Saskatchewan.[1] The province had endured more than a half century of struggles and problems during its early development phase, with many harsh times that often tempered the dreams of its pioneers.[2] Thus, the prospect of new opportunities was greeted eagerly and created new hope for the struggling province.

This caused some excitement within the government, and Phelps wanted it followed up. The department made special efforts to determine the extent and quality of the resource and continued its efforts for some years.[3] Enthusiasm was tempered, however, as it was recognized how difficult it would be to penetrate some underground water-bearing formations safely. Discussions also commenced on who should develop the resource. The Douglas CCF government still had considerable faith in public ownership in spite of difficulties encountered in some early ventures. The initial government position was that there had to be some degree of public ownership, a position Phelps would press vigorously.

The impetuous Joe Phelps was defeated in the 1948 election. He had accomplished much but left a legacy of problems, many in the resource sector. He was replaced by the more cautious, careful J. H. Brockelbank as minister of natural resources. A veteran of World War I, he carved out a farm for himself from bush in the northeast area of the settled portion of the province, became active in the CCF, was elected an MLA in 1938, and was Leader of the Opposition for a time. In government, he became the "gray eminence" and was often the troubleshooter who dealt with special problems or issues. His shrewd, low-key approach was invaluable to the government. One of his jobs was to smooth out relations with the private resource industry, which had become "rocky" because of Phelps' style and his heavy emphasis on public ownership, some of it spelled out in government publications. After the government's near defeat in the 1948 election, the CCF modified its emphasis on public ownership, and more recognition was given to the role of private enterprise. Brockelbank personified that stance. In time, both Tommy Douglas and Brockelbank, or "Brock" as everybody affectionately called him, became highly respected in the resource industry.

But policy shifts, and Brock's presence could not make some serious problems go away. The Government of Saskatchewan was coping with serious financial constraints. The province had just emerged from the ravages of the 1930s drought and depression, followed immediately by wartime dislocations and aggravations. The provincial debt was staggering in relative terms, with gross debt of $213 million when the annual budget was just over $30 million. A portion of the budget had to be allocated to debt repayment, while the demand for services was high. In spite of these problems, the government explored the possibility of a joint venture in potash with a private firm, but there were no takers. The federal Liberal government was also approached with the proposition of a joint-development project. The idea was rejected flatly by Hon. J. A. Glen, a Liberal cabinet minister from Manitoba.[4] After the government had decided that private investment was the only route open to it, a private firm did approach the province about a private-public project, but by that time the government was not prepared to reverse its position.

The Saskatchewan government set up an internal potash committee in 1949 headed by Brockelbank, as minister, to manage all activity concerning potash development. After exploring all options, the minister concluded at a meeting on November 22, 1950, that the government would have to abandon its insistence on crown participation. That was a key turning point. This left-wing government encountered a predominant attitude in the outside world that the role of government was largely to stay out of the way except when help was needed. The mining, oil, and gas industries had long enjoyed tax advantages, modest royalties, and substantial assistance in development. The Saskatchewan government did not have the clout to change the established pattern of development found in those extractive industries throughout North America, the same as in many other parts of the world.

Pursuing private-sector development was not easy either, and progress was slow. Apprehension about the existing political environment was one factor, but beyond that, problems anticipated from the water-bearing formations encountered before reaching potash were recognized as staggering. Some of these formations had water under high pressure (as much as 1100 lbs. per sq. inch) that were very difficult to control and could quickly flood a mine completely. The risks involved could result in the complete loss of large capital expenditures. Potential investors were understandably cautious. In any case, it generally takes time before a new resource is developed, as companies assess matters and make decisions. A demand–supply balance at the time in international markets also reduced pressure for new capacity. On the other hand, Saskatchewan was eager and anxious to see the resource developed. Douglas, Brockelbank, and others also had to mollify ardent CCF supporters who were uncomfortable with the new approach. I remember Brock saying at CCF Council meetings, "In our

13

first term, we took steps to share the economic pie more evenly. Now, we have to create a bigger pie."

It took almost a year before the first potash exploration permit was issued to Western Potash Corporation Ltd.[5] It first tried to develop a solution mine, requiring less investment, where water would be pumped down to the potash to brine it out. When that failed, it commenced sinking a mine shaft at Unity in late 1952. It took some time for the shaft even to reach 280 feet (potash was well over 3,000 feet underground at that location) as water-bearing strata were already posing serious problems. Progress was painfully slow, and by 1960, the mine shaft had only reached a depth of 1,800 feet, barely halfway to the potash. At that level, the major water-bearing formation, the Blairmore sands, was encountered. In spite of previous experience in managing water veins, the miners could not cope with the rush of water, clay, shale, and sand and had to scramble for the surface as the shaft flooded to within 360 feet of the surface. That was the end of that mine. Reaching potash was not going to be easy.

Fortunately, other things were happening. In 1951 and 1955, two major potash producers entered the Saskatchewan scene. They had more financial and technical strength than the first developer, but it still took them a long time to reach their goal. The first, Potash Company of America (PCA), started a mine east of Saskatoon, struggled with severe water problems, and finally commenced operations seven years later in 1958. It was in production for only a few months when more water problems forced it to shut down, and it took another seven years before it resumed operations in 1965. International Minerals and Chemical Corporation (IMC) started a mine shaft (25 feet outside diameter; 18 feet inside diameter) nine miles northeast of Esterhazy, but it too encountered flooding in 1958. Many techniques were tried in order to overcome the problem. "For some time, we thought the project might have to be abandoned altogether," said Merv Upham, general manager, with a grimace in June 1962 while showing the facilities under construction to Hon. Russ Brown, Minister of Industry, and myself, a candidate in the 1962 federal election. Finally, the problem was solved with the help of a German company, Thyssen Mining Construction, that used a unique "tubbing" process comparable to tunnelling under a river. The 200-feet water-bearing formation was frozen and the shaft was sunk through the frozen formation. Then cast iron tubbing was installed and wooden wedges were pounded between it and the frozen surface. The mine went into operation in autumn 1962, more than seven years after work had started.

Government actions and statements both to the industry and to the public underlined its commitment to private-sector potash development. I was on a platform in Esterhazy, near the IMC mine site, in March 1958 with Brockelbank during a federal election campaign. In response to a barbed question about his view of public versus private ownership of mining, Brock stated his view clearly that such developments were best left to the private sector. He said there were all sorts of problems for government or public enterprises in undertaking that sort of activity.

Brock was a long-time friend and colleague of my father[6] and, in fact, was a pallbearer at his funeral. I knew him as a friend as well. After the meeting that night, he and I had a drink of Scotch whiskey in his hotel room. He "let his hair down" and outlined his difficulties and frustrations with potash over the past 10 years. He said, "We couldn't develop it ourselves so we had to get the private sector to do it. They have had a tough time. In the meantime, we have done everything we can to help and now all we can do is wait. If we could just get the industry up and running, it would make such a difference to Saskatchewan. We have done a great deal for the province but there is still so much more to be done."

When success finally came, it was greeted with a mixture of relief and elation by all concerned. The successful companies could salvage their investment, which had doubled from original expectations, but the first company lost everything. The government was anxious to see more development now that it was shown the water problem could be overcome. The province's economy was improving because of oil and natural gas development, a steel mill, a cement plant, et cetera, but improvement was still not as fast as desired, and comparisons with the Alberta boom were a constant aggravation. The government continued to pursue geological investigations to determine the extent and quality of the potash beds. A proposal was developed and costed out for a publicly owned mine. It was rejected because of the risks and the amount of money required. Another proposal was prepared in the early 1960s but was shelved when the CCF lost the 1964 election.[7]

Royalty rates were a source of friction for some time as the producers pushed their position to the limit by testing the government, thinking that in its desperation to see production the government might give producers potash virtually for free. Finally, the government "drew the line" and rates were confirmed at a level of two to three percent of the value of production, similar to rates in New Mexico, the only other significant producer in North America.[8] The concept was that potash companies would be allowed to recover a major portion of their capital investment first, and royalties would be increased later. These rates were guaranteed until 1981 for the two companies that overcame the water problem. Later, other companies were guaranteed the same rates to 1974 as an incentive to undertake development. While these measures contributed to the euphoria of the moment, they helped to set the stage for difficult issues later. Once the water problem was solved, things began to move. By early April 1964, three more mines had been announced. Kalium (PPG) was building a solution mine at Belle Plaine, a consortium of three companies planned a mine at Allan, and a French-German enterprise started to build a mine at Lanigan. At the same time, IMC added a second mine at Gerald, east of Esterhazy.[9] There was a feeling that big things were happening. The mood was set already in 1962 when the IMC mine was opened. A *Leader-Post* editorial exclaimed: "Thursday, Sept. 20, will be a date to remember. It will mark the official opening of a new industry of extraordinary importance not only to Saskatchewan but to Canada. ... From Saskatchewan's point of view, the most noteworthy aspect of the development is the strong stimulant it will provide to our economy ..."[10]

In 1964, the CCF government, now led by Woodrow Lloyd, lost the election. The aftermath of a bitter dispute about the introduction of medicare, ongoing dissatisfaction about the pace of economic development, the impact of structural changes in agriculture, and generally poor farm prices all took their toll on the incumbent government. The new Liberal government, led by Premier Ross Thatcher, was elected on a platform of promoting economic development more vigorously and was stridently private enterprise in outlook. Thatcher was a CCF Member of Parliament from 1945 to 1955 when he left the party, became a Liberal shortly after, and in 1959 became Saskatchewan Liberal leader. As a strong supporter of private enterprise, he criticized crown corporations vigorously. He made some adroit and shrewd moves that helped on the road to political power during his transition and after becoming leader. A key move was to persuade a leading federal NDP Member of Parliament to switch to the Liberals.

With an aggressive personality and an ideological mindset, he set his sights on certain targets. He fired a host of leading civil servants he considered politically tainted but was particularly interested in David Cass-Beggs, general manager of Saskatchewan Power Corporation, the electric and natural gas utility. Cass-Beggs was a "socialist" from Wales and an electrical engineer. He gained fame by designing the electrical system for flying suits that enabled Allied pilots to make sharper turns than German pilots and was a key factor in winning the 1940 Battle of Britain. He came to Canada, taught at the University of Toronto, and was a CCF candidate. Douglas recruited him to help plan the expansion of Saskatchewan Power after World War II, and in particular he designed the electrical features of the imaginative rural electrification program undertaken in the 1950s. Subsequently he became general manager and built the corporation into a strong entity. He was a colourful figure and, to Thatcher, he was symbolic of the public enterprises he hated so much. He had to go. He was fired within a month.

Cass-Beggs later related that before he was fired, he was called into Thatcher's office to discuss corporation affairs. Thatcher said electrical rates had to come down. Cass-Beggs responded that the performance of the corporation had improved so much that if rates didn't go down they would end up with embarrassing surpluses. That did not impress Thatcher, and he was still fired.

Another of Thatcher's enemies was Saskatchewan Government Insurance (SGI). It had introduced a universal auto insurance plan and also engaged in general insurance, both of which forced private industry rates down sharply. Jim Dutton was general manager in 1964 when the government changed. He was on Regina City Council, was not politically identified, and had good standing in the community. He told Allan Blakeney and myself in personal conversation at a social function that whenever Thatcher raised the question of scrapping auto insurance, he would simply point out that anything in its place would have to be comparable in cost to the public system. End of discussion. Thatcher had to assign a minister-in-charge of SGI. He gave the job to Dave Boldt, an MLA from Rosthern who was known as a very conservative-minded person. Over time, however, Boldt began to appreciate the merits of

SGI and eventually became its strongest supporter. Thatcher was still determined to uproot SGI. He and Boldt got into a raging argument in Cabinet that was so fierce that Boldt collapsed and had to be carried out on a stretcher. After seven years in office, Thatcher did not succeed in changing SGI despite his vows, commitments, and exclamations. In some other areas, however, Thatcher had more success, and had his way in part because of his vigorous and aggressive personal style.

Potash was the centrepiece of the new government's strategy, and Thatcher pushed it vigorously. This contrasted with the CCF strategy of moderately paced development designed to keep in tandem with market growth. Guaranteeing existing royalty rates to 1981 for all producers was the first step by the new government. New companies were encouraged to commence construction as rapidly as possible. There is also potash in western Manitoba next to Saskatchewan. Hudson Bay Mining and Smelting planned to build a mine in Manitoba, but Thatcher enticed them to build in Saskatchewan instead, one half mile from the border, by offering them free electrical power for three years. The ultimate step was a threat that any company that did not make development commitments by October 1, 1967, would not have the benefit of the extended royalty guarantee. Why October 1, 1967? It's a funny thing: a provincial election was held on October 11, 1967!

# CHAPTER 3
## Oversupply Crisis and Government Intervention

"**W**alk out of this room and I guarantee you that I will close your mine in this province and I'll see to it that it never operates again,"[1] thundered Premier Ross Thatcher to US executives at an October 3, 1969, meeting he had called to deal with the potash crisis. The industry executives were very nervous about US anti-trust laws and threatened to walk out of the meeting. In addition, the idea of interfering with the free market was completely foreign to their way of thinking. But, Thatcher's threat stopped them cold. The premier had no time for industry concerns about US anti-trust laws. "Here in Canada now, you do what Canadians say,"[2] he exclaimed.

Everybody agreed that something had to be done.[3] The price of potash was plunging steadily. Dale Eisler, in his book on Thatcher, noted, "The battle over market shares led to a price war, the price of potash plummeting to $12 a ton from $23 a ton in early 1967."[4]

Since potash development was the centrepiece of Thatcher's economic development strategy, he faced serious economic and political difficulties. Vigorous and prompt action was required, which certainly fitted the premier's style. The political problem was addressed by shifting the blame from him to the companies. This is the curious way Thatcher explained things: "Seldom in the economic annals of Canada have we seen such responsible corporations get into such an economic mess. Lack of co-operation and lack of planning have brought major companies to the brink of disaster."[5] Such accusations were questionable, since it was Thatcher's very aggressive potash development policy that had created the problem in the first place. There is no evidence, though, that companies got into a fight with him over his remarks, and for good reason, as their only hope was to rely on government action.[6]

New, lower-cost production from Saskatchewan coupled with a growing oversupply of potash had begun to affect potash mines in New Mexico, the only other major producing area in North America. Job losses there led to a political threat of a countervailing tariff on Canadian potash imports. Two-thirds of Saskatchewan's production went to the United States. A US Tariff Commission hearing and the likely prospect of such duties on Canadian potash imports propelled Saskatchewan into action.[7] IMC spelled out the three developments that highlighted the problem in 1967:

1. A bill was introduced in the US Senate to restrict potash imports from all sources to a maximum of 25% of US consumption.

2. Another bill was introduced in the US House of Representatives to levy an 8% duty on potash imports.

3. Precedent-shattering anti-dumping proceedings were initiated against potash importers.[8]

It is not totally clear who introduced the idea of a production-price control system, known as pro-rationing. It involved developing a formula for sharing markets when there is surplus productive capacity. The trick is in finding an acceptable formula. The concept is standard in the oil industry in Canada (including Saskatchewan) and the United States. It was one of the options considered by an internal Saskatchewan committee in 1968. Consideration of the option, no doubt, continued as problems grew. At some point in 1969, the Department of Mineral Resources commissioned a staff study to explore the option more fully.

When it became apparent that US action was imminent to curtail potash imports, meaning Canada effectively, Premier Thatcher assumed leadership of the situation and worked vigorously to protect

Saskatchewan's potash industry.[9] He had in his hand the pro-rationing proposal fleshed out by officials. Industry leaders urged the premier to take action; however, US owned companies would have had to be very circumspect because of concerns about US anti-trust law. It was not easy pulling together a disparate group of companies each with its own interests and competing with each other in the same markets. For example, after operations started, Central Canada Potash, owned jointly by Noranda (Canada) and Central Farmers Industries (CFI), a Chicago-based wholesale co-op, had its entire output committed to CFI. Previously, CFI was a major customer of IMC.

Plant managers in Saskatchewan had little authority, and most decisions were made by head offices, mostly outside Canada. This was noted by Cliff Kelly, who was successively plant superintendent, plant manager, and vice-president of Kalium mine. He pointed out that even when he signed a submission to the government, he did not prepare it.[10]

Matters did not proceed smoothly. For example, Boyd Willett, an American who was chief executive officer of Kalium, kept on his recreation room wall a framed copy of an exchange of correspondence between him and Premier Thatcher following the meeting noted above, together with a newspaper clipping pasted between the letters.[11] His letter to the premier, dated October 20, 1969, read:

> Since attending the meeting in your office on October 3, 1969, I have had an opportunity to review with my principals and counsel your telegram of September 26 and the matters discussed at the *October 3 meeting which I attended at your request.* [emphasis added]
>
> We wish to inform that counsel have advised that in their opinion Kalium cannot lawfully participate in collective action with respect to the production, exportation and pricing of potash. Under the circumstances, we are unable to participate in formulation of the proposed program. Accordingly, we are sending copies to each of the companies represented at the October 3 meeting.

Premier Thatcher's response, dated October 24, 1969, was short and to the point:

May I acknowledge your letter of October 20th.

Your company may take any attitude it sees fit.

However, may I be permitted to say that I was somewhat annoyed at the wording of your letter. Your words at the meeting were very different.

Our government is only trying to help the potash industry and your sudden waffling leaves me cold.

Between the two letters was a newspaper clipping from the *Wall Street Journal* dated June 30, 1976, with the headline, "U.S. charges 8 Potash Makers with Conspiracy." The subheading read, "Indictment Alleges Scheme To Co-ordinate Canadian, U.S. Output and Prices." Kalium was not named in the indictment nor was any related company, a matter that obviously gave Mr. Willett great satisfaction and a feeling of vindication. The framed material also included a cartoon showing a boardroom with the chairman saying to the others present, "All in favor of waffling say 'Aye.'"

International Minerals and Chemical Corporation (IMC), the company that first overcame the water problem encountered in shaft sinking, later developed a second mine nearby and was widely regarded as the "industry leader." Suggestions were made that it played a lead role and that pro-rationing was largely for the benefit of IMC because of difficulties it had at that time. Richard A. Lenon became president in 1970 and chief executive officer in 1972. Meeting him more than 30 years later, I could see that even well into his retirement he was a congenial and impressive man. Coupled with a large body frame, his presence would have an impact. He gave me the IMC perspective: "the company was having a difficult time in 1969; it lost money for the first time in history. Twenty million in the next year and only made four and a half [the following]. That was a very critical period and it never had anything like that before or since. It's the only time when the debt exceeded the equity."[12]

Lenon drew attention to the 1969 IMC *Annual Report* where then president Nelson White stated,

... the government of Saskatchewan has expressed great concern with the economic situation in potash and its effect on the development of the world's largest potash ore body in that province.

Saskatchewan's Premier has been extremely active on this matter in the last few weeks, meeting with officials of the Canadian national government, with federal officials in Washington, and with the Canadian producers.

He has mentioned the possibility of the government controlling production and setting prices at what he terms "a reasonable level."

... Government intervention in itself is not generally desirable because such intervention once begun, too often tends to continue indefinitely. On the other hand, a "reasonable price" on potash could mean some earnings improvement.[13]

IMC had a major stake in Saskatchewan's potash industry. The excerpt from the 1969 *Annual Report* was a carefully crafted statement that balanced the need to respond to shareholder concerns while not exposing the company to anti-trust problems. IMC, however, was better able to weather the storm than other producers in part because of lower relative capital costs as confirmed by the table in Appendix E. Having been on the scene first gave it some advantages over other firms.

While most of the potash companies agreed something had to be done, it was difficult to get these diverse groups of competing companies to agree on a course of action. Pro-rationing was one clear option, but Kalium and others were concerned about anti-trust laws; Central Canada Potash didn't need pro-rationing; Cominco and Hudson Bay Mining and Smelting had other concerns. It is doubtful pro-rationing would have come into being without the persistence and determination of Premier Thatcher.

The proposal put forward at first involved companies sharing production based on market size, plant capacity, and markets secured by each operator. There was also to be a floor price determined by the minister. The regulations, with little change from the first proposal, were announced in November 1969 to be effective January 1, 1970. The stated objective of the government was to achieve a minimum price of US $18.75 per ton as soon as possible.[14] See Appendix C.

The federal government took a keen interest in what was happening because of its jurisdiction over interprovincial and international trade, as well as pricing issues. Pro-rationing of production was not a concern for the federal government as long as it did not extend to any other form of control. The federal Liberal government made special efforts to work things out smoothly with the provincial Liberal government.

Industry and Commerce Minister Jean Luc Pepin travelled to Regina in November 1969 to meet with provincial ministers. His department had already been actively involved in US anti-dumping investigations and made representations to the US government. Efforts continued following a finding that there had been dumping. Documents also show that Nelson White, then chairman and president of IMC, met with Mr. Pepin and his deputy minister because IMC was being charged in the case.[15] Later, Justice Minister John Turner also travelled to Regina to discuss the potash regulations and press for changes. A particular concern reported by Saskatchewan Deputy Attorney General Roy Meldrum, who was at the meeting, was that the federal Justice Department wanted to be "in a position of not having to make an adverse report to Trade and Commerce [Department] at the present time."[15] They wanted to avoid having control of the situation turned over to the Supreme Court.

Further particulars of the meeting between Justice Minister Turner, accompanied by a federal lawyer, Premier Thatcher, Saskatchewan Attorney General Darrel Heald, and his deputy minister Roy Meldrum are revealed in a memorandum to Deputy Mineral Resources Minister Cawley:

> ... Mr. Heald was handed a copy of the regulations by Mr. Olson [A federal Justice Department lawyer] who was here with the Minister of Justice on which Mr. Olson had made certain pencilled notes of changes which he would suggest be made in the regulations in order to make them less open to attack by anyone. When Mr. Turner was discussing the regulations with the Premier and Mr. Heald he did not indicate that his concern was more than that the province not set a minimum price for potash for the reason that he and his staff considered that such a provision would be beyond the powers of the province. ...[16]

Deputy Attorney General Meldrum was a consummate civil servant. A highly skilled lawyer, he quietly applied his skills and knowledge to support the activities of his political masters. (He was famous for his 10-page legal memorandums—long paper, too.) He wrote to D. S.

Maxwell, deputy minister of justice in Ottawa, on December 2, 1969. The letter was headed, "CONFIDENTIAL—WITHOUT PREJUDICE." Mr. Meldrum defended the regulations prepared by Saskatchewan, clarified certain events at the time of the visit by the federal justice minister, and reported on actions taken by the Saskatchewan government since federal representations made during ministerial visits. Thus he placed on record that the federal government was not being ignored.[17] Early in the new year, federal officials again pressed the province to make changes to the regulations, pointing out pressures on the government and the consequences of not acting. Attorney General Heald was known as the one cabinet minister who could stand up to Thatcher in Cabinet meetings. He was an able lawyer who later became a Federal Court judge. He relayed federal representations to the premier and stated, "I recommend that we make these changes and avoid such Court proceedings. ... I think it is imperative that this be considered immediately."[18] Subsequently, Heald wrote Pepin, reporting to him that it was the government's intention to make changes exactly along the lines proposed by Mr. Olson with one addition.[19] A key feature of the changes was to describe the licences to be issued to potash producers as producing licences rather than disposal licences.

While acknowledging the changes made, federal authorities still pressed Saskatchewan to withdraw a ministerial order establishing a minimum price for potash. If this change and the changes to the regulations were not made, federal officials indicated that the matter would be referred to the Supreme Court of Canada to determine its validity. Finally, on March 4, 1970, Attorney General Heald notified Mr. Meldrum by memorandum that he had received word from Mineral Resources Minister Cameron that he would agree with the further changes requested as long as there was a clear understanding the federal Department of Justice would not ask for further changes. Mr. Heald asked Mr. Meldrum to pursue the matter with Mr. Olson.[20] The federal reply was that if the proposed changes were made, they would be considered as valid, but if they were not made, the matter would be referred to the Supreme Court. One final compromise was developed whereby the amendments would be enacted immediately but would not take effect until July 1, 1970.

While the federal government was co-operative and wanted to reach an accommodation, it was insistent on certain changes being made in the regulations. The persistence with which federal officials pursued the matter suggests dissatisfaction and/or discomfort with the response of the province to its representations and some lack of confidence that the changes would actually be made. The inescapable conclusion then is that in spite of pressure from Attorney General Heald, certain key actors, most likely Thatcher and Cameron, were reluctant or unwilling to make the changes and didn't want to be pushed around by the federal government. At this time, I was the Member of Parliament for Regina East and was aware of potash problems. I raised questions in the House of Commons, thus putting pressure on the federal government. Question period in the House of Commons was regarded by the government as a good barometer of public interest and concern. Questions raised centred on issues of pricing, marketing, licensing, and constitutionality. Answers given suggest that at some points the federal government didn't really know what was happening. In my research for this project, I learned that constitutional questions on the potash issue were the most sensitive for the government.

The situation appears to have been settled finally in a "Personal and Confidential" letter from a federal legal official, E. R. Olson, to Mr. Meldrum dated March 10, 1970.

> The amendments proposed by Mr. Heald in his recent letter to Mr. Pepin when enacted would result, in our view, in the Regulations being prima facie within the legislative jurisdiction of the province. ... In view of this opinion, I cannot see what further amendments could possibly be asked for reasons of constitutional law ... The foregoing does not, of course, deal with the Ministerial Order fixing sale price. We have discussed this Order and considered a number of ways in which its present characterization as a trade regulation could be changed to one of production or conservation control. ... our clients here are very anxious to see the implementation of the adjustment which you and I have been able to work out ...[21]

A variety of cross-currents were at work as the pro-rationing program was introduced, but all the players knew production had to be curtailed. Central Canada Potash, reluctant at the outset, wanted a limited program with a termination date. IMC and some other companies were happy. Mineral Resources Minister Cameron was quoted in the *New York Times*, November 27, 1969, with an astonishing statement coming from a person who was the guardian of Saskatchewan resources: "The move Saskatchewan is taking now will be the salvation of New Mexico's potash industry. This will give them an umbrella. They'll gain $6.75 a ton."[22] While the tug of war between the province and Ottawa dragged on, the threat of measures to protect US mines overshadowed the well-being of Saskatchewan's potash industry. Tensions rose. There were even suggestions that some ministers and officials would be arrested if they entered the United States.[23]

Indications are that while there were difficulties, once it was in effect, the program functioned without major incident for the remainder of the Thatcher government administration to June 30, 1971. Events over the previous seven years had altered the course of potash industry development. The dominant role of Premier Thatcher, with his driving personality, spurred the development of the industry and then found a way of coping with the crisis created as a result. But many uncertainties still remained for the future, and it was evident affairs had to be managed carefully if potash was to be the salvation of the Saskatchewan economy.

# CHAPTER 4

## The Dynamics of Potash Politics

Saskatchewan's two dominant political parties in the previous 40 years were far apart in their philosophical outlook. The Liberal party over time became increasingly right wing and free enterprise in stance. The New Democratic Party (NDP), formerly the CCF, looked on collective action through government, co-operatives, and community action as important tools for progress. These differences were reflected in their initial positions concerning potash development, but both were fully aware that potash had the potential to improve Saskatchewan conditions dramatically. After having pressed for some degree of public ownership initially, the CCF government had to give in and make way for private sector development in the 1950s. Having done so, the government then worked closely with the private sector while mines were being developed. It wasn't until things began to unravel during the late 1960s under a Liberal government that positions began to shift.

During its period of Opposition from 1964 to 1971, the CCF first, and renamed the NDP under the leadership of Woodrow Lloyd, succeeded by Allan Blakeney, placed heavy emphasis on policy development. The outcome was an NDP policy paper, *New Deal for People*, released in February 1971 as the party's manifesto for the next election. Among many other issues, it addressed potash directly. When government, the NDP

promised to shake up potash affairs and ended the manifesto by saying, "an NDP government will consider the feasibility of bringing the
potash industry under public ownership." The paper blasted Thatcher's
Liberals for making "deals with U.S. potash interests whereby American mines run at full capacity while Saskatchewan's American-owned
mines lay off one-third of their workers." Pro-rationing would have to
go, and the party vowed to "end the present government collaboration
in a potash cartel that restrict [sic] Saskatchewan output and jobs."[3]
The industry also felt the sting of the party's criticism as the manifesto
lashed the mine owners for showing "unconcern about jobs for Saskatchewan miners."[4]

Some potash companies took a "wait and see" approach, but IMC
took the NDP program seriously. Richard A. Lenon, president and later
chief executive officer of IMC, saw trouble coming and even envisaged
the possibility of expropriation or nationalization. He wanted to protect the corporate interests of IMC. He was concerned that big changes
might be coming. He harkened back to a previous time: "we had a good
relationship with Douglas, [premier of Saskatchewan, 1944–61] pretty
good, cause he was out trying to do something for Saskatchewan, bring
in some money besides wheat ... The propaganda that came out of the
Blakeney approach was very disturbing to me... ."[5]

The stage was set for big things to happen. An election was coming
soon. The incumbent government was having difficulties, while the
main Opposition party was proposing major changes in the management of potash affairs. From a distance, Lenon, a key industrial executive, was not at all happy about what he saw.

The public also came to appreciate the importance of potash. Thus,
the introduction of pro-rationing brought about widespread disillusion-
ment. Its introduction was accompanied by a lot of rhetoric and publicity (sometimes called BS). It was widely recognized that the industry
was in deep trouble. In a short space of time, the dreams and hopes of
many were shattered. To make things worse, while the Saskatchewan
industry was in shambles, New Mexico operations prospered. For the
incumbent Liberal government, the centrepiece of their economic strategy was crumbling. Coupled with deteriorating agricultural conditions,
this situation put the political future for the government in jeopardy.

On the other hand, the NDP Opposition searched for alternatives.
Allan Blakeney was deputy leader of the party when pro-rationing was

introduced in 1969. He became leader of the NDP in July 1970 and premier of Saskatchewan in June 1971. He developed a keen understanding of the Saskatchewan scene and recognized that with a strong emphasis on co-operation, the tradition in the province is not one of fear of government but instead one of the use and control of government powers for the public benefit. Two other factors also played a role. One was a surge of nationalism in Canada because of growing foreign ownership and control of the economy. A special federal study was undertaken followed by legislation that would tackle future developments, leaving existing operations untouched. I joined my colleagues in attacking this measure vigorously in the House of Commons:

> ... this bill is making a mockery of Canadian nationhood. ... It is the type of bill that places Canadian nationhood in jeopardy. Canadians have a right to expect more forthright leadership from the government than is demonstrated in this bill. The government of Canada, whatever its political persuasion, has an obligation to provide more effective leadership to the nation than has been demonstrated in this bill. ...
>
> ...we are dealing with a matter which affects the future of this nation, that the future of Canada is at stake, and that the decisions we are making now will affect the nature and substance of Canada in the future ...[6]

Later, under pressure in a minority government situation, stronger legislation was introduced and passed as the Foreign Investment Review Act (FIRA).

In Saskatchewan a growing militant wing within the NDP known as the "Waffle" pressed for more vigorous government intervention and public ownership in the Canadian economy. The Waffle candidate made a strong showing at the 1970 leadership convention. Blakeney tried to make peace with them after he was elected leader but found them very difficult to deal with. In time, they disappeared as an entity, but they did have an ongoing influence on policy development.

Mr. Blakeney, with the benefit of hindsight, reflected on potash affairs: "Mr. Thatcher favoured ... pro-rationing, reducing production, maintaining profits, and reducing employment and we questioned that priority. I'm not sure we were right, but he didn't even contemplate the possibility that it might have been wrong ..."[7] Having served on the Board of Directors of Potash Corporation of Saskatchewan myself, given its objectives as a crown corporation and recognizing the milieu in which it functioned, I considered that the best interests of the shareholder, that is, the province and its people, were served by ensuring the well-being of the corporation first as opposed to other public considerations; for example, on employment.

In December 1969, Blakeney prepared some notes on potash affairs, presumably for discussion with his colleagues in the Legislature. Some excerpts illustrate the picture as seen from a critic's view:

> Clearly the problem originated when the government ... encouraged potash companies to establish in Saskatchewan without taking any precautions to ensure that there was a sufficient market or that if Saskatchewan producers started displacing U.S. producers in a large way there would not be protective tariffs or dumping duties. ... the Saskatchewan government took no steps to secure orderly development of this resource. ...
>
> This price drop has been brought about by Canadian producers, principally IMC, more or less blasting their way into the U.S. market. ... IMC and possibly PCA and Kalium put great pressure on U.S. producers. ...
>
> Apparently the Canadian producers made the mistake of not selling to the small Canadian market, principally in Ontario, at the same low prices as they were selling in the U.S. In the summer of 1969 the U.S. Treasury Department ruled that potash from Canada was being "dumped" into the U.S. ... the U.S. Tariff Commission ... recommended special dumping duties. ...
>
> The Canadian mines are more efficient than the Carlsbad mines ... Threatened also was the relatively cozy price arrangement which previously prevailed. The problem as seen from Carlsbad was to stop IMC from breaking price. ... New Mexico and the industry then induced Thatcher to do the job of controlling imports and supporting the cartel price ...[8]

Blakeney then went on to point out that the plan would hurt production, jobs, and royalties, increasing profits (or reducing losses). It was a trade-off of profits for jobs and also made the Saskatchewan government an instrument of price-fixing for an international cartel. From there, he criticized the lack of planning and questioned other potential impacts. He also pointed out the contradiction of the Thatcher government strengthening a major highway and then letting IMC wreck it by allowing it to truck potash to railhead at the North Dakota border when potash was selling for only $12 a ton, but then after the highway was ruined forcing prices up to $18.75.

The discussion of potash in the NDP manifesto, *New Deal for People*, was placed within the framework of a discussion of "Resource and Economic Development." It pointed out that "Saskatchewan's natural resources are the rightful heritage of the people of our province—not the preserve of private interests."⁹ This was followed by proposing a comprehensive economic development program emphasizing the role of public ownership and co-operatives, reviewing existing royalty and other arrangements, and reclaiming, where feasible, the ownership and control of foreign-owned resources. Statements such as those contained in *New Deal for People* had not been advanced since the early days of the CCF government elected in 1944. A much more cautious and conservative approach was in vogue in subsequent years. This new approach marked a sharp turn in thinking. Difficulties in both potash and agriculture made the public more receptive to such proposals. This parallels hard times after World War I and the 1930s drought and depression that made the public more ready to accept far-reaching proposals.

Allan Blakeney explained, "we had this block of social issues and we wanted to get more money out of resources. That was the short run objective. The longer-run objectives that I had were to see whether we could make those resources a basis for a diversified Saskatchewan economy."

IMC's relations with the Thatcher government, while sometimes rocky, were generally tolerable. *New Deal for People*, as they saw it, had the potential to turn everything upside down. IMC had its own problems and it didn't need another one.

IMC apparently was the only company that took steps in contemplation of a possible change of government. They had some mixed feelings because most of the potash companies didn't care that much whether Thatcher was re-elected after the way he had treated them. However, potash was a key investment in IMC's diversified operations, and as the largest and most well-entrenched firm, it was the industry leader. It naturally wanted to protect its assets. Lenon pointed out, "we had $200 million in the game."[10] He commissioned a poll to find out what support there was for the NDP proposals and had some concerns with the results. So, as he said, "I began to move some political chips."[11] He had high-level contacts and operated in a style that might be expected of a chief executive officer of a multinational private industrial or mining company.

How IMC dealt with these developments after Lenon saw the polling numbers reveals some of his attitudes and style. He describes the actions he took or contemplated:

> I discussed matters with influential Canadian Board[s] of Directors, the American Ambassador and a good contact in the Prime Minister's office. Internally, I remember telling my associates that if we had serious trouble I would "call for the Mounties" ... The key top level would not have worked for the government. As a coincidence, I was elected to the position of Chairman and CEO the same day as Blakeney became Premier. I did not sleep much that night.[12]

It appears their strategy was to rely primarily on high-level contacts in corporate and government circles in an attempt to outflank this new "problem." But at no point did they take the step of contacting Blakeney or someone in the NDP directly and simply talking to him. They could have drawn on a reservoir of goodwill and good relations in the past. Had they done so, they may well have gained a different understanding than they seem to have gained. If they had done so, IMC and the remainder of the industry may have approached issues differently. To illustrate, Blakeney provided some elaboration on his proposals in a reply to one letter sent to him by a Saskatchewan citizen who expressed concerns about NDP intentions on potash after *New Deal for People* was released:

> We are disturbed about employment in the potash industry and want to do everything we can to get the industry rolling again. To do this we will consider all alternatives including public ownership or some joint ownership between the province and

a potash company. We are by no means saying that the potash companies will become public corporations. We are simply saying that we will look at the feasibility of this proposition. Other propositions will, of course, be considered.

In any case, if we do go into the public ownership of potash it does not necessarily mean that we would 'take them over'. Public ownership could be achieved by buying a potash plant from the previous owners.[13]

It would appear IMC regarded "public ownership" in the same terms as "expropriation" and worried that public ownership would be "a big steal,"[14] which suggests they thought they would not get adequate compensation. They did have a legitimate concern because their Saskatchewan plants were a profitable and key segment of their operations. However, it appears they "assumed the worst" without looking into matters adequately. While the company would be aware of such state action in other places and, indeed, may have encountered it in its own corporate operations, the likely mindset was that it was unthinkable on the North American scene, including the United States and Canada. The conclusions reached from an incomplete analysis would have affected their approach. References were also made to "powerful Canadian Board[s] of Directors,"[15] meaning high-level Canadian corporate executives. No doubt, they played a role in influencing IMC's course of action. Was their advice focused on IMC's corporate interests or, it might be speculated, were they concerned more about their own operations in Canada?

IMC appears to have played an important role in the way potash affairs unfolded. The company was doing fine when it had the CFI market, but when the latter switched to potash from the new plant in which it, CFI, had a stake, IMC ran into trouble. It had financial difficulties, and some of the measures taken by the United States to curtail Canadian imports developed as a result of IMC "blasting its way into U.S. markets." IMC also persuaded the Saskatchewan government to strengthen the heavy-load side of Highway 9 from its plants to a railway at the North Dakota border so it could sell its potash at a lower cost. The highway was wrecked as a result of the truck haul.

When the Saskatchewan general election was called for June 23, 1971, I made plans to spend three of the four weeks campaigning in

Saskatchewan and the other week in the House of Commons in Ottawa. I spent the first week in Saskatchewan. After only a few days, it became clear to me that there was a mood for change and that the NDP message was catching on. I kept in touch with my wife and family in Ottawa. My wife was anxious to find out what was happening. I responded, "I'm not saying this out here but I think it is shaping up to be a massive NDP win like the CCF win in 1944." She gasped at my response. Previously, there had not been any perception that such a change was in the making. I spent the second week of the campaign back in Ottawa. On my return to Saskatchewan for the last two weeks, I stopped in Winnipeg for a plane transfer. I went to the VIP lounge. The only person there was David Dombowsky, deputy provincial treasurer, whom I had known for some time. (David was later president of crown-owned Potash Corporation of Saskatchewan.) After some chit-chat, I said to him, "Well, David, after June 23rd, you're going to have new bosses." He was startled by my statement. Wrapped up in his own demanding work within government, he was not tuned in to what was happening "out there."

Potash affairs did not play a major role in the election campaign in spite of events since 1969 and the contents of the NDP program. However, it did have an underlying influence in that events of the past few years left an impression that things were not being well managed. Allan Blakeney and the New Democratic Party won a resounding victory on June 23, 1971.

Blakeney became premier and his government took office on June 30, 1971. Little did I envisage that in another year and a half, I would be working for that government.

# CHAPTER 5
## New Realities

I t was June 23, 1971, election night in Saskatchewan! The NDP won 45 of 60 seats. I was at the NDP victory celebration being held in a closed-down grocery supermarket in Regina. I could hardly believe my eyes when I saw Premier Ross Thatcher mount the platform with Allan Blakeney, former premier Woodrow Lloyd, and several of the victorious candidates. Thatcher went to the microphone to speak. He had generated such animosity because of his policies and his style that some "Boos" broke out. Blakeney put his hand up telling them to stop. Thatcher's first words were, "I want to congratulate Allan Blakeney on a magnificent victory." He then went on to make a short speech and ended by saying, "Allan, it will only take us a few days to clean out our offices and you can take over." Blakeney visibly winced as those words brought home fully what was ahead of him.

Twenty years after coming to Saskatchewan, he was premier of the province. Now, he had to form a government and then get on with implementation of the ambitious *New Deal for People*, on which he had been elected. He had no difficulty in finding members to make up a good Cabinet, but the civil service, so necessary in managing programs effectively, had been stripped of many talented people by the previous administration. Blakeney was well equipped to lead the province, manage an overview of affairs, and oversee a wide range of ongoing activities as well as introducing new programs. In discussions or debates in any forum it was difficult to match his keen insight.

Blakeney was an engaging and jovial person. Relatively short in stature, a feature of most Saskatchewan premiers over time, he would readily break out in a distinctive, raucous laugh that became his hallmark. However, if someone had not thought through a matter clearly, he or she could expect the sting of his sharp, incisive, analytical mind. He did not hesitate to present his view clearly, including saying "bullshit" to Prime Minister Pierre Trudeau in a face to face meeting.

He was a native of Nova Scotia, graduated in law from Dalhousie University, and was awarded a Rhodes scholarship taking him to Oxford in England. Following his return, he spent a year in Edmonton but then moved to Saskatchewan because he was attracted by the exciting new programs being implemented by the CCF government led by Tommy Douglas. He became corporate secretary of the group of growing crown corporations, a unique feature of the Douglas administration. After several years there, he was appointed chairman of the Saskatchewan Securities Commission, and then went into private law practice. He was elected an MLA in June 1960 and was immediately appointed minister of education. Tommy Douglas had identified him as a potential future leader. This was followed by a stint as provincial treasurer and, after the controversial introduction of the medical care plan, he was named minister of health. When the CCF government was defeated in 1964, he survived as an MLA and resumed his law practice. The next change for him was in 1970, when he was elected leader of the Saskatchewan New Democratic Party, the successor to the CCF.

Cabinet formation is the single most difficult task facing a prime minister or a premier. Blakeney had a steep road ahead of him. He had veteran members to draw on for his Cabinet, but there were also a large number of new, untried members, some of whom it could be expected would make good cabinet ministers. Provincial finances were tight because of economic difficulties, and there were many promises to keep in the election manifesto, *New Deal for People*. When he and Thatcher met later, before the change in government in the traditional meeting between the outgoing premier and his incoming successor, Blakeney was told by Thatcher that there was money in the Liquor Board fund not yet taken into the budget, "to pay for some of the things you want to do." Liquor sales in Saskatchewan had been operated by a government agency ever since prohibition days, and profits could be transferred to the provincial treasury when expedient. Blakeney decided on a small Cabinet at the outset in order to leave room for new members later.

G. R. (Ted) Bowerman was appointed minister of mineral resources. Bowerman was also designated minister of Northern Saskatchewan, a new department to be set up that would pull all government activities in the sparsely settled northern part of Saskatchewan into one department. That is where Ted's heart really was. That was his primary assignment, and it was a demanding task. Bowerman was a big, burly, and energetic man who had spent time in the north. He was a "no nonsense" type of person and worked as a "smoke jumper," one of a crew of men who parachuted down to the site of forest fires and put them out. Subsequently, he farmed west of Prince Albert and had been an MLA for four years. The new department was not yet a reality, so he was slotted in as mineral resources minister at first. He had to do his job there too, so the obvious thing was to rely on the established bureaucracy for support.

Now that the stage was set, both government and the potash industry had to face new realities. Industry was anxious about what the government would do, and government had to determine what to do first. Initially, the premier fielded a parade of potash officials at his door. Allan Blakeney recalled the first contacts by potash firms after becoming premier:

> ... I don't recall any reaction by them about the possibility of public ownership, that they didn't sort of raise the issue. And if they did I don't remember it and therefore it wasn't raised very forcefully. I remember many contacts with respect to the nature of pro-rationing—were we going to continue the Thatcher pro-rationing scheme. ... what were we going to do about this pro-rationing policy, which if you look at the *New Deal for People* we said we would end our participation in the potash cartel. It was that policy which they wanted to urge us against. ...[1]

Ralph Cheesman, who was later manager of the Saskatchewan Mining Association, provided the industry perspective on the situation. He said, "They certainly didn't have a grand strategy. ... I think they just said let's wait and see what happens. ... the industry still needed pro-rationing to keep it viable and so this was the obvious thing to discuss with the new government ... it wasn't a grand strategy; it was an economic requirement."[2] Dr. Cheesman also noted that industry people found the new premier "agreeable" to work with.

R. A. Lenon, by then president and CEO of IMC, commented on his first contact with Allan Blakeney after he became premier. He said, "I had a visit with him and obviously pro-rationing was one thing on my mind, and I was always the great advocate of Canpotex [joint off-shore sales agency] ... And we didn't resolve very much but it didn't end unfriendly. I guess you could say he agreed to listen to what I was talking about."[3]

The new government had an extraordinarily heavy agenda at the out-set. In addition to taking over the reins of office, it convened a special session of the new Legislature near the end of July to pass legislation to remove measures by the previous government considered particularly repugnant, such as medical deterrent fees and repressive labour legisla-tion. If that wasn't enough, the premier regularly reminded ministers of things that required attention. As an example, he sent a memorandum on July 22, 1971, to Bowerman on potash pro-rationing, thus indicat-ing that potash had considerable priority and he wanted some action from him. He noted that some potash companies wanted to keep pro-rationing, observed that there were complaints of IMC undercutting prices, and asked that the matter be investigated. He went on:

> Would you also prepare a submission to Cabinet so that we
> may get some definite decision on a continuation of the potash
> pro-rationing program or, alternatively, a dismantling of the
> program.
>
> It seems clear from the activity in the potash world that
> it is necessary for us to put out a policy statement on the pro-
> rationing program before long. ...[4]

Bowerman replied promptly on July 27, reporting on action taken, noting that on July 23 he submitted a report to Cabinet entitled, "The Saskatchewan Pro-rationing and Price Stabilization Program," with the recommendation that there be no major changes in the program.[5]

Bowerman watched the potash industry closely. Administrative problems with the pro-rationing program became steadily more acute.

Some of those difficulties were identified in a sharply worded letter he sent to the industry. He pointed out that the pro-rationing program faced considerable pressures and stated bluntly, "The continuous attempts by certain producers to circumvent established procedures and to obtain special concessions or advantages have now reached the point where the program may be in jeopardy."[6] He then went on to spell out particulars: sales not reported; employee layoffs; mishandling of Canadian aid tenders and offshore sales; and other miscellaneous matters. After pointing out the alternatives, he concluded by asking for an expression of unqualified support for the program.

Evidence that Premier Blakeney continued to take an interest in potash affairs is seen in department correspondence sent direct to him rather than through the minister. Immediate issues had to be addressed, but longer-term issues also required attention. An entrenched culture was encountered within the Department of Mineral Resources. A former deputy minister of finance, Garry Beatty, commented: "I think they were perfectly good technical people. ... it was one of attitude and these were attitudes that had built up and passed on over many, many years since the formation of the Department. ... I wouldn't call it intransigence exactly but it was a self-stultification in there amongst the personnel. It wasn't incompetence, it was just they had a fixed view of the world ..."[7]

In fairness to the officials concerned, it must be observed that they had functioned for well over 20 years with the type of policies then in place; they were managing a difficult program where the consequences of a program cancellation would have been severe; and the new government had not yet determined a precise course of action.

The premier maintained a keen interest in the future of pro-rationing and expected action from the minister. One memo to the minister stated: "I am assuming that if there are to be any changes in the government program on potash pro-rationing you will put forward some general ideas for discussion. In short, I am assuming that the ball is in your court for the time being although, of course, I would be happy to discuss any ideas or thoughts you might have."[8]

Bowerman's response identified a number of ways for increasing potash revenues, such as revoking royalty guarantees and increasing various fees or taxes. Blakeney then suggested, "It seems to me that we will simply have to say to the potash companies that we do not feel bound to maintain the pro-rationing program if they intend to insist upon the special agreements fixing royalty to 1981."[9] The department continued to promote the merits of pro-rationing but wanted the formula changed to one based on capacity only, which would hurt one firm, Central Canada Potash, in particular. Bowerman took their proposal to Cabinet.

After meeting with the industry on December 8, the government announced on December 10 that pro-rationing would be continued, but that it was considering a change in formula. It looked as if Cabinet may have had concerns and wanted to have the proposed change tested with the industry first.

Shortly after, Premier Blakeney was asked by a London, England, based firm that monitored world potash affairs as well as other commodities, the British Sulphur Corporation, why the government had decided not to change pro-rationing. "We made a careful evaluation of the programme and decided that removal of the controls could result in a return to the chaotic conditions prevalent in late 1969 which would hurt the industry and in turn employment and the province's economy," Blakeney told them. He went on to say:

> Maintaining the programme allows the province to obtain greater benefits from its resources. We are not, however, happy with our share of world markets and we will, therefore, continue to review the programme and if necessary make changes to increase our percentage of world sales. We believe it is inequitable that the Saskatchewan potash industry operates at half capacity while other world producers operate at or near full capacity. Producers throughout the world are sharing the benefits of a world-wide improvement in potash prices and in our view all producers should share in the necessary production cuts.[10]

In early January 1972, Blakeney appointed Kim Thorson as minister of mineral resources.[11] He won a by-election after the death of Russ Brown, the member elected in 1971. A lawyer, he was known for his careful, astute handling of matters. His election gave Blakeney a chance to relieve Bowerman of his heavy load with two portfolios. In recalling his first days in his new post, Thorson said, "what is in my memory is that pro-rationing was a difficult problem ... that was the main issue ..."[12]

Prior to the change of ministers, it was evident that other options were already being considered, including revoking the royalty guarantees and increasing mineral taxation. Potash issues were a priority for Thorson as he settled into his portfolio. In February, he reported to the premier that he had established a task force including himself; specific recommendations would be available in a week or ten days that would take into account producer representations; he planned to review the recommendations with George Cadbury[13] in early March and then follow up further. Blakeney marked the memo "BF March 5/72" ["BF—Bring Forward" meant he was keeping on Thorson's tail]. On March 6 he asked Thorson if there was anything to report. Thorson responded with a summary of activities. During the session of the Legislature that spring, he also introduced legislation that was enacted and was designed to give the government the ability to establish a potash marketing board.

On June 13, 1972, Thorson announced two major changes to the pro-rationing program at the Second Marketing Conference of the World Fertilizer Institute held in White Sulphur Springs, West Virginia. One was the implementation of the new pro-rationing formula based on plant capacity that officials had been advocating for the past year. The second was the introduction of a potash pro-ration fee of 60 cents per ton of muriate (KCl). At the then level of production, that would produce some $4 million in revenue.

A curious event occurred that closed one possible avenue of opportunity. Federal minister of industry, trade and commerce, Jean-Luc Pepin, wrote Thorson on May 11, 1972, concerning the recent amendments made to Saskatchewan's Mineral Resources Act. He noted that Mr. Thorson was reported to have said the amendments had a potash marketing board in mind. Pepin pointed out, "Since Saskatchewan's potash enters both interprovincial and international trade, it is difficult to see on what basis the Province could regulate or control this trade without impinging on the *Federal Government's responsibilities*."[14] Mr. Pepin then went on to suggest "some mutually acceptable way to deal with this matter." He proposed informal and confidential discussions between federal and provincial officials concerning marketing board possibilities.

Thorson replied sharply on June 16, 1972 by saying, "our Government is not aware of any need for such discussions on the matter of marketing potash. I do not know what purpose such discussions would serve."[15] He continued the tone of his reply by saying, "I trust there is no thought on the part of the federal government that it would initiate any move that would have the effect of disturbing the arrangements which the Saskatchewan Government has made to improve the quantity and value of sales of potash produced in our province. We believe that our efforts in the future, which may or may not include a more formal marketing structure than presently exists, will also be successful."[16]

It is difficult to understand why Mr. Thorson would "slam the door shut" so abruptly on federal overtures at that time. Saskatchewan had made numerous public references to the possibility of a marketing board and now had legislation in place. Given Canada's constitution and the location of potash markets, it is difficult to fathom a provincial marketing board without federal involvement. Options for a reply might have been to say either, "let's do that" or "we'll keep your letter in mind." I discussed this correspondence with Mr. Thorson recently. He did not recall it but was also puzzled why he would have used that tone in his response. We both surmised that his reply was drafted for him by the department and was signed in a mountain of correspondence without getting a careful review.

The reaction of Central Canada Potash (CCP) to the changes in pro-rationing was predictable. They were unhappy about pro-rationing from the beginning and accepted the initial plan reluctantly. They repeated their position to the new government and made clear their opposition to the new formula in industry consultations. The announced changes went into effect on July 1, 1972. It did not take long for a reaction. On July 14, CCP applied to the Court of Queen's Bench for a writ of mandamus requiring the government to allow it to produce all the potash it needed. That application was turned down on February 5, 1973.[17] The department issued a stern warning to CCP that they were producing more potash than allowed and threatened them with cancellation of their lease.[18] Pressure was escalated when CCP launched an action against the Saskatchewan government on December 11, 1972, to have the pro-rationing regulations declared ultra vires and claimed damages.

Allan Blakeney commented that, in hindsight, "going with flat pro-rationing was on balance a mistake."[19] He elaborated, "This would then have prevented Central Canada Potash from leading the fray against the pro-rationing and may have let that issue disappear." He went on to point out, though, that the conflict would have occurred in any case because of the two basic issues, the first and most important being that the province wanted a lot more money and, secondly, it also wanted ownership participation.

In contrast with the CCP approach, IMC had a long record of a carefully managed relationship with the government, illustrated by its publishing a booklet on the Canadian potash industry emphasizing the need for a continuing strong relationship between potash produc-ers and the Saskatchewan government. It concluded that pro-rationing regulations "have been a dramatic success."[20] Later, though, Lenon expressed IMC unhappiness about the change to flat pro-rationing by saying, "we were being screwed."[21]

It was evident the new government was not finding it easy to change the state of affairs. It had to cope with immediate problems and was groping for its longer-term policy. It did achieve one short-run objec-tive in the form of a modest revenue increase. But it was still relying heavily on incumbent personnel who were committed to the existing program and who pressed for a change in the pro-rationing formula that then got the government into trouble. Allan Blakeney knew there was going to be a big fight, though, and that there was much more to come. He was determined that things were going to change. Something more needed to be done. He was casting about for ways and means of changing the status quo. Among the steps taken, he found the chance to get another actor in the scene, namely me. My misfortune opened a new opportunity for both him and myself.

# CHAPTER 6
## Defining Goals and Finding New Directions

Allan Blakeney and his government had been in power for more than a year. Many promises in the manifesto, *New Deal for People*, had already been implemented. But some things were missing. Some fundamental issues still needed to be tackled in spite of what had been accomplished. A key moment was coming up. The New Democratic Party took itself seriously, and its annual convention was more than just a time to party and socialize. The government was expected to report to members on its performance and plans for the future. I had belonged to the party and been active in many executive and/or leading roles since I was a teenager. I had just been defeated in the federal election but that did not stop me. I was at the convention along with many other committed members.

Premier Blakeney recognized the need by emphasizing resource development policy in his report to the NDP annual convention on November 17, 1972. "The public interest—not private gain—must be the basis of an alternative strategy," he declared.[1] He revealed that the government was working on a development strategy for major resources, that public ownership of key industries in the resource sector was being studied, and that resource development was only one element in a total development strategy.

He cautioned that resource industries are highly capital intensive, need large investments, have markets mostly outside provincial borders, require the best technology, and experience world demand that is generally rising faster than new discoveries.

Next, in the methodical way Blakeney had of addressing matters, he identified the choices for development. First, he pointed out was partnership arrangements with private enterprise; then, private development but with much more rigorous public supervision and greater returns through royalties and taxes; and third, co-operative development. Finally, he expressed a special interest in public enterprise where the public interest would be served by the government developing a resource.

Blakeney then zeroed in on the last-mentioned option and noted that socialists have an obligation to pursue this option when the benefits are clear and there is a reasonable chance of success, but he also noted some of the problems:

1. Large capital requirements and the need to make best use of available capital.

2. Making sure a public enterprise gets the best technology.

3. All of the marketing issues that need attention.

4. The timing of development taking into account the generally increasing value of resources.

I listened closely to that speech, as did the more than 500 other people who were at the convention. Many of them or their forebears had been members of the CCF when it was in power from 1944 to 1964. They were comfortable with the management of power, and they approved the framework their leader and premier was setting out for the future. They were satisfied with his plan for Saskatchewan in coping with its serious economic difficulties. His well-crafted and carefully thought-out statement identified resource development as a government priority. Blakeney delivered the speech while fighting a heavy cold. He carried a bottle of Vicks VapoRub with him at the convention and whenever needed took the lid off and took a sniff.

I was comfortable with his carefully laid-out plan that provided a framework for my work. Experiencing defeat in the federal election following more than four years of very hard work was disillusioning. I was very fortunate now to have the opportunity to participate in such constructive and creative work, and it would reinvigorate me quickly. I would have hardly believed that in less than a year the government would spell out the goal of public ownership of the potash industry, and it gives me satisfaction that I played a role in reaching that decision. I would also not have believed that within a year the federal government would be getting its sticky fingers into potash affairs, including revenues.

Premier Blakeney demonstrated his ability to lead the province in that speech. He had an amazing capacity to oversee a broad range of issues with rapidly changing scenarios and problems. These skills served him well in his position of premier, where he had to maintain an overview of the government while monitoring a large number of issues that sometimes required his intervention. Garry Beatty, former deputy minister of finance, also observed, "If Blakeney was good at anything, he was certainly good at lifting his eyes up off what was on the government's plate and looking at the horizon and he was constantly taking steps that would provide information and intelligence about what lay over the horizon ..."[2]

Many years later, Blakeney placed potash affairs in the perspective of government goals and objectives when I interviewed him, "we had this block of social issues and we wanted to get more money out of resources. That was the short-run objective. The longer-run objectives that I had were to see whether we could make those resources a basis for a diversified Saskatchewan economy."[3]

Next, somebody had to do the job. The man he put in the "hot seat" was Mineral Resources Minister Kim Thorson. He had been active in the NDP and was practicing law in Estevan when the MLA there died suddenly. I was in Blakeney's office just before the by-election was called, and he was enthusiastic about his potential candidacy. Shortly after Thorson was elected, he was appointed to Cabinet. He quickly immersed himself in potash affairs after his appointment. Pressure from the premier, together with the obvious need to address immediate issues, made potash a priority.

Thorson was a conscientious, hard-working minister who strived to do his best. He recognized the importance of potash, constantly pressed the industry to do better in marketing, and took part in a Canadian delegation to China in 1972 when the first potash was sold to that country. He commissioned a consulting study on potash and was concerned about the longer-term picture. Thirty years later in an interview he talked about a Cabinet submission he prepared identifying all of the options, "… I certainly recall struggling with it and labouring. I don't think it was something that I just whipped up in an afternoon. I think I drafted, I reviewed it with some people in the department, thought about it myself and finally sent it to Cabinet."[4]

Out of nine options, he recommended keeping pro-rationing with increases in the pro-rationing fee and working toward equity in existing mines. Other courses of action such as a marketing board were examined. It is clear there were ongoing discussions about potash in Cabinet, but an acceptable and feasible course of action was not emerging quickly. Thorson appeared to have difficulty in determining a way to go. His term as mineral resources minister covered a period of almost two tumultuous years during which he had to contend with immense pressures for change countered by resistance to change, searches for new policy directions, limited resources for managing affairs, and other intervening issues such as the looming energy crisis. Blakeney appointed Elwood Cowley as minister of mineral resources in late 1973, transferring Thorson to Industry because planned oil legislation would have placed him in a difficult political situation.

It was clear to Premier Blakeney, judging by his interventions, statements, and other activities that more needed to happen. It was at this point that I came into the picture. I was defeated in the 1972 federal election after having been a Member of Parliament for over four years. I was an economist, had worked previously for central agencies in the Saskatchewan government, and was a research officer in the office of the Leader of the Opposition in the Saskatchewan Legislature from 1964 to 1968. A long-time activist in the New Democratic Party and its predecessor, the CCF, I raised potash questions on the floor of the House of Commons on numerous occasions. Now, I was resuming a professional career.

On my first day at work, I had a number of meetings with officials and, in particular, with Premier Blakeney. He wanted me to study and review a range of resource policy questions and wanted particular attention given to the development of a long-term policy and strategy for potash. He stressed, "I want a potash policy that ensures the resource provides the greatest possible long-term benefits to the province and that best serves Saskatchewan looking well into the 1980s."

I will never forget that statement. When people say, "All politicians think about is the next election," I fire back at them, "Not at all." Then I recount Blakeney's words. I am a little sensitive on this point myself because I consider that I did more than just think about the next election when I was a Member of Parliament. (In fact, I should have thought about it a little more.) I had colleagues who thought about more than their self-interest, and I have to say there were many members of other parties who were similarly motivated.

Things ran into a snag quickly. Thorson objected when "planners" got involved in potash because it conflicted with his initiatives. He urged the premier to have me concentrate on oil refining and distribution and said he would be happy to work out terms of reference with me on oil policy studies. Kim and I got along fine, but he still thought this was intruding on his territory. Matters got sorted out after a while, and Cabinet decided that I should study certain specific potash questions together with Mineral Resources and submit a report to Cabinet. Thorson's recommendation to pursue acquisition of equity in mines was accepted, but Cabinet wanted more studies on pro-rationing and marketing. Blakeney then wrote Thorson, "This will confirm our understanding that you are to co-ordinate our internal government studies re the potash industry and re the oil industry."[5] He then underlined the need for staff co-operation between the Department of Mineral Resources and me. (That was a pretty strong statement meaning, "Get along, fellows!")

By this time, I had already had dealings with the department and encountered their resistance to changes in the status quo. A consulting study commissioned the previous summer favoured most of the existing structure. The report never played the role it might have, as the author was killed in an automobile accident just before a planned trip to Regina. In the meantime I continued my studies. The department had a number of meetings with the industry. I attended those meetings and was identified by the deputy minister as "the premier's representative." Some 30 sets of eyes turned my direction saying mentally, "Who is this guy? What's this all about?" I am sure inquiries were made and got the answer to the first question. One group, Noranda of CCP, went further. They came to see me. We had several meetings. They outlined their grievances about pro-rationing changes made in summer 1972. They pointed out their market was guaranteed when they undertook construction. Their mine would operate at full capacity. Now they were restricted to the pro-rationing formula and the mine was losing money. I acknowledged that they had a good case and said I would make their position known.

Some time later, I attended a meeting in the premier's office when a group of top Noranda officials presented their company position to the premier and the minister of mineral resources. While in Parliament, I was the regional development critic for the NDP. I severely criticized a federal government program of grants to private companies for new development, some large, some before plans were even prepared. As an example, I drew attention to a large grant made to Noranda, one of Canada's largest mining companies. The company response was made by their treasurer, Kendall Cork. He was at the meeting. When the meeting concluded and people were mixing informally, I introduced myself to him. I said, "Mr. Cork, I don't believe we have met before but I believe we have had occasion to refer to each other's name," and then explained. He pointed his finger at me and exclaimed, "It was YOU." After a short conversation, he tried to brush it off by saying, "After the issue came up, I had to go look up to see how much the grant was." By this time, the premier had come into the picture and interjected, "Oh, come, come."

Ongoing relationships between government and industry were not always easy. Some upper-level industry officials suggested they were smooth but, in fact, there were difficulties. One cause was that local officials had little authority. Cliff Kelly, a Kalium official, said that when he signed submissions to the government, they had been prepared elsewhere.[6] Decisions of any magnitude were made at head offices located far from Saskatchewan. Head-office personnel were generally present for negotiations or meetings of any importance with the government. The industry rarely spoke with a unified voice. Allan Blakeney observed this and made dealings with them much more difficult than with oil or uranium. He said, "They were really unsophisticated and they were hampered again by the fact that the negotiators appear to have been told that they had to stick to the lowest common denominator." One step Blakeney took to help smooth matters was that he often spoke favourably of Canpotex. This was an industry association formed with Department of Mineral Resources encouragement to manage all overseas potash sales. Not all producers joined at the outset, but they eventually did, in part because of pressure from the department. It is not clear at this time whether Blakeney's support was because of his approval of the concept or whether it was for any other reason. At that time, it was not looked on as being a cartel in nature. See Appendix H.

Some companies, such as IMC, made a special effort to foster good relations with the government. Nelson White, chairman of the board of directors, and R. A. Lenon, president, told a news conference in Regina in June 1972 that, "Regulations on potash production and pricing instituted by the Saskatchewan government in 1969 saved the industry from disaster and have put it again on the threshold of a bright future."[7] Mr. White also said recent changes in regulations had been for the good as they resulted in clarification and streamlining, while recently increased payments (pro-rationing fees) were understood and not unique to Saskatchewan. He then added that IMC's relations with the NDP government had been excellent. The depth, loyalty, and commitment to the company of top officials was illustrated when I interviewed Richard Lenon in his home in 2003 as part of my thesis research. He was retired but still thought of company interests and invited me to have a telephone conversation with Nelson White, his predecessor as CEO, then 97 years of age.

The Cabinet directive asking for a study of marketing and acquisition of equity was issued on January 23, 1973, but it was not until June that the report was submitted (DMR-Burton report). The complexities of the issues, together with difficulty in reaching agreement, slowed its progress. Agreement was reached eventually on the recommendations and much of the analysis, but there were still significant differences. Four options provided a framework:

- Proceed with a marketing agency only.

- Proceed with a marketing agency and at the same time attempt to acquire ownership in one or more mines.

- Proceed with steps to acquire equity in mines only.

- Leave marketing and ownership as is with/without the pro-rationing program.[8]

The first recommendation would require all companies to file individual financial statements. Next, it was recommended the government determine the possibilities for government ownership in the potash industry through acquisition of equity. Finally, it was recommended Cabinet authorize planning and preparation for a crown-operated marketing agency, but defer decisions on implementation until studies were completed and prospects for ownership were clearer. A concern was that while a marketing agency had both benefits and advantages, there were serious risks and unknowns.

Differences of view were spelled out. Essentially, I regarded a marketing agency more favourably, even with potential problems, while the department didn't like the idea. The fundamental differences were, I argued: first, maintenance of the status quo would result in the province continuing to be a residual supplier in world markets; and, second, the capital-intensive nature of the industry required a high rate of utilization of facilities if the industry was to reach its potential. A marketing agency could better accomplish this, but the department differed. Despite ongoing interest in a marketing agency, however, it was agreed that a plan had not as yet been fleshed out in order to make it a viable option.

A bone of contention was the question of companies providing financial statements to the government. The companies prepared a composite industry statement for 1971 and 1972 supplied through a chartered accountant. The statement was of little value because of the known huge differences in performance by the companies and their widely varying accounting practices and capital structures. After much discussion within government and with the companies, the DMR-Burton report submitted in June 1973 made a firm recommendation that companies be required to submit annual financial statements. The companies refused steadfastly. The issue became more acute later when the potash reserve tax was introduced, and the government responded to industry protests by saying adjustments could be made but the financial statements were necessary in order to assess matters adequately.

The former manager of the Saskatchewan Mining Association explained the companies' resistance to financial statements: "They were very concerned that it would affect their competitive edge; in other words ... they in turn did not trust the government ..."[9] Government suspicions about financial presentations were supported subsequently in a comment by Ryan Willett, son of a former president of Kalium

Chemicals. His father, Boyd Willett, thought the sale of Kalium to IMC was a mistake because PPG, the former owner, had loaded a growing number of overhead costs onto Kalium, a profitable operation, resulting in tax benefits. These costs then had to be absorbed elsewhere.[10]

Following the completion of the DMR-Burton report, I turned my attention to the next step. I prepared a "Proposed Strategy for Potash," reviewed it with five senior government officials, and submitted it to Premier Blakeney.[11] A draft critical path was also attached with a policy of working to public ownership of the industry. I proposed conducting marketing agency studies, pursuing equity acquisition prospects, and requiring filing of financial statements. Additionally, I proposed increasing the pro-rationing fee again, publicly declaring government intentions to control new development and expansions, establishing contact with major potash buyers, and investigating possible expropriation procedures.

This is the first recorded mention of expropriation. While only an internal staff paper discussing options, a standard practice, it reveals a realization of the potential for major conflict and an awareness that serious problems could be in store if the government pursued the course of action proposed. While only an initial attempt to design a tentative strategy, it was the product of serious discussions and was an effort to move the agenda ahead. The potential difficulties were also recognized, such as effective countermeasures or retaliatory action by the industry; unsatisfactory discussions with the federal government on a marketing agency; and no results in trying to acquire equity. This was a dramatic development in the context that it occurred just two years after the Blakeney government assumed office.

In the meantime, I took another step to secure more in-depth analysis of potash affairs. Professor Arne Paus-Jenssen, an economics lecturer at the University of Saskatchewan, had an interest in potash. After my discussions with him, he was prepared to undertake a potash study. I approached Minister Thorson, who agreed to the study. Blakeney also approved.

The study was to provide basic economic analysis of the potash industry; study the influence of the pro-rationing pricing system on demand and supply; determine the extent to which Saskatchewan was a residual supplier; examine the influence of pro-rationing pricing on potash prices, markets, and competitive position; assess the implications for pricing policy of the analysis; and establish the influence of exchange rate changes on marketing, together with implications for future policy. A second study would examine the US potash industry cartel, the impact on US marketing of any major Saskatchewan initiatives, and the implications of Combines Investigation legislation on potash affairs.

The report analyzed the economics of the potash industry and was sharply critical of existing policies. For the most part, it confirmed what the government's instincts already told them. Key comments were:

- The present influence of the pro-rationing scheme is to support the industry and to hold a price umbrella over all the producers.

- ... the evidence suggests that the pro-rationing scheme is presently retarding the rate at which Saskatchewan's market share could expand due to the support price system. The existence of the floor price cannot but help sustain marginal producers elsewhere.

- The introduction of a marketing board for potash will not solve the problem ... a marketing board may reduce further Canada's share of the world market.

- ... the Province should not permit the price of potash to increase nor should the Province initiate revenue raising policies which will tend to increase the price of potash. We consider the imposition of a pro-rationing fee to be a move in the wrong direction. ... the resulting price increase will increase the risk of attracting new producers as well as prolonging the life expectancy of the marginal producers.

- ... a policy of low and only slowly increasing prices reflecting increased costs would appear essential to insure a dominant position for Saskatchewan potash in world markets.

- If, however, it is considered preferable to retain the production controls ... the province can at least insist [on]
  some of the financial returns presently captured by the
  firms, which would not be possible without the controls,
  be turned over to the province. A marketing board is one
  possibility, new taxation is another. But it is important
  to choose a method of increasing revenue which will not
  have undesirable side effects both in the short-run and the
  long-run.[12]

The Paus-Jenssen study then presented a tax proposal. After reviewing the problems and deficiencies in existing tax policies and establishing objectives, it concluded a restrictive approach was better than a
competitive approach. Four tax-policy options were examined: public
ownership, income tax, severance tax, and property tax. He preferred
a property tax approach. He suggested the tax should be based on the
size of the ore deposit, price of the finished product, mining costs of
the ore, and costs of refining ore into finished product. This was better
than a marketing board because it would achieve the same results, it
would be less cumbersome, it would clearly be under provincial jurisdiction, and it would avoid the expenses of a marketing board. The
study set the stage for the potash reserve tax.

For the first time, the government had a solid, independent analysis of the state of affairs and a proposal that, if implemented, would
result in meaningful change. Until that time, Thorson depended on
department staff, Blakeney wanted more action, and I was trying to
find a way. I recall one occasion just prior to a meeting with officials.
Tensions were present and we were waiting for someone to arrive. To
put in the time, we had an "exciting" conversation on the problems of
dog "poop" on lawns.

Minister Thorson announced on July 5, 1973, his intention to make
changes in pro-rationing and was particularly critical of companies
with mines in other places as well as Saskatchewan that did not cut production. He threatened drastic action if Saskatchewan's position did
not improve. He also said other proposals were under consideration.

This got the attention of industry. On August 13, C. J. (Cliff) Kelly,
by then plant manager at Kalium, sent Thorson a 25-page brief in preparation for a meeting. The brief was a well-prepared, comprehensive,

and reasoned presentation defending the existing state of affairs and making the case for keeping things as they were. It described the 10-year development of potash production in Saskatchewan as very good, argued that pro-rationing had been effective, and concluded that prospects were good for future market growth. It warned that price reductions would not increase sales, but if the government felt more aggressive selling was necessary, three alternatives were suggested: abandon pro-rationing; compete for added sales without price requirement; and allow Canpotex to compete for offshore sales at lower prices. Each option had its problems. In the end, Kalium recommended the program be kept intact at least until the end of the current potash year (June 30, 1974).[13]

Thorson met potash producers on August 30, 1973, and announced technical changes in the pro-rationing program: that the pro-rationing fee would increase from 60 cents per ton of muriate to $1.20, that financial statements would be required on a confidential basis, and that no additional productive capacity would be recognized or authorized until a sound plan for government participation in the industry has been developed. Firms responded verbally and were invited to submit their written responses after studying the government announcement in detail. Eleven of the 12 companies responded. They were unanimous in their criticisms of the proposed changes in pro-rationing, some of them severe. Four were willing to submit financial statements, none objected to it, and seven made no comment. One, Central Canada Potash, expressed willingness to explore prospects for a joint venture with the government; three objected to the proposition, while seven made no comment.[14]

Thorson then had to act. The department suggested going ahead with the pro-ration fee increase and filing financial data but delaying pro-rationing changes to July 1, 1974. I recommended approving the fee increase, filing financial statements, and announcing government interest in industry participation. I also suggested a decision not to proceed with pro-rationing changes immediately was perfectly rational if the objective was not to rock the boat too much right then. I pointed out industry sensitivity to pricing questions, emphasized the need to underline government dissatisfaction with a residual supplier role, and commented on the marketing agency proposal. I then sent a memo to Blakeney on September 26 attaching a copy of my submission to Thorson and expressed my frustrations by saying, "I must also state frankly that I have encountered a great deal of resistance in the Department of Mineral Resources to any proposals for change in the existing situation."[15] I asked Blakeney for direction on future activities in view of the inflexible position of the department.

Thorson announced his decision on October 2, 1973. He included the increase in pro-ration fee, the requirement for filing financial statements, and government participation in new developments. However, the pro-rationing changes would not take effect until July 1, 1974.

The Cabinet Planning Committee met in October to review the status of potash. The keystone of government potash policy since 1970 was pro-rationing, sharply criticized in the 1971 NDP program, but not as yet changed. Now Cabinet had the Paus-Jenssen study and considerable internal work to support decisions. Before the meeting, held around the Cabinet table and attended by several ministers and officials, I was sitting directly across from the premier. I gazed at him steadily trying to signal my dissatisfaction with the submission. He caught my signal. He started flipping through papers and looking about. Whenever Blakeney was uncertain, or unhappy with what was before him, he had a habit of scratching the back of his head. This time, he scratched vigorously. By the time the meeting started, he had the picture. When he saw that the department was stalling by saying more study was needed before a recommendation could be made, he blurted out, "Why does some of this stuff have to be studied forever before we can get some idea of where we are going?" I kept my mouth shut. J. G. Wotherspoon, the deputy minister, had to try and respond. The premier's salvo, as it turned out, set the tone of the meeting and influenced its outcome. Later, I talked to Jack Messer, a cabinet minister who was there, and told him what I had done and what took place. Jack replied, "Yes, old Jack's (Wotherspoon's) tie was flapping about two inches above his chest."

All good internal government reports start off with a recitation of the options. Having done that, the submission soon revealed sharp differences between the Department of Mineral Resources and Planning and Research of Executive Council, represented by myself. The department officials urged delays and further studies before making decisions, while I pressed for more aggressive action and establishing public ownership of potash as a goal. The department wanted to see the present program kept in place until a new policy was in place, while I pressed for some steps to start then.[16]

There was no doubt about the outcome of the meeting. The Cabinet Planning Committee minute stated, "Further work on potash policy should be based on the premise that the objective of government policy is public ownership and control of the potash industry."[17] The minute recognized the need for further research on strategy, timing, and immediate programs needed before further action could be determined. The minute directed that work proceed "with all deliberate speed" toward the goals established. A delegation of Wotherspoon, Meldrum, and me was authorized to meet with federal officials on potash marketing. This, so to speak, "cut them off at the pass," as Mineral Resources wanted to go alone.

Thus, for the first time, the goal of public ownership of the potash industry was clearly spelled out. That was a significant shift in policy to occur in just over two years. Using expropriation as the means was, of course, an entirely different matter. Expropriation was clearly rejected in a number of places in the documentation. Recognizing that time was required to accomplish the goal implicitly involved the concept of negotiated acquisitions. At the same time, the thought of using means such as increased taxation, taking royalties in kind, et cetera, indicated the approach was not a passive one. The underlying reason behind the goal of public ownership was the conclusion that private sector development would always require the province foregoing some of the benefits and returns it contended rightfully belonged to the province. Furthermore, the province now considered that it could mobilize the capacity to develop and manage the industry.

Government pressure increased. In late October, Thorson said publicly that provincial takeover of all potash below ground was a possibility, and other changes might be made after the potash year-end on June 30, 1974. He also said the government was still thinking about a marketing agency and dropping the floor price in the current plan.[18] On the other hand, companies were pleased Thorson announced on November 2 that potash quotas were being boosted again in the current year due to buoyant demand, and he was going to make a personal appeal to the railways to provide enough cars to cope with extra traffic.

While this was taking place, the oil crisis, also called the energy crisis, unfolded rapidly during the latter part of 1973 and early 1974.

Saskatchewan introduced legislation, called Bill 42, designed to capture virtually all of the windfall profits from oil price increases for the province. Preparations for this legislation and its presentation, followed by planning for a Federal-Provincial Energy Conference, required all of the available resources of the government. I was heavily involved in both of these activities. Potash had to go on the "back burner." Blakeney explained: "there were just so many battles you could fight at once and this was certainly going to be a major battle. ... with respect to potash, we had not reached the time, had not reached the belief that it was time to make the major move forward in potash."[19]

In spite of these demands, I completed a comprehensive potash policy study together with a Mineral Resources official and submitted it to the government.[20] It reviewed the development, structure, and role of potash in the Saskatchewan economy. After reviewing developments since the current government came into power, it pointed out little had changed in fact. References were made to a study prepared recently for the Manitoba government by Professor Eric Kierans, a former federal Liberal cabinet minister, entitled *Report on Natural Resources Policy in Manitoba*. He pointed out that if Manitoba continued its existing policies, the same problems would emerge as those afflicting the potash industry in Saskatchewan. He emphasized that many industries such as potash trace the source of their strength to control of raw materials. He called for a radical new resource policy with exploration and development to be carried out by a crown corporation.

The DMR-Burton policy study emphasized the residual supplier position of Saskatchewan resulting from existing policies. The department eventually recognized and accepted the need to change its stance. It was concluded that retaining existing private-sector policies would not serve Saskatchewan's best interests in the long run. The mixed approach also contained a host of problems and would fall short of the basic goal. It was concluded that a long-run policy of working toward public ownership was the only way of ensuring that the industry would best serve Saskatchewan's interests. This was based on the premise that private-sector ownership would always demand that a portion of returns that should remain with the people of the province would go to private owners instead, and the private sector would also retain its economic power. Kierans also emphasized these points.

Demands of the oil crisis delayed the start of implementation until February–March 1974. Taxation proposals under study and government sharing in ownership were the major items. A tax based on the Paus-Jenssen report and guidelines for government participation were being developed. In the meantime, potash demand became more buoyant and helped ease existing strains.

Cabinet approved pursuing prospects for involvement in mine expansions and investigating a new mine. The minister of mineral resources, now Elwood Cowley, was to take action. He was also to inform potash companies of the government's taxation, marketing, and participation proposals. This was in no way a "takeover." The government wanted to take part in future expansions. The idea of negotiating for the acquisition of existing facilities had not yet taken shape, while the option of expropriation was explicitly rejected.

Two other factors began to overshadow potash affairs. First, a series of court actions by potash companies were designed to frustrate government actions. Second, the federal government stepped up its interest and involvement in resource affairs. It was designed to curb provincial initiatives to capture windfall profits created by escalating prices and counter their efforts to capture a larger share of increasing values.

The July 1, 1972, application by CCP to the Saskatchewan Court of Queen's Bench for a writ of mandamus to allow the company to produce all the potash it could was turned down, and the Supreme Court of Canada dismissed the appeal. CCP did not stop there. On December 11, 1972, it launched another court action, asking that the pro-rationing regulations be declared ultra vires and that the company be awarded $2 million in damages. On November 13, 1973, the Attorney General for Canada, in an unprecedented application, was added as a co-plaintiff on the side of the company. On May 6, 1975, the Saskatchewan Court of Queen's Bench ruled the regulations were ultra vires and awarded the company $1.5 million in damages. The Saskatchewan government appealed the decision, but it was not dealt with before other events superseded the situation.

The Government of Saskatchewan was outraged. After an understanding was reached between the previous Liberal government and the federal government that the federal government had no further difficulty with the regulations, now, that position was changed. Allan

Blakeney was still furious almost 30 years later: "We became angry later when they thought that things our government did were unconstitutional but the things that the Thatcher government did were not. ... we didn't know that they would later take the view that the constitution changed depending which government was in power."[21] Federal officials must have known they were on questionable ground. They first broke the news to Saskatchewan when Wotherspoon, Meldrum, and I went to Ottawa to explore marketing agency possibilities with the federal government. It was later learned the officials deliberately arranged for a pleasant, mild-mannered, female federal lawyer to tell us the federal government was going to enter the CCP court action as a co-plaintiff. Who would get into a heated argument with such a pleasant person?

Both Saskatchewan and Alberta passed legislation during this period to capture for the provinces significant portions of the windfall revenues from higher oil prices. Previously, the federal government expressly kept its hands off resource revenues except through income tax. Now federal policy changed and new tax measures were imposed, transferring a significant amount of revenue to Ottawa. The final straw came when the federal budget on May 6, 1974, announced provincial royalties, provincial mining taxes, and other similar payments could not be treated as an expense in calculating taxable income.

When the budget was reintroduced in November 1974, after a federal election, the measures were reintroduced with some modifications, but the principle was kept intact. Most of the changes benefited resource companies. Alberta and Saskatchewan, in particular, protested this action vigorously but to no avail. It was pointed out that Canada's constitution from the outset had placed resources under provincial jurisdiction and as an offset to areas kept under federal control. Inconsistencies were pointed out such as royalty on freehold land being deductible from income while royalty from an adjacent crown-owned property was not, but, again to no avail.[22]

The federal government's action had a serious impact. It was of particular concern as it was announced just after the province introduced its potash reserve tax. Federal actions created a problem for both the province and the potash industry. Federal intrusion complicated an already complex state of affairs between the province and the potash industry. Provincial potash policy had evolved over the previous three years to the point where there was a significant increase in direct returns to the province. Now these efforts were being stymied by federal intrusions into provincial areas of jurisdiction, making it even more difficult for the province and the potash companies to reach a settlement.

# CHAPTER 7
## The Potash Reserve Tax

The Paus-Jenssen report changed the state of affairs. Until its submission, the government was groping for a course of action and was only tinkering with the existing system. Resistance by the producers, resistance by officials, locked-in royalty commitments, and uncertainty about a clear course of action frustrated the government. The report, along with its recommendations, clarified many issues for the government and proposed a clear course of action that would change things dramatically. The Department of Mineral Resources shifted its stance after the report was presented and proceeded to flesh out the proposal into a plan that could be implemented. It became one feature of a comprehensive policy that covered a range of issues.

The tax plan prepared was based on the Paus-Jenssen proposal. It would be levied against each producer in a manner similar to a property tax. When the plan was completed and presented to the minister of mineral resources, Elwood Cowley, he was told that it was estimated the tax would produce $60 million in additional revenue annually. In today's terms, that would be the equivalent of more than $800 million. "Sixty million dollars," Cowley exclaimed. "Sixty million dollars," he kept repeating. I could see him visualizing what the government could do with that much more revenue. At that time, the government was still pressed to finance the demands on its resources. I could almost see the dollar signs in his eyes.

Cowley announced the draft potash policy at a meeting with producers in Regina on April 29, 1974. The potash reserve tax was the centrepiece. He reiterated previously stated aims as well as introducing new items. They included government participation in future development, changes to pro-rationing including dropping the minimum price feature, improving markets for Saskatchewan potash, and recognizing that producers require a reasonable rate of return. A strategy was urged that would discourage development of reserves elsewhere. Planning for industry expansion needed to start now and should be paced with market growth. Companies were invited to submit their comments after review of the proposals.

The new potash reserve tax would be based on the assessed valuation of potash deposits. This valuation would be determined for each individual potash facility, taking into account productive capacity, scale of operation, ore grade, capital cost, a base price, and assumed life of the operation. A mill rate increasing with price levels would be applied to the value to produce a lump-sum figure independent of production or sales. Annual adjustments for cost increases would be made with a ceiling on all taxes of 90% of net income. Financial statements were requested again so adjustments could be made if the new policy created problems requiring attention.

I had a feeling of real satisfaction at this point. A way had been found through all the difficulties. Saskatchewan would be a better place as a result. I hoped, perhaps unrealistically, this policy package would set the stage after further negotiations for the accomplishment of goals. Allan Blakeney felt the same way: "We felt that those policies had the potential to give us a major participation in the industry and a substantially greater return for our resource."[1]

The industry reaction was predictable. "The Government proposal now under discussion will, quite predictably, serve only to destroy or materially impair the great progress that has been made to date,"[2] asserted Dr. C. L. Randolph, president of the Canadian Potash Producers Association (CPPA) in a carefully prepared letter to Blakeney and Cowley on May 8, 1974. Most industry participants at the April 29 meeting restrained themselves, although some had to give vent to their feelings. Now all of them were responding in full force. "The potash industry is currently emerging from a depressed period which may well have produced disastrous results ..."[3] stated the letter as it blasted the government proposal. Potential US anti-trust problems were avoided by making no comment about dropping the minimum price requirement. They disliked government participation, asked for clear criteria, and thought it should not be tied to expansion. The industry objected to government in marketing and found the new tax proposal highly objectionable. A meeting with government was requested.

About the same time, the federal Liberal government was defeated in the House of Commons and a federal election was called for July 8. I was nominated as a candidate in an attempt to regain my former constituency. I have wondered whether there were some "Machiavellian" minds among government officials, and industry as well, who were hoping I would win so I wouldn't be around causing so much trouble in my efforts to change the status quo. Ironically, the person who had defeated me in 1972 was a Regina lawyer, Jim Balfour, Conservative, who was on the Board of Directors of Duval Corporation, one of the private potash companies. Had I not been defeated in 1972, I would not have been available to Blakeney to help give matters a push. Undoubtedly, he would have found some other person or way to get things moving, but timing may have been later and events may have taken a different course. As it turned out, I was defeated in 1974 again as the Liberals regained a majority and the New Democrats faced a severe setback. I went back to work and continued where I had left off. I was greeted with varying kinds of smiles.

Randolph's May 8 letter was followed up with a formal, comprehensive brief on July 17, 1974. Much of its contents focused on the potash reserve tax. The industry contended that it was much too excessive, as well as being unsound in concept, and had some specific unsatisfactory features. Complicating things were the federal budget provisions disallowing royalties and other provincial payments as deductions from taxable income. The industry's solution was to do nothing until these difficulties were resolved. Their alternative was that total federal and provincial tax take not exceed 50% of pre-tax income. They threatened that unless Saskatchewan was attractive to investors, investment would be placed elsewhere, whether in potash or other activities.

Obviously, they were sabre-rattling and threatening, but this didn't make Allan Blakeney flinch: "... I wasn't worried all that much about whether we lost legal actions because in real politics if the public thinks you are doing the right thing in dealing ... with foreign corporations

... a way will be found to accommodate this ..."[4] He emphasized that the province was entitled to a share of the increasing value of resources and that this was the way to get Saskatchewan out of the "next year" syndrome, just as Alberta was doing with its petroleum industry. He also pointed out that the industry was happy to have the province intervene when there were difficulties, but when things were better they just wanted the province to back off.

An interview with R. A. Lenon in 2003 provided an industry perspective. The introduction of the potash reserve tax was the point when he became really uncomfortable. He supplied me with tables that outlined the impact of the tax at that time along with the further impact of federal budget measures. The tables illustrated the effect on a hypothetical mine about the size of the first IMC mine, producing one million tons of $K_2O$ per year with an investment of $78 million. Prices shown were from $50 per ton to $90 and the outcome when royalties and all other provincial payments are 1) totally deductible from taxable income, 2) partially deductible, and 3) not deductible. I did further calculations to determine the percent rate of return on investment applying the numbers supplied.

Analysis revealed that when the potash reserve tax was fully deductible from taxable income, the return on investment (ROI) comes out to a very narrow range of 16.8–17.8% over a full range of prices between $50 and $90 per ton. While the level of return on investment is debatable, and there may be other problems with the tax plan, this very narrow range of ROI applied to the full range of prices suggests the essentials of the plan were well constructed and accomplished the objective of capturing for the public purse revenues beyond those required for a reasonable level of profit. However, when provincial levies were not deductible from taxable income or were only partially deductible, the impact on company finances was severe. The ROI is only 10.7% at a price of $50 per ton, drops as the price increases, and is a loss when the price is just over $70 per ton. When provincial levies are partially deductible, the ROI ranges from12.7% at $50 per ton to 1.2% at $90 per ton. (See Appendix F.)

The companies were alarmed and dismayed by the combined effects of federal and provincial measures. If the federal government had not moved to disallow provincial resource payments, the province and the companies may have eventually reached a settlement. (Mr. Lenon talked about contacts in "high places" including the prime minister's office. Did this cause problems for companies he did not anticipate?) The CPPA brief made it clear the industry expected the province to back off completely because of the federal initiative. Their first target was to fight the provincial tax plan.

The then manager of the Saskatchewan Mining Association, Ralph Cheesman, said that when the potash reserve tax was unveiled, the companies became really alarmed but were still willing to negotiate. He pointed out one side effect of the federal action to disallow royalties. Public support for Blakeney and the government increased because of objections to federal intrusion into areas recognized constitutionally as being under provincial jurisdiction.

An analysis of the industry submission revealed a mix of legitimate concerns along with assertions that could be questioned. However, companies' refusal to submit financial statements became increasingly the centre of conflict. There did not appear to be much room for negotiation given the industry's complete rejection of the government's April 29 proposal, its refusal to submit financial statements, and its position that nothing should be done until difficulties with the federal government were resolved. Blakeney's response to industry complaints that the tax was needlessly complex was, "I'll take your system if I get the money."

In the meantime, potash markets had improved markedly. The result was that on August 21, 1974, Mineral Resources Minister Cowley announced that production allocations under the pro-rationing program were being expanded to the full rated capacity of all mines in Saskatchewan. He also announced that the minimum price rule for selling potash had been dropped as prices were already well above the stipulated minimum price. It is curious, but not known, why the minimum price order remained in place for so long after it was such a central feature of federal-provincial negotiations in late 1969 and early 1970.

On October 23, 1974, Cowley announced the new Saskatchewan potash policy.[5] The centrepiece was the new potash reserve tax, which it was now expected would produce an added $87 million in provincial revenue in the next calendar year. The original proposal was changed, resulting in a 28% reduction in the amount of revenue that would be collected. However, sharply higher potash prices in the meantime increased revenue expectations to a significantly higher level than the

$60 million originally forecast. The stated intention of the government was to allow producers a fair rate of return, but without their financial statements that could not be determined satisfactorily.

The structure of the tax was kept the same as in the original proposal, but the range of prices addressed was changed from $34.50–50.00 per ton to $35.00–90.00 because between April and October, prices rose from $40 to $60 per ton, resulting in a $134 million increase in industry revenues. Under the existing tax regime, the government would have captured an extra $3 million, while the industry would have kept the other $131 million. In contrast, the potash reserve tax would result in the government getting $91 million while the industry would keep the remaining $43 million. These numbers do not consider the impact of additional income tax that may have been payable, but this could very well be offset by tax loopholes. The industry submission on July 17, 1974, included a composite financial statement for all Saskatchewan potash producers which showed that on December 31, 1973, they had deferred income taxes of $49,149,000, and it was projected that the amount would increase to $57,335,000 by June 30, 1975. Studies have found that, often, in reality, most of these amounts are never recovered for the public purse.[6]

Three charts attached to the October 23 statement illustrated the government view of affairs. The first showed that prices escalated rapidly from 1973 to 1975 but, even with the new tax, industry revenues after new provincial taxes would be more than double the levels in 1971 and 1972 (before income tax). The second chart showed industry revenues would increase moderately as prices rose from $40 per ton to $90, while government revenues increased substantially. The third chart showed that with projected sales and current prices, gross industry revenue after provincial taxes would be $324.5 million. Provincial revenues from existing levies would be $22.5 million while the reserve tax would add another $87 million, bringing total provincial take to over $109 million or 25.2% of gross revenue.[7]

Cowley also reiterated the government's position on the need for industry expansion and the government's interest in playing an active role in the industry. The following day, CPPA President Randolph expressed his disappointment with the government announcement and underlined the essentials of the July 17 brief.[8]

The introduction of the potash reserve tax was a key development in the ongoing saga of government-industry relations. It coincided with a period of rapidly escalating product prices that promised to be a boon for the industry and was in sharp contrast with the gloomy outlook a short time previously. This initiative occurred not long after the government's dramatic action to capture windfall gains from the oil industry. Both Saskatchewan and Alberta had passed legislation resulting in a substantial portion of the increase in oil and gas prices going to provincial treasuries. Now the same thing was happening with potash. The potash industry had difficulty coping with developments. Most of the industry had a mindset that saw government as a nuisance at best and something to be tolerated. The idea that a government wanted a piece of the action was unthinkable except for the European-owned firm, Alwinsal. The thought of letting government take a peek at their financial statements was virtually beyond reality. They did not have the same experience and outlook as the oil and uranium industries, which by then had no difficulty with such requirements.[9]

Correspondence and presentations from the industry, individually and jointly, were obviously prepared with care and showed considerable sophistication and deference up to a point, but on some major issues, they demonstrated little understanding in coping effectively. For example, their suggestion that the government hold off on any new taxes until difficulties with the federal government had been cleared up was simply not realistic. This would leave the province a prisoner of both the industry and the federal government. (It is not known how much pressure the industry put on the federal government to change its position.)

Given the government's objectives, it was inevitable that there would be a clash between industry and government. Different responses at certain junctures may have helped ease some difficulties, but given the government's objectives, the industry's outlook, and earlier locked-in arrangements, it would have been virtually impossible to avoid the conflict.

The formulation of a tax to increase government revenues was hampered by long-standing royalty commitments with the industry, problems with the pro-rationing fee, and limited information and resources for delving into a relatively unexplored area. The potash reserve tax was the first plan developed that might work and provide substantial revenue. The producers identified a number of conceptual problems that had some validity as determined later. The failure of the industry to supply financial statements made it virtually impossible to develop a plan that took account of widely varying corporate situations and that could be implemented equitably while ensuring the achievement of government objectives.

Some years later, Professor David L. Anderson analyzed the difficulties with the reserve tax as it was structured in a study for the Centre for Resource Studies at Queen's University, Kingston.[10] The study noted that the tax was introduced as a property tax but by nature was a type of profits tax. Problems were pointed out with the mechanics of the tax, although it had a number of advantages from the government's point of view. It was concluded that tax rates were extremely high, especially with federal non-deductibility, and analysis of its impact conflicted with the stated desire for expansion. Anderson noted that after further study and negotiations an acceptable tax plan was developed and implemented. It was based on "the principle of economic rent extraction." He called for further study of economic rent, rates of return, incentives for investment, and efficient corporate performance. Based on the sequence of events that occurred, Anderson also identified policy implications to be considered for the future:

1.  meaningful industry-government negotiations require frank disclosure of the relevant facts, and of the intentions of all parties;

2.  provincial governments must exercise discretion and responsibility in utilizing their power;

3.  tax agreements with unrealistically low royalties or mining taxes may lead to nationalization proceedings;

4.  rate-of-return schemes of taxation offer a number of advantages for resource taxation, provided they are project specific.[11]

Anderson's study was carried out after the potash reserve tax had been replaced with a new tax plan that applied to all potash firms including the crown-owned Potash Corporation of Saskatchewan, which by that time was the leading potash producer in the province after having acquired a number of mines. The directors of the crown-owned firm, including myself, found ourselves in an interesting position in that we had an interest in lower tax payments to the provincial treasury so it would show higher profits (surpluses) in our operations. In the case of the crown-owned firm, the province would, of course, be the eventual beneficiary of those funds regardless of what route was utilized.

The Anderson article addressed the management of affairs where the industry is essentially privately owned. The question of whether the industry is best owned publicly or privately was not addressed.

# CHAPTER 8

## A Crisis Looms

Tensions grew after the potash reserve tax was implemented. Administrative procedures and arrangements had to be developed, and not having company financial statements made it more difficult to ensure tax objectives were met. In hindsight, in my view, it is apparent now that more than the financial statements by themselves was required to produce a fully satisfactory plan. The government made it clear, repeatedly, that it was prepared to make changes if a review of financial information made it advisable. As things stood, the industry was expected to pay its taxes. The industry, on the other hand, felt that its submissions had been ignored, that consultations had been inadequate, and that the tax was much too high.

The companies made their first payments on the due date, December 20, 1974, but under protest. The companies then had to decide what to do next. The then chief executive officer of IMC, Richard Lenon, said many years later, "They [the companies] thought we could negotiate."[1] The then manager of the Saskatchewan Mining Association, Ralph Cheesman, spoke in the same tone: "… they still felt there was room for negotiation … they did not declare war at this stage."[2] A cynical view would suggest their idea of negotiations might have been to persuade the government to return to old arrangements as nearly as possible.

There was one item, though, on which all of the companies except one drew the line. That was on government participation in industry expansion. There was no way that could be tolerated. Richard Lenon of IMC said to me, "That would have been rejected out of hand."[3] They may have had a variety of reasons for their stance, but it was evident that position was part of their strategy for withholding expansion, and that was their biggest bargaining weapon. Ralph Cheesman discussed the exception: "... Central Canada actually came to the government and offered the joint venture. They acted again independently of the other companies but they came and said okay, we're willing, we'll sit down and talk about a joint venture."[4] I learned of this matter from Department of Mineral Resources officials soon after I went to work for the government in December 1972. The department advised against pursuing this opportunity because in its view that mine, located at Colonsay, was at more risk of flooding than all other mines. I had no reason to question that assessment at the time as they were the experts. They may have been right, but looking at it now, more than 40 years later, the mine, now owned by Mosaic, is still in operation in 2012 without having had any catastrophes, while some other mines have experienced severe flooding.

If things weren't difficult enough, a federal budget introduced on November 18, 1974, added more problems. The removal of provincial royalties and other payments as deductions from taxable income was first introduced on May 6 and was left intact. A minority federal Liberal government was defeated in Parliament earlier, but now it was re-elected with a clear majority. These federal measures had serious financial consequences for potash producers, and for the provincial government they constituted a serious invasion of provincial areas of jurisdiction. The potash industry reacted by announcing $200 million in expansion plans were being deferred. (They had not yet been announced.)

The Saskatchewan government continued to emphasize that it was prepared to review the potash reserve tax as soon as companies submitted financial statements so the impact on individual companies could be assessed adequately. Several steps were taken to extend a hand to the industry, the first being amending regulations to protect the confidentiality of financial information provided. Then Mineral Resources Minister Cowley announced on December 30, 1974, that legislation would be amended to ensure that royalties and other provincial levies would remain deductible from provincial taxable income. The potash industry in early 1975 drew attention to a problem on the non-deductibility provision in tax law. In some cases, a price increase could produce more than the same amount of additional federal and provincial levies. The province responded by ensuring that an increase in price did not result in total federal and provincial taxes increasing by more than 90% of the increase in profits.[5]

In late January 1975, another potential problem emerged. A news report indicated that a US federal grand jury was investigating the potash industry for possible anti-trust violations. It was reported that one or more potash companies had been ordered to appear before a grand jury in Chicago on February 18 with documents in hand.[6] In response to an inquiry, the Canadian embassy in Washington confirmed that a federal grand jury in Chicago had been investigating price-fixing by US companies but went on to add:

> No Canadian-owned companies are under investigation, although United States and possibly other foreign-owned companies with operations in Canada are being considered. The central question at issue appears to be whether companies operating in the United States conspired illegally to fix the price of potash, using the Saskatchewan government-controlled price as a base; neither the actions of the Saskatchewan government nor the operations in Canada of any company are in question in the investigation.[7]

While this development was not of direct concern to the Government of Saskatchewan, it was of great concern to potash companies with operations in the United States as well as Canada. Kalium and its parent, PPG, had no worry, though, as they declined to be involved in planning pro-rationing.

The Saskatchewan government created a new crown corporation on February 5, 1975, Potash Corporation of Saskatchewan, to provide an instrument to manage any participation in the industry that might flow from the October 1974 policy. This removed all doubts the industry may have had that the government meant business. I was appointed to the board of directors along with several other senior government officials.

Senior potash company executives continued to voice their objections to the potash reserve tax and appealed for change. On February 10, 1975, the Canadian Potash Producers Association presented another brief to the government. As an alternative, they proposed, again, a tax on profits, allowing no more than 50% of profits in total taxes by the two levels of government.[8] Subsequently industry officials met with the premier and the minister of mineral resources. Much of the discussion centred around the question of a fair rate of return but there was disagreement about the numbers. It was agreed to set up a joint committee to resolve that issue.

The basic differences between government and industry still remained. The industry wanted a profits tax with a ceiling, while the premier preferred the reserve tax but was willing to consider changes.[9] Essentially, the industry view was that the tax burden was too high, the tax was too complex, and inequities and mechanical difficulties made it inappropriate. The province countered with a roster of reasons why it preferred the reserve tax over a profits tax. It argued it is too easy to evade a profits tax because the province has no control over depletion as well as many cost items. Transfer pricing, and many other techniques used to evade a profits tax, was another concern. Lump-sum taxation encourages economic efficiency in an industry with a significant degree of economic power. An objective is to reduce the influence of tax measures on marginal production decisions. It was also pointed out that incentives for greater efficiency are built into the reserve tax formula. The objective of the reserve tax is to allow producers a reasonable rate of return and to capture a significant portion of the economic rent or windfall gains resulting from much higher prices in recent years. Finally, it was noted the reserve tax varies directly with market price conditions, and the reserve tax is easier to administer than a profits tax.[10]

There were no informal exploratory conversations between government and industry such as adversaries having lunch together or going for a beer after work. Hovering over things was a provincial election expected shortly. A joint committee meeting was held on May 2, 1975, preceded by preparatory activities. Some changes had been made in response to industry requests, but the industry reaffirmed its opposition to the tax in principle, and alterations would not change that position. They were not going to file financial statements and bluntly said they did not trust the government, fearing it would tax them to the limit and eventually drive them out of business. Tentative plans were made for another meeting, but it never occurred.[11]

To add to the turmoil, Mr. Justice Disbery of the Court of Queen's Bench of Saskatchewan handed down a decision on May 6, 1975, that the Saskatchewan pro-rationing regulations were ultra vires and awarded the plaintiff $1.5 million in damages. The case had been launched in December 1972 as the first step in fighting the pro-rationing plan. The Saskatchewan government filed an appeal immediately. Federal intervention as a co-plaintiff had compounded tensions.

Some 30 years later, former premier Allan Blakeney was still indignant about federal government actions on this issue. He commented:

> It is ... believed by me and ... others that John Turner [federal justice minister in 1969] was fully informed ... when pro-rationing was set up and that they were raising no objections with Ross Thatcher. Then when we are continuing the Ross Thatcher policy under an NDP government, it somehow gets to be unconstitutional and the same Department of Justice in Ottawa decides that they are going to intervene to declare unconstitutional that which John Turner, the minister of justice, said was okay under a Liberal government.
>
> ... I think [it is] unprecedented up to today for the federal government, in a constitutional case between a resource company and a province, to intervene as a co-plaintiff. They have intervened as an intervener lots of times to simply defend the constitution. That is fair game but to intervene to defend the interest of Noranda and to call evidence if Noranda somehow doesn't know how to conduct a case. This struck me as belligerent ... my views were not softened by the fact that the then minister of justice was a Saskatchewan minister, Otto Lang, whom I think did not share the philosophical view of our government. ... this is no place for the minister of justice in Canada to carry on his opposition to our particular political views through making the Government of Canada co-plaintiff.[12]

On June 11, 1975, a provincial election in Saskatchewan returned the incumbent New Democratic Party to power. Nine days later, on June 20, all of the potash producers, except Central Canada Potash, launched a joint action against the Government of Saskatchewan asking the courts to declare the potash reserve tax ultra vires. Cliff Kelly, then plant manager at Kalium Chemical, said the companies held off filing the action until after the election because they wanted to avoid any impression that they were trying to influence the outcome of the election.[13]

Most of the tax installment due on June 20 was not paid. One company was already in arrears. Most producers had stopped paying the pro-rationing fee, which was due monthly. They had also stopped sending in their monthly production and disposition reports.[14]

Clearly, they were challenging the government on all fronts. Some of their actions were intolerable in a democratically ordered society. The fact that the statements of claim required for the court action were complex, taking considerable time for preparation, indicates that a course of action was determined some time previously. The government knew it would have to determine a firm course of action carefully.

Allan Blakeney said he probably did not anticipate the host of legal issues that developed. He also cast events in the context of the provincial election held at that time:

> I tended to believe that we would get a negotiated deal with the potash industry. … they became very hard to get along with … this is a huge overstepping the bounds in a battle. And I said, but oh well they're just wanting to show that they're angry and in a fighting mood and that they are doing this in order to ratchet up the dispute prior to an election that we might or might not win …
>
> It was widely known that we would have an election in June of 1975. … They would just wait us out. And they did, and I didn't get too excited … let's relax on this. Just keep expressing our indignation but don't ratchet it up any more until after the election and then they'll know they have to deal with us for the next four years if we're elected. And they'll come and they'll sort this out. I really confidently expected that.
>
> After the election … they became more aggressive by joining in more legal action. So a bunch of the companies which had urged me and importuned me to institute flat pro-rationing then joined the action of the Central Canada Potash in opposition to pro-ration as a whole. I said, my, oh my, this is a bit

much and I did exactly as you wanted and now you are suing me for it. ... I reached the conclusion that the potash industry was taking us on. That they were not going to negotiate some sort of a settlement ...[15]

Richard Lenon was blunt in explaining why the industry changed its position: "you couldn't just let it go like it was in the amounts that were involved potentially ..."[16] He pointed to anti-trust concerns as an underlying factor. He described the US Department of Justice investigations that started in 1975, said they would take paper away by the truckload, and emphasized this was a major concern for the industry. The impact of the anti-trust investigation was not fully appreciated in Saskatchewan at that time, though it was being monitored.

A confrontation was occurring. Both sides were entrenched and something had to happen. Allan Blakeney described the impact on his outlook and his view of what was taking place: "... it was not until the potash industry ... declared war on the government after the 1975 election. ... I felt that once the 1975 election was over that they would simply say, no, we have to make peace now, let's get on with this. But not a bit of this. They carried on. ... This caused me to do a real turn in my thinking after June of 1975."[17] He went on to explain that when production went up from 50% of capacity to 90%, profits would go up, and the province wanted more. Some time between the 1975 election and August, he concluded, "I think these people are not going to negotiate."

It was obvious to people interested in potash that an impasse was developing. I maintained my ongoing involvement in potash affairs, including attending meetings, monitoring developments and, now, working on the newly formed crown corporation, Potash Corporation of Saskatchewan. After a holiday in early August, I reviewed affairs when back at work and sent a memorandum to the new minister of mineral resources, Hon. Ed Whelan. I outlined the impasse that was emerging and suggested some overarching measure may be required to change the situation. I noted my availability to assist in whatever course of action the government may want to pursue.

David Dombowsky had a unique perspective based on the extensive contact he had with the potash industry while president of crown-owned Potash Corporation of Saskatchewan. The industry in his view considered Saskatchewan as worse than a Third World country. They could not brook a province, here in the North American market economy, doing what it was. They thought they had to draw a line in the sand. If it happened in Africa or South America, that was different. But they weren't going to allow it to happen in Canada. The industry, he thought, expected the government would back down in the face of an onslaught. He didn't think they believed in their wildest imagination that the province would take more drastic steps.

Richard Lenon of IMC voiced a similar underlying tone. He looked on Canadian and American people as "brothers" and said, "... some day we'll sit down and settle the thing."[18] After having delayed payments earlier, as of September 30, 1975, IMC had paid all of its potash reserve tax, in contrast to some other companies, and was up to date on all other matters except for a lag on the pro-rationing fee.

The federal government kept the pot boiling when it brought down another budget on June 23, 1975, that offered no relief to either the companies or the province on resource taxation. A *Financial Post* article suggested some softening of positions as a result:

> John Lorne Carpenter, new President of the Canadian Potash Producers Association, welcomes the promise of Saskatchewan Premier Allan Blakeney to relieve the tax burden on the province's resource producers.
>
> Blakeney made the statement after Ottawa's June 23 budget was brought down. While saying that relief from the combined burden of federal and provincial taxes still should come through federal tax changes, Blakeney added: "There comes a time when you have to address yourself to the realities, as we now are."
>
> This could portend some benefit for the potash mines from the provincial side. As it is, there was next to nothing for them in the federal budget.[19]

Statements such as Blakeney made would have enabled skilled negotiators to open a dialogue. That did not occur. A review of events and developments over time also suggests that the situation cried out for a skilled mediator. That may still not have produced a settlement. The government was determined to increase its share of returns from the resource to much higher levels and had also decided it was going to participate in the industry. The industry was not prepared to have the government as a partner and still wanted to keep the bulk of profits in this very lucrative industry. Concessions from both were essential.

Ralph Cheesman, former manager of the Saskatchewan Mining Association, observed that the companies regarded their stances as "bargaining chips" or "bargaining tools." When private companies regard measures that flout the law as "bargaining chips" or "bargaining tools," there is a fundamental flaw in their thinking. It means they consider themselves on a par with government and that rules that apply to everyone else don't apply to them. The government could not ignore the actions of the companies unless it was to capitulate. The companies stopped expansion plans and had a right to do so. They could not cease production because they had too much money invested and fixed costs were relatively high. A standoff had developed.

# CHAPTER 9
## The Decision—Public Ownership

*"Where the terms for an agreement for sale can be reached between my government and a selected potash company, it will not be necessary to invoke the legislation. Where such an agreement cannot be reached, however, the Legislation will enable my government to expropriate the Saskatchewan assets of that company."*—(Excerpt from the Speech from the Throne read by Lieutenant-Governor George Porteous opening a session of the Saskatchewan Legislature, November 12, 1975)

The world now knew what the Saskatchewan government was going to do about the potash impasse. Opposition Liberal members of the Legislature literally gasped when they heard these words. Many years later, David Dombowsky, who was appointed to manage the crown initiative in potash, still chortled about some of the little vignettes that occurred.

Dave Steuart was the leader of the Liberal party. He was a small, feisty man and a mean scrapper in debates or encounters, and usually won. The only person who could best him was former premier Woodrow Lloyd, who would flatten him by saying in debate, "If the sawdust Caesar from Prince Albert will just sit back and let his feet dangle, I'll get on with my speech." Steuart was deputy premier and provincial treasurer in the Thatcher Liberal government in 1971. His deputy minister was David Dombowsky, and they had had a good relationship. Now Dombowsky in his new role wanted to see the drama about to unfold and seated himself in the legislative gallery where he had a good view of

Opposition members, and they saw him. When Porteous made his dramatic announcement, Steuart looked up at Dombowsky and mouthed the words, "you son of a bitch." Later, Steuart told him the Liberals had heard rumours but they never dreamed the NDP would actually do it.

A rapid succession of events had led to this landmark development. Legal actions taken by the potash industry, if successful, would have effectively blocked all initiatives taken by the government. The industry said it would like to negotiate, but it appeared it would accept very little change. The government, on the other hand, was prepared to negotiate only if financial statements were submitted, and it would not back down on the principle of the potash reserve tax.

The government faced serious difficulties because of the court decision striking down pro-rationing, and other pending cases had the potential for even more. Open flouting of the law by producers was intolerable for any government. The choice was clear—either the government had to surrender to the industry or it would have to find some overarching course of action that transcended the industry blockade.

The industry position was that they had invested large sums of money in developing the mines. This was done at considerable risk, including the distinct possibility that the investment made in any one of the mines could have been completely lost as, in fact, occurred at the first mine at Unity. It also maintained that the deals made with government should be honoured. Historically, they got their way with governments and were not used to the idea of governments, particularly those in North America, including Canada, demanding a significantly higher return from resources. Allan Blakeney summed up where the industry was: "But the potash people were not agreeing with our fundamental concept, that as the price and value of this resource went up, the amount of taxes we got had to go up."

As the argument continued, I looked into the question of what assistance the industry received, directly and indirectly, from government or other public sources. The list was impressive. A considerable amount of money had been invested by government and other public bodies in the infrastructure and other activities associated with potash development. My list is in the records:

## Summary—Government Assistance to the Potash Industry

1.   Some of the services provided to the potash industry by the Department of Mineral Resources include:
    – geological reports and other technical information;
    – advanced work on rock mechanics in potash mines;
    – introduction and administration of the pro-rationing program;
    – collection of information and publication of reports on potash production and sales;
    – encouraged and assisted in the formation of Canpotex.

2.   The Saskatchewan Research Council is involved in research in a number of areas related to potash.

3.   Government agencies assisted potash companies in dealing with freight rate problems.

4.   The province is active in mine pollution control and mine safety while the University of Saskatchewan is conducting respiratory studies on potash miners.

5.   The Government of Saskatchewan upgraded the road from the IMC mine to the U.S. border (140 miles) in order to allow potash to be hauled by truck. Other roads have been built near potash mines to facilitate development.

6.   Special grant, loans and other assistance had been provided to communities affected by potash developments. [schools in particular]

7.   Special assistance was provided to ensure that a number of mines had adequate water supplies.

8.   In summary, the province has been ready and willing to assist the potash industry in any way it could ever since the industry came into the province.[2]

Potash got special attention in the 1975 provincial election. The NDP election platform stated, "New Democrats will continue to act to see that Saskatchewan people get the greatest possible benefits from our resources. ... This may well involve new approaches to public ownership, to joint ventures between the government and private enterprise, and to resource royalties and taxation. ... Speed up direct government participation in exploration for and development of potash ..."[3]

While the direction of policy was clear, the platform did not identify specific plans. Certainly, there was no hint that drastic measures such as expropriation were going to be pursued. Nevertheless, it was obvious that the NDP, if elected again, had declared both its intent and its willingness to take more aggressive action in order to achieve its goals.

Few were surprised when the NDP government was re-elected in June 1975. The economy had improved greatly, the weather was good, and everybody was busy with their lives, while many planned for their summer holidays. It was general knowledge that there were problems between the potash industry and the government, but most people were not that worried. That began to change, though, when the industry suddenly stepped up pressure on the government by refusing to pay its taxes, initiating legal action to strike down the reserve tax, refusing to expand, et cetera. Blakeney reviewed the state of affairs in late June from the government's perspective:

> But my surprise after the 1975 election, that there were no overtures of any kind and that our own overtures were more or less rebuffed, that indicated that this was a point of no return. That we were now ratcheting it up. That we had to take more vigorous action. ... And we then were playing our next card. When did government contemplate nationalization legislation? Some time in July or August. ... I remember John Messer saying while he was for it he was kind of surprised that his colleagues were for it ...[4] [Messer was known as one of the more aggressive cabinet ministers.]

Blakeney described how far the government thought of going, its options, and the basic features of its conflict with the industry. He emphasized that at no time until mid-1975 was nationalization contemplated. Until then, they thought of purchasing assets or taking part in expansions. One choice was to build a new mine, a potential one having been identified and studied at Bredenbury. When it was apparent the industry wasn't going to deal with the government, it was concluded, "we had to engage them fairly seriously." It had been decided much more money should go to the public purse, so if that couldn't be done through taxation then it could be done through ownership.[5]

An initial decision was made in early September 1975 to pursue the public ownership option. Planning was to proceed, with the final decision left open for later. Blakeney explained, "… I saw no resolution of the impasse with the potash companies. … their position was in part, in a major part, a consequence of the 1974 federal government budget. … [that] put the potash companies in a bind. The potash companies expected us, the Government of Saskatchewan, to unravel the bind and to fight their battle. … I felt this was not the role of the Government of Saskatchewan. …"[6]

I interviewed five other former cabinet ministers[7] at the time to get their perspective. All confirmed their resolve to proceed with the decision with much the same reasoning as Blakeney, but Gordon MacMurchy added, "in terms of the opportunity to get into the potash business, which attracted me not only from the point of view of the old CCF philosophy that's within me but from the point of view of being in a very profitable venture … we didn't sell the policy on the fight with the federal government, the fight with the potash industry. In the final analysis we sold the policy on the benefits to the province."[8] MacMurchy was a lean, lanky, "no nonsense" kind of man with a big square jaw who grew up as a farm boy, took over the farm, and was a local legend for his hockey prowess. If a player got into a corner with Gordon, chances were he did not come out the winner. He had a deep, rich voice that carried a ring of authority with it. He became president of the NDP party organization prior to 1971 and in Cabinet was a key rural spokesman.

Roy Romanow, who had given Blakeney a close run for party leadership and later was premier of Saskatchewan, summed up the situation by saying, "The government's choice was very stark. You could acquiesce to the industry or you took the position that you are the democratically elected institution in our society authorized by the people to make the appropriate decision."[9]

In a letter to me in 2004, Allan Blakeney placed the government's decision to proceed with public ownership in another dimension:

... the moves we made in the potash industry were meant not only to assist in our dealing with the potash industry but to be instructive for other people involved in resource issues, notably the oil industry, the uranium industry and particularly the federal government. In many ways the move was meant to thwart the federal government as much as to resolve issues with the potash industry. Without the Turner budget I do not think the public ownership of potash would have occurred. The federal government was indicating by their use of the corporate taxation device that they were willing to use unorthodox methods to get a share of rising resource values. By using public ownership we were indicating that we were willing to use unorthodox methods to keep our share of rising resource values.[10]

He expanded on those comments later: "we were almost equally angry or perhaps more than equally angry at the federal government for imposing the same rules not only on potash companies but on oil and gas companies. Then it was clear that we were in a three-way conflict involving the federal government and the potash industry. ... this was a declaration of war against the producing provinces ... actions of the federal government [were] hostile ... I certainly in my mind was really turning to what weapons we had in this war that we hadn't started but we were certainly in."[11]

Cabinet debated and mulled over the issue for the most part of two months. They thought about more than the specific potash issues and federal government actions. Roy Romanow discussed some of the political implications that came up:

... we had next door in Alberta a province which was building up an entirely different model of economic development with the consequent social and other values. The Conservative government of Peter Lougheed was basing its approach on a free enterprise model, full stop, period. We were supposed to be social democrats or democratic socialists who believed in a mixed economy of which the crown corporations played an important role and that if we didn't as part of this, ... expanding it to areas like Saskatchewan Mining Development Corporation, SMDC, or Sask Oil, ... if we didn't do this that in the march of history the position of social democracy would be eroded away by the Lougheed initiatives, the booming economy ...[12]

Elwood Cowley was the minister delegated to oversee the potash initiative. He was a "happy-go-lucky" type of person but had a very keen analytical mind. One reason for his demeanour may have been that his father won a $100,000 Irish Sweepstakes ticket in 1937 in the depths of the drought-depression, relieving the family of the grinding burdens facing most families then. This would be worth many more times in terms of present day dollars. He explained how Cabinet would have looked at the politics of the situation while decisions were being made during summer 1975:

> ... I think it had to do with two things. One, the industry's actions up to and including the election, and the other was the results of the election which, while we won a comfortable majority, were very disappointing for the government. We'd done all these wonderful things we thought and done them all reasonably well, we thought, with a few little problems. And I think we got the lowest percentage of the popular vote since 1938 and we were able to get re-elected by virtue of a wonderful three-way split ... we'd been, we thought, very pragmatic. We had curtailed some things we might have liked to have done because we didn't think they were acceptable, etc. and lo and behold, folks didn't seem to like what we'd done anyway all that well. And, so it's where do we go from here and I think that, as much as anything, hardened the battle lines from our per-spective. After the '75 election [it was], "Okay! You guys want a fight!" If we're going to spend this next term doing what we did the last term, it didn't seem to be all that successful so let's do some things that will really make a difference and let's get in there and go to it. That's an oversimplification but I think there was a real sense of that emerged around the Cabinet table.[13]

Quite surprisingly, there was virtually no speculation or reports in the media that the government might be considering any type of far-reaching action. A keen observer would have discerned that some-thing major had to occur. If anything, one would expect reporters to

be snooping around trying to find out what was going on. While preparatory efforts were carefully camouflaged, it was impossible to hide
everything. If they had seen lights on and curtains drawn in a basement
room on a Sunday evening in the Legislative Building, they would have
known something was up and would have pursued it. A CBC reporter
in Regina, Bob Allison was an energetic, enterprising reporter. But he
was transferred to Halifax in summer 1975. Had he been there, I think
he would have smoked something out. As it turned out, the reporters
and the media were asleep at the switch.

Blakeney also consulted a number of informed Canadians elsewhere
whose advice he valued. One former Saskatchewan government official,
later a senior official in Ottawa, related to me in conversation that Blakeney asked him to set up a meeting with Maurice Strong, former president of the Canadian International Development Agency and then a
senior United Nations official. The meeting took place in the majestic
and august Metropolitan Club in New York. Over dinner, Blakeney
reviewed the sequence of events in Saskatchewan and outlined some of
the options the government might pursue without making mention of
the ultimate step. Finally, Maurice Strong said, "Why don't you say it?
Nationalize them!"[14]

Events kept rolling along while the government considered its course
of action. On August 7, 1975, the new minister of mineral resources,
Ed Whelan, sent letters to the producers demanding payment of the
reserve tax. These were followed by another letter demanding payment
of the pro-rationing fee. His actions were publicized, and he revealed
a number of steps the government could take. Within days, the companies replied, remitting payments but requesting assurances that the
monies would be returned to the companies if their court challenge
was successful. Whelan replied it would not be in the public interest
to respond to their request since the matter was before the courts. The
companies then resorted to the courts to get assurances but encountered difficulties.[15]

Third-quarter payments were remitted in late September. By September 30, $83 million of the almost $95.5 million payable to that time
had been paid. Almost $8 million of the outstanding was owed by
Central Canada Potash, who claimed cash flow problems. Three others
owed about $1 million each, three had paid in full, while the remaining
five accounted for the other $1.5 million, some of which may be due to

differences in making calculations. The companies also owed $3,750,000 in pro-rationing fees. One company, Alwinsal, was fully paid, another had paid to May, while the rest had not remitted payments since March or April. Royalties were fully paid, but there was a mixed picture concerning reports required by the Department of Mineral Resources.

On October 2, 1975, all producers except Central Canada Potash and Alwinsal commenced a new court action to have the pro-ration fee and its regulations declared ultra vires. While this action contradicted their previous positions, R. A. Lenon said it was done as part of the bargaining process. Two companies, Central Canada Potash and Alwinsal, submitted their financial statements, one in late August and the other in mid-October. But the impasse still continued. No negotiations were under way and contacts were minimal.

As soon as Cabinet had made its decision, a task force was assembled that would report to a Cabinet committee chaired by Elwood Cowley. It was headed by David Dombowsky, who was already president of the Potash Corporation of Saskatchewan. It included a number of senior civil servants possessing a variety of skills and one external lawyer, John Beke, a Regina lawyer with considerable corporate experience. Others included Don Ching, a lawyer with government and corporate experience; Garry Beatty, deputy minister of finance, who was to work on financing; Ken Lysyk, Deputy Attorney General, who was in charge of preparing legislation; Roy Lloyd, head of the Budget Bureau, who dealt with establishing an evaluation process; myself, who headed a section in the planning and research office of Executive Council and studied marketing; Bruce Lawson, the premier's press secretary, who addressed public relations and publicity; and Doug Karvonen, head of the potash division in Mineral Resources, who worked on both evaluation and marketing. In retrospect, it was a pretty formidable crew.

We had to work in utmost secrecy and could tell no one unless authorized. Next, we had to find a place to work and ensure the secrecy demanded of us. We found room 43, a self-enclosed vacant suite of offices in the basement of the Legislative Building across the hall from Cowley's office. Some renovations had just been made for new occupants. There was no trouble telling the Department of Public Works to take down their changes because the suite was needed for other requirements. The only problem was this could start the rumour mill rolling since potash was in the news. So an elaborate cover story was created. Public Works officials were told in a very "confidential" sort of way that it had been learned the federal government was intending to introduce wage and price controls and the province needed to prepare for it. I was the one who came up with the idea. Why did I think of it?[16]

A key issue in the 1974 federal election had been a federal Conservative proposal for wage and price controls. This was opposed by the Liberal government. The Liberals won the election, but I was defeated by the Conservatives in my constituency. On election night, my wife and I had just returned home. I took off my coat, tie, and shoes and sat down in my favourite chair to recover from having had the s—t knocked out of me, when the doorbell rang. It was our neighbours across the street. He was president of the Conservative constituency association that defeated me. Their words when the door opened were, "We'd rather have you as neighbours." We socialized with them and other neighbours regularly. One night, later, over a beer, he said to me, "It's only a matter of time until the Liberals will have to bring in wage and price controls." Those words stuck with me and came to mind when we were looking for a cover story. In fact, that is what the Liberals did do later.

Each of us had a key to the doors of the Legislative Building so we didn't have to sign in at the front door after hours or deal with commissionaires, and we could go at any time of the day or night. There was no nameplate on the door of our suite, few people knew the telephone number, we did not enter or leave as a group, we checked to see if anyone was in the corridor when we entered, we did not leave papers on our desks for cleaners to see, and we did not eat together in the cafeteria.

Each maintained his own office and appeared there regularly. But room 43—it became known as "the bunker room"—is where we were really working. Not everything could be hidden though. One ministerial assistant noticed that his boss regularly wrote "Room 43" in his desk diary. One time when I was in a corridor, another civil servant pointed at me and said to a colleague, "There's someone who knows what's going on!" One day I was in my regular office when my director stormed in and said, "John, I know potash is important and I know $500 million is a lot of money (a reference to a proposal under study for a new PCS mine) but does everybody have to be working on potash?" Then he recited a litany of attempts to contact people but how he kept being told, "He's working on potash." I gave some excuse. As soon as he left I called the premier. "Allan, re the project I'm working on now." "Right."

"A problem! Gerry Gartner came storming into my office today," and I described what had occurred, but that we were instructed to tell no one unless authorized, so I could say nothing. He replied, "I have to see Gerry about some other matters so I will talk to him." Next morning, I was in Gerry's office. When we were alone, he said, "The premier just gave me a crash course on potash."

Activities in the bunker room were highly organized as well as feverish. Special assistance was obtained as necessary. A Toronto law firm, Davies, Ward and Beck, assisted in drafting legislation when it was recognized that international law required special attention. I made a trip to London, England, to consult a world-class potash intelligence firm, the British Sulphur Corporation, on the question of whether marketing should be managed as a joint venture or independently. Garry Beatty, deputy minister of finance, investigated financing issues that should be anticipated. He described his concerns:

> Is it conceivable that the US capital market would close to us just at a time when we needed it although we ... had substantial revenues in the Heritage Fund. ... Saskatchewan had never done an issue in the US capital market. We'd always done private placements up until that time so I had to prepare to get Saskatchewan up and able to do a public issue because we certainly wanted the U.S. capital market, the public market. ... you need a very extensive prospectus. ... you'd seen how the US government behaved in relation to certain other governments that wanted to do things. ... what if the US capital market decides it doesn't want to loan any money to this province. ... and the investment bankers on Wall Street are very well-informed people. They know what's going on in all parts of the world.[17]

The premier and key cabinet ministers were involved in meetings regularly as activities were pursued day and night, including a number of Sunday evening meetings. By the end of October and the early days of November, sufficient progress had been made in developing a plan and resolving key issues so that a final decision could be made in time for the opening of the Legislature.

Jack Kinzel, a superb writer who was one of the premier's staff and secretary to the Cabinet Potash Committee, described what he considered a key moment in making the final decision. He had prepared a draft of the Speech from the Throne opening the Legislature. He gave particular attention to the section on potash. He took it to the premier and said, "Do I leave it in?" The premier thought for a few minutes and replied, "Yes." The decision having been made, the premier's press officer, Bruce Lawson, called nationally known news media reporters and invited them to be in Regina on November 12 for a "national story." They knew him well enough to be there.

The government announced its new potash policy on November 12, 1975, in the Speech from the Throne read by the Lieutenant-Governor in opening the first session of the Saskatchewan Legislature after the 1975 election. In the section of the speech dealing with potash, there was first a litany of events on government-industry relations, followed by identification of the options and confirmation that the government intended to get into the potash business. All of this was a lead up to the dramatic moment spelled out at the beginning of this chapter.

Most of the potash industry was shocked and surprised by the announcement. Cliff Kelly, then plant manager at Kalium, responded with a firm "Yes" when asked if the announcement was a surprise to the industry.[18] Ralph Cheesman answered the same question by saying: "Yes, it was a surprise and for a while they were just stunned. The first person I think to respond with comment was Peter Jack [Manager, Potash Company of America]. Who really, he responded in a very hurt, I mean, how can they do this to us, we've been trying to discuss things, we've been trying to work together and now they do this to us. It was a rather plaintive response."[19] Richard Lenon of IMC said he was not surprised by the announcement.[20] This was consistent with his concerns and perceptions since 1971 (see Chapter 4), plus his activities in governmental and diplomatic circles to protect corporate interests.

These reactions of industry personnel to the government's announcement of its momentous decision reveal two essential points. The comments by Peter Jack suggest that there were some in the industry who just did not understand that the government could and would introduce such far-reaching changes. The comment by Lenon, together with other IMC actions, indicates that the company looked on itself largely as on a par with government and conducted itself accordingly. Both of these attitudes help to explain the difficult relations that had developed.

On the other hand, it took the government some time to develop its policies on resource development and management as well as its capability to implement them effectively. Public opinion had to be taken into account as well. Saskatchewan was settled originally mostly by rural people who had a conservative outlook on life, and while new and innovative things were done later based on new ideas, old attitudes were still there and played a significant role. The incredibly difficult times encountered by many people made them look for better ways of coping with problems. Co-operatives, a wide variety of community initiatives, and then government action laid the foundation for what was described as the "Saskatchewan spirit." The population became relatively well informed on a wide variety of issues. Allan Blakeney once commented that it was not at all unusual for a Saskatchewan farmer to hook his thumbs in his overall suspenders and give his view on the constitution. In Regina, in the 1930s, a group of federal civil servants, prohibited from being politically active at that time, organized themselves to assess the state of affairs, propose solutions, and print publications under the pseudonym of Watt Hugh McCallum, a takeoff on a commonly used phrase, "Whatcha m'callum." These things laid the foundation for a more radical approach to public affairs and the organization of society.

The government's 1975 decision on potash was a striking example of this new approach. It was a watershed event that was unprecedented and would not have been generally predicted or even dreamed of until it occurred. It was not the government's intention at the outset and went much beyond the tone of the 1971 NDP election platform. Some had no difficulty with the move. The *Leader-Post* published a picture at the time of a Kamsack, Saskatchewan, farmer in his work clothes and a head covering looking like a bowler hat pulled down to his ears so that they stuck out. He was quoted saying, "NDP government is good for me. Nationalize the whole god damn works!"

On a more sophisticated level, a government publication printed after the 1975 potash decision answered the question, "Why is Saskatchewan Acquiring Control of its Potash Industry?" by saying:

1. To guarantee a fair and lasting return to the people of Saskatchewan from their resource;

2.  To guarantee orderly expansion of the industry so Saskatchewan can keep up with growing world demand and maintain its position as a leading world supplier of potash.[21]

Another question on the reasons for public ownership was answered by saying: "Attempts to achieve the goals of assured returns and orderly expansions through normal government means such as regulation and taxation have succeeded with other Saskatchewan resources, but failed in the case of potash. Public ownership seemed the only sensible solution. The alternatives would have been to give up control of our potash resource, or allow the uncertainties and stagnation to continue indefinitely."[22]

Three major factors brought about the 1975 decision to acquire potash assets by extra-ordinary means, if necessary. The first was the difficulty the NDP government led by Blakeney encountered in securing greater benefits, primarily revenue from Saskatchewan's potash resources. Participation in expansions was a secondary means for achieving that goal. The inability of the potash industry to cope with the demands of the new government and its eventual refusal to pay its taxes, along with court actions and other measures designed to thwart the government, was the second factor leading to the government's action. The third factor was the action of the federal government by intervening in a company court case against the Saskatchewan government as a co-plaintiff and then disallowing provincial royalties and other provincial payments as a deduction from taxable income. It can only be speculated whether industry representations to the federal government persuaded it to take these actions. However, R. A. Lenon, president of IMC, did make mention of the contacts he had in "high places" including the prime minister's office. Hmm! I wonder!

Let's step back and take a look at some of the things that brought affairs to this pass! The successful completion of the IMC mine in 1962 broke the "logjam." New mine announcements followed shortly after, encouraged by the confirmation of low royalty rates for all to 1974 and to 1981 for the two that solved the water problem. A Liberal government was elected in 1964 by promising accelerated economic development with potash as the centrepiece. Changes were coming! On a personal level, my wife and I went home on election night knowing changes were coming in our lives—not the least of which was the birth of our second child, expected shortly. I still remember at three o'clock in the morning, our almost-four-year-old daughter crawled into bed with us, something we didn't normally allow, but we didn't have the heart to kick her out that time. The bed was kind of crowded for the rest of the night.

Seven years of Liberal government under Ross Thatcher featured a potash crisis that almost brought the industry to its knees. When an NDP government returned in 1971, it coincided with a wave of nationalism in Canada. The federal government had conducted studies on foreign ownership in the Canadian economy and a Foreign Ownership Review Act was passed by Parliament. Other studies also expressed concern, in particular, about the extent of American ownership in the economy. This mood drew attention to American interests in the potash industry and supported contentions that public ownership of potash merited consideration.

Premier Allan Blakeney was the dominant personality on the potash scene leading up to 1975 events. He was determined to see conditions improve in Saskatchewan. His view was that the province should get better returns from its resources. He was committed to the implementation of the NDP program, *New Deal for People*. His ability to think through issues clearly served him well in dealing with complex and difficult matters, and he did not flinch when faced with difficult situations. In the final analysis, the decision to proceed with the 1975 legislation happened only because the government, and its leadership, was determined to achieve its goals. It took strength and courage to venture into uncharted waters.

In the past, other industries such as oil and uranium learned how to work with government. That was not the case with potash. The industry encountered an unprecedented situation and seemed not to know what to do other than dig in its heels. One difficulty was that senior executive management of most firms was located outside the province, for the most part in the United States. Their goals and objectives often differed, as well as their management styles. Corporate interests in these multinational operations extended beyond potash. The industry view was that the original royalty agreements as amended by Premier Thatcher were "cast in stone." They did not comprehend that the pro-rationing program implicitly changed "the rules of the game" on royalties.

The importance of the US anti-trust investigation for potash companies was never fully appreciated by Saskatchewan authorities.

While the province rightly said this was not its law or concern, the US companies could not ignore it. The US anti-dumping case against the companies a few years previous was a major problem at that time. The anti-trust investigation was even more of a problem and caused them a great deal of concern.

An outstanding question is whether the dispute could have been settled if federal non-deductibility had not been introduced. Blakeney's answer to that question was "yes, but it is a very hesitant yes." Two key ministers, Romanow and MacMurchy, did not agree. Blakeney, of course, would have had the final say. In my view, I do not think a settlement would have been reached because of the rigid position of the industry, although the situation may have played out differently. Former ministers interviewed were still happy with the decision they made many years later.

I look back now on the role I played as one of the high points of my life. At the outset, I was virtually alone in the bureaucracy trying to determine a more precise course of action in order to improve the position of the province. As events unfolded, others joined in and roles were shared. Some people have said the 1975 events would not have occurred had it not been for my efforts.

That overstates matters, but there is enough truth to the assertion that it leads to the statement.

The government's action was unique in Saskatchewan history. Some who were involved, such as Elwood Cowley, said a particular combination of factors came together that made it possible. It is not possible to anticipate anything similar happening in the foreseeable future.

# CHAPTER 10
## Getting Started

*"All the things you have to think about."*

The potash legislation had passed the Legislature. A lot of other things had also happened. But that still didn't mean that any real change had taken place. Much more was required.

The Potash Corporation of Saskatchewan (PCS) could now function with its own legislative charter just like SaskPower and Sask-Tel. A corporation with the same name had already been established earlier in the year under the authority of the Crown Corporations Act. The board of directors consisted of five civil servants including myself. All five of us were born and raised in Saskatchewan, took our university training in the province, and had virtually all of our work experience to that date in Saskatchewan. We were devoted to building a better province. Executive personnel had been hired, and some amazing plans had been developed for a new mine near Bredenbury after having explored possibilities for a joint venture with existing producers. Between February and August, a fully fleshed out plan for a "state of the art" $500 million mine had been prepared and reviewed by the board of directors and the premier as well as some ministers. The corporation was folded into the new PCS, and plans for the new mine were put on hold.

Saskatchewan was quite accustomed to crown corporations. Some were of long standing while others were created more recently, primarily during the Douglas government era. Turning to PCS, the November 12 announcement turned everything upside down. David Dombowsky, who had been chairman of the board, was appointed president and chief executive officer and another board member, Don Ching, became executive vice-president. Three cabinet ministers were added to the board, with Elwood Cowley as chairman while Roy Romanow and Jack Messer were members. Three other members of the previous board continued in their positions. An important decision was made to locate the head office in Saskatoon, closer to most of the mines than any other major centre.

It was obvious. The future of the Blakeney government now hinged on its potash decision. That decision towered over all other decisions made by the government. Everything was at stake. They had to make it work. Publicly owned potash mines would have to operate under a glaring spotlight. Since potash was regarded by many as Saskatchewan's hope for the future, the debate would be whether public operations did any better than private operations in achieving the province's goals. The legislation was subjected to a lengthy debate in the Legislature. Dave Steuart, then Leader of the Opposition, related long after the event that he considered the crunch point in the debate was when potash executives were no longer sitting in the legislative gallery. Their major concern was whether compensation features were adequate, and they were greatly relieved when they learned it would be "appraised market value."

An acquisition strategy was ready to implement as soon as the legislation was passed. A host of policy and operational matters required attention in anticipation of the needs of a major new industrial complex. Personnel recruitment was another priority item, as a wide range of expertise was needed. A firm skilled in conducting evaluations was contracted. Recruiting marketing expertise proved more difficult but was eventually dealt with. Atlanta, Georgia, was chosen as the marketing headquarters at the outset. Subsidiaries were created later to market potash and to oversee transportation and storage facilities needed.

Exploratory discussions had already commenced between PCS and some private firms before the legislation was passed. Duval, near Saskatoon, was prepared for an evaluation; Alwinsal at Lanigan was ready for discussions; IMC at Esterhazy discussed the possibility of a joint venture (IMC did not want to give up its crown jewel). Hudson Bay Mining and Smelting at Rocanville was prepared to talk. The others maintained their hostility and would not talk. The PCS approach was to attempt negotiations rather than expropriations. Finally, on October 29, 1976, almost a year after the province embarked on its new policy, the Duval mine was acquired for US $118,500,000 cash and US $10 million in a time payment. (At that time, the Canadian dollar was worth approximately US $1.06.) Funds were drawn from the Heritage Fund, a special fund created after the energy crisis when new legislation enabled the province to capture the windfall profits from higher oil prices.

It was time for a celebration. A big banquet was held in Saskatoon to mark the occasion, and President Atgood of Duval handed over the keys of the operation to Hon. Elwood Cowley, chairman of the Board of Directors of PCS. It was an exciting moment for all concerned. It was the culmination of many long hours of work. It was a Saskatchewan business, and all of the benefits would go to Saskatchewan people. It was a moment of personal satisfaction for me. This trail started for me almost four years previously. The frustrations I experienced earlier could now be set to rest. We were looking ahead to the future. Supervisory and management staff in almost their entirety continued to work at the mine. The labour union organized at the mine, United Steel Workers, supported what had been done.

Prior to the banquet that night, a small reception was held, attended by members of the Boards of Directors of Duval and PCS, senior management of both companies, and spouses. Introductions were being made, and David Dombowsky introduced President Atgood to my wife and me. He noted during his introduction that I had been a Member of Parliament. Atgood, an American, commented that he had not met many Members of Parliament. The only one he ever met was Jim Balfour (on the board of Duval and the candidate who defeated me in 1972) and asked if I knew him. Fortunately, a PCS official interjected, "That was exactly the wrong thing to say!" I then responded, "Yes, he's the bastard who defeated me." For the rest of the night, Duval board members teased Atgood about how he had put his foot in his mouth. Meantime, Atgood and I had a good chuckle over the matter, albeit he still looked somewhat uncomfortable.

Public opinion was much against the government's action at the outset. Opinion polls were in the order of 80–20 against. This was anticipated. Blakeney said on one occasion, "People like the results of change but they don't like the process of change." The government lost the public relations battle at the time, and it was concluded that the only way to change public opinion would be a good performance by the new corporation. Nevertheless, it was recognized steps had to be taken to ensure a better understanding by the public of what had been done.

One step was to establish a potash secretariat. It was designed to act as staff to the Cabinet Committee on potash. It was not to be a permanent body. There were a host of matters that demanded attention. Somebody had to look after them, and many of them were "governmental" in nature. They were not directly related to the mandate of PCS, which was to acquire and operate a potash business. If PCS had been assigned some of these matters, they would have detracted from its job of pursuing the critical and specific mandate it had been given. The secretariat was headed by Jack Kinzel, who was secretary to the Cabinet Committee on potash. I was named director of external relations. My job was to deal with all governmental matters concerning potash involving issues or matters outside Saskatchewan, and I continued to be a member of the Board of Directors of PCS. Other personnel dealt with the many demands for information on the government's actions, prepared and published a publication, as well as performed many other assorted activities. The secretariat continued in existence until mid-1977, by which time affairs had stabilized to the point where a special organization was not required to manage them. I moved on to another assignment but continued as a board member.

Ken Lysyk, Saskatchewan-born Deputy Attorney General, was a highly competent lawyer, and he had ensured that full care was given to international issues in drafting Saskatchewan's expropriation legislation. Later, legal officials in the US State Department were reported to have acknowledged the extent to which international law was taken into account in the legislation introduced. Public statements by political leaders were just as important as the letter of the law in order to avoid conflicts with international law. Premier Blakeney and Attorney General Roy Romanow, both lawyers, were always very careful in their public statements to stress the prime objectives of government policy:

1. An assured fair return from the resource for the people of Saskatchewan; and,

2. Orderly expansion to ensure the province's position as a potash supplier and to enhance its economic growth.

International law stipulates that a state may only do certain things to aliens or alien corporations if they are in accordance with international law, even though such things are being done to its own citizens or corporations. Expropriation is one of the areas in which international law has been purported by some to derogate from the supremacy of the state. International law is weighted heavily in favour of investor countries and is regarded so especially in the United States. It is not law in the usual sense because there is no effective way of enforcing it. Customary practice on expropriations has become more broadly defined as a result of actions taken mostly by a number of lesser-developed nations. Any actions taken now by Saskatchewan could then also affect and add to the trend of custom or practice. Public statements would play a greater role than strictly legal terms in determining the acceptability of the Saskatchewan legislation. There are other considerations encompassed within international law that also play a role, including non-discrimination, adequacy of compensation, effectiveness of payments, and arbitration provisions.

The United Nations approved a definition of state powers to expropriate on December 12, 1974: "Each state has the right ... to nationalize, expropriate or transfer ownership of foreign property, in which case appropriate compensation should be paid by the state adopting such measures taking into account its relevant laws and regulations and all circumstances that the state considers pertinent. ..." Canada abstained on the vote, and efforts were made by it and a number of other industrial countries to modify the resolution. Canada does not have a clearly defined position, but its attitude has tended to be closer to that of an investor country, in part, because Canadian-owned assets could be affected.

The long-held official position of the United States has been that payment for American-owned property expropriated by foreign governments must be "adequate, prompt and effective." The general US stance is against expropriation but insists that, in addition to the compensation requirements, any taking of American private property must be non-discriminatory and must be for a public purpose. In 1976, the US State Department announced a new policy that reserved the right to take expropriation cases to international tribunals even where a settlement had been reached.

It was the morning of November 12, 1975, the day of the big announcement. Premier Blakeney telephoned Prime Minister Trudeau to inform him of Saskatchewan's plans to introduce potash nationalization legislation. The prime minister immediately noted the international implications of such action. After further discussion of the province's plans, Trudeau ended the discussion by saying, "Well, good luck." Other steps were taken to brief federal officials of provincial plans.

Subsequently, a very satisfactory liaison and line of communication was developed with the Department of External Affairs. Officials kept in touch with Saskatchewan personnel regularly. I was the person through whom most contacts were channelled. The approach of the department did not reflect the negative attitude some federal cabinet ministers displayed toward the new Saskatchewan policy. The stance of the department was to protect the rights of Canadians to do what they wanted in Canada in managing Canadian affairs.

An important consideration was that American firms owned the great majority of potash productive capacity in Saskatchewan. More than two-thirds of our production was shipped to the United States. (The ratio is now 57–58% due to market growth elsewhere.) It was anticipated US capital markets would be required to meet a portion of capital financing needs. To top things off, in 1975, Canada-US relations were probably at their lowest ebb for a long time due to a raft of irritants and difficulties. These included positions and stances taken by Canada to protect its sovereignty, identity, and other future interests. The United States had begun to push back. Potash would become one more item and had the potential to become a focus for US retaliatory activity.

The United States, very quickly, sent an *aide-mémoire* to Canada, a procedure in international diplomacy that is not as strong as a diplomatic note. Concern was expressed about Saskatchewan's intentions. The public purpose was questioned as well as the negative effect on investment and concerns about further Saskatchewan actions. Canada was reminded of US policy that "any expropriation be for a public purpose, be neither arbitrary nor discriminatory, and ... [include] compensation which is prompt, effective and adequate by international standards." The United States also wanted to know what action the Canadian government might take.

Despite its provocative and possibly impertinent tone, issuing the *aide-mémoire* was probably the least that the US could do in response to the pressure that no doubt was placed on it. Canada asked Saskatchewan for its comments on the *aide-mémoire* and made available a draft reply. I was charged with coordinating consultations prior to sending a response. The draft was excellent in our view, and our suggestions for change were essentially editorial in nature. I was charged with taking the reply to Ottawa, where I met with External Affairs officials and, on the instructions of Premier Blakeney, conveyed Saskatchewan's pleasure with the tone of the draft response followed by a review of our suggestions. I then raised one sensitive matter. A federal grand jury had been convened in Chicago to investigate potash anti-trust charges and wanted to talk to 157 Canadians. Saskatchewan instructed its officials not to co-operate. But Dave Steuart, Liberal leader of the Opposition, whose name was on the list, said openly he would go to Chicago. The Saskatchewan government didn't think that was a good idea but had little influence with him. I presented this problem to Jerry Shannon of External Affairs. He replied, "Leave that with us." Not long after, Steuart dropped his stance. I expect External Affairs briefed their minister, Don Jamieson. He picked up the phone and said, Liberal to Liberal, "Dave, we don't think you should do that."

The Canadian response to the *aide-mémoire* noted that the legislation had been enacted and that Saskatchewan's intentions had been outlined repeatedly. The United States was also reminded that some issues are properly federal-provincial matters, but Canada was prepared to discuss matters that did affect US interests. (Diplomatically, that says, "Mind your own business.") The Canadian response went on to counter a number of statements made by the United States and gave assurances on other items. It was also pointed out that US policy on expropriation differs from general international practice. Canada finally asked the United States to assist in avoiding some misunderstandings that had occurred.

In early 1976, a new US ambassador to Canada was appointed, Thomas O. Enders. He ranked high in the US State Department and was known as a pleasant, articulate, tough, and direct-speaking spokesman. It would be reasonable to conclude he was appointed to address problems in relations with Canada. He lived up to his reputation in addressing Canada-US issues and on potash said:

"... Nor do we contest the right of your authorities to expropriate—or buy into—U.S. enterprises for authentic public purposes, provided it is paid for fully, promptly and effectively. But we are concerned where takeover is used to gain a quasi-monopoly position. Saskatchewan's proposal to acquire half the potash capacity in its province would give it control of one-third of U.S. potash supply. Although welcome, statements that this power would be used benignly are not adequate reassurance.

In July 1976, Enders paid his first official visit to Regina. He met with Premier Blakeney, and they exchanged views and comments reiterating what had already been said. The Government of Saskatchewan then hosted a luncheon attended by 75–100 people that had all the elements of a diplomatic function. Both Enders and Blakeney gave delightful talks that could be described as "tiptoeing through the tulips." Blakeney talked about the long-standing relationship between Canada and the United States and told that where he grew up on the south shore of Nova Scotia, they looked on Boston, New York, and Washington in much the same way people in Saskatchewan often looked on Toronto, Montreal, and Ottawa. Enders, in his reply, emphasized that the United States had lessons to learn from Saskatchewan's experience in implementing and managing a medical care system.

Later, Enders met with Elwood Cowley and Roy Romanow along with three officials including myself. He reiterated the position he presented to Blakeney and at the luncheon: first, that the payment for a takeover must be "prompt, effective and adequate." Then he pressed US concerns about the potential quasi-monopoly position and the inadequacy of Saskatchewan assurances it would not take advantage of its position. After some discussion, Cowley and Romanow asked Enders if he would spell out what he considered would be an adequate assurance. Enders agreed to do so, but Saskatchewan never heard further from him. The visit was regarded as highly satisfactory by the province.

Potash was on the agenda of a number of agencies in Washington, and developments in Saskatchewan were reviewed. It is noteworthy that in assessing Saskatchewan legislation, State Department lawyers concluded that compensation features were fair. Developments were monitored constantly. Ambassador Enders did not hesitate to criticize US agencies when he thought it necessary. His actions, however, may have been more questionable than appeared to be the case when he was in Regina. For example, he sent a telex to the Secretary of State in September 1976 criticizing a US Department of Justice plan to indict a large number of Canadians in its investigations. He stated: "This occurred at a time when we were beginning to build in constraints on Regina that would have made it difficult for Saskatchewan to go beyond voluntary purchases of U.S. companies."[1]

In mid-1976, I went on a mission to Washington, accompanied by Brian Kaukinen of the PCS management team, to discuss potash affairs with a number of US government agencies. The trip was designed as a low-key level of activity in which meetings were held with mid-level officials in the Departments of Commerce and Agriculture, the US Bureau of Mines, an official on the Senate Committee on Agriculture, and finally with the senior deputy assistant secretary of state, Julius Katz. That took me into the upper levels of the State Department. The meetings were arranged by an official at the Canadian embassy who accompanied us. A representative of our Washington law firm was also along.

The most memorable moment for me was at the meeting with Katz. He was very suave and diplomatic, but during the meeting, we were joined by Richard Vine, a senior official ranking at about the same level as Katz. Vine had already made some abrasive public comments on potash and was more aggressive than Katz in his stance. While I was discussing Saskatchewan's actions, Vine interjected by saying "greed." I responded instantly and sharply, "I cannot accept that term and I trust it is not used otherwise." Vine did not continue his approach.

Two conflicting concerns were raised in the meetings. Some were worried prices would be increased artificially, while others thought prices might be dropped artificially. It was concluded potash was a low-priority item in Washington, but developments should still be monitored. On a side note, in a little spare time, I went to the US National Archives where I found and copied a ship list for the ship on which my great-grandfather and two brothers had travelled from Antwerp to New York in 1845, cleared Ellis Island, and gone on to settle in Wisconsin north of Milwaukee.[2]

The US Justice Department convened a grand jury in early 1975 and charged eight potash companies with breaking anti-trust law by participating in the pro-rationing and pricing plan in 1969. The grand jury investigation proceeded without much attention for more than 18 months, but came to the fore when it was decided they wanted to interview 157 Canadian individuals including past and present Canadian and Saskatchewan government officials, Canadian judges, and potash company officials. They were described as "unindicted co-conspirators" and included two deceased persons, one of whom was the late premier Ross Thatcher. This brought a sharp reaction, and Saskatchewan officials were instructed not to co-operate. Premier Blakeney immediately contacted External Affairs Minister Allan MacEachen, expressing concern about the implication that Saskatchewan or its people broke US law and objected to the naming of Saskatchewan people and the direct approaches being made. He asked for consideration of appropriate action. The Canadian ambassador called on the State Department within two days. This and other actions caused US Justice to moderate its approach. The ensuing furore eventually subsided, and the judge decided not to pursue criminal charges but did leave the door open for a large number of civil class action suits.

Some years later another previously unknown initiative came to light. Mr. Svend Robinson, an NDP Member of Parliament from Burnaby, revealed in a House of Commons committee meeting[3] that the Central Intelligence Agency (CIA) of the United States was trying to get information on what compensation Saskatchewan was prepared to pay for the potash industry and financing arrangements for same. He had obtained, from his own sources, a document issued in May 1976 prepared by the Economic Intelligence Committee of the US Intelligence Oversight Board that included key intelligence questions issued by the director of Central Intelligence, then George H. W. Bush, who was later president of the United States of America.

It is clear Saskatchewan could have faced major problems in pursuing its potash policy if it had not taken adequate account of international law and other international and extra-provincial considerations. Evidence is that careful handling of international issues helped to avoid many potential difficulties and smoothed the way for the implementation of Saskatchewan's policy. Careful management of relations with the Government of Canada, in particular, was also very helpful.

Sound management of its acquisition program followed by good and effective management of its operations laid the foundation for PCS to be a first-rate business enterprise designed to benefit the people of Saskatchewan.

# CHAPTER 11

## Saskatchewan's Golden Opportunity
*The Story of the Potash Corporation of Saskatchewan from Construction to Destruction (1975–1989)*

P CS grew rapidly from 1976 on into a strong entity clearly destined to give Saskatchewan the economic strength it had lacked for so long. It is difficult to understand how the people who were charged with the reins of power in 1982 could from the outset undermine and sabotage this new pillar of strength for the province to the point that, in the end, it was a burden on the people of Saskatchewan. While some members of the Grant Devine Conservative government were convicted for other things they did and spent time in jail, in my view, the really criminal act for which they have never had to accept responsibility was their betrayal of the trust granted them by the people of Saskatchewan in what they did to the Potash Corporation of Saskatchewan.

The years following 1976 were an exciting time with a whirlwind of activity for all concerned. Saskatchewan had not seen anything like it before, even with its colourful history of innovation and unique efforts to overcome problems. Both board members and management were faced with a steady barrage of decisions and situations resulting from a growing scale of operations and an ever-expanding dimension of factors that had to be taken into account. For my own part as a member of the board of directors, it was an exciting and challenging experience that, looking at it now, I value as one of several highlights in my life. Something worthwhile was being done for the people of Saskatchewan to build a more secure foundation for the province's economy.

Rather than providing a long recitation of the complex set of negotiations and events that established PCS as a major force in the potash industry, the following sets out the essentials. A reputable evaluation firm was contracted to guide the company in its efforts. PCS was governed by the legislation enacted and government policy pronouncements. All of the purchase agreements concluded addressed taxes owing to the government. All were negotiated without use of the expropriation powers.

| MINE | EVALUA-TION | PURCHASE DATE | COST | OTHER DEVELOP-MENTS |
|---|---|---|---|---|
| Cory (Saskatoon) | Early 1976 | Oct. 29, 1976 | $128,500,000 | |
| Sylvite (Rocanville) | End of 1976 | April 22, 1977 | $144,000,000 | |
| Alwinsal (Lanigan) | End of 1976 | Nov. 1, 1977 | $76,500,000 +$9,000,000 taxes paid | |
| CCP (Colonsay) | Under way 1976 | | | Discussions dropped June 1977 |
| IMC (Esterhazy) | | | | Exploratory discussions |
| Amax (Esterhazy) | October 1977 | Jan. 9, 1978 | $85,000,000 | IMC also evaluated |
| US Borax (40%) & Swift Can. (20%) (Allan) | n.a. | January 11, 1978 | $85,800,000 | Texasgulf retained 40% |

PCS was now the single largest producer of potash outside Russia and East Germany and owned 40% of Saskatchewan's productive capacity. Further acquisitions were going to be more difficult without using expropriation powers. It was acknowledged within the industry that the private owners had been treated fairly. Financing was largely drawn from a Heritage Fund established by the government from extra revenues obtained by levies on higher oil prices. PCS joined Canpotex, a consortium of Canadian potash producers that managed offshore North America sales. Soon after their acquisition, capacity increases were undertaken at three mines, Cory, Sylvite, and Alwinsal.

Negotiations with IMC, the industry leader, were more tricky. Essentially, IMC did not want to sell because the mines at Esterhazy were key components of its operations. Doubtless, it was recognized they might have to accept some changes. While they suggested some options for PCS involvement, they gave commercial concerns for not wanting it to be known that an evaluation was under way. An alternative advanced was to pursue acquisition of the Amax potash interests and leave existing IMC-Amax operating arrangements in place. Amax held potash rights adjacent to IMC leases and contracted with IMC to do its mining. Arrangements were made for the Amax evaluation, thereby requiring evaluation of the IMC operations, but IMC avoided being evaluated directly.

By year-end 1977, PCS was faced with three conclusions if it was to achieve the government's announced objective of 50% ownership of the industry. First, if expropriation was used, IMC would be the target. Second, if expropriation was not used, IMC would be its major competitor, and to compete effectively, current negotiations and expansions would have to be completed and adjustments in provincial taxes would be necessary to reflect investments. Finally, if current negotiations were not concluded successfully, expropriation of IMC should be the priority. Early in 1978, two more purchases were concluded. IMC thus avoided the prospect at that point of being targeted, while PCS had less reason to continue its aggressive approach. In the meantime, royalty and taxation issues were getting sorted out between the government and the industry, thus lowering tensions.

The scale of operations that resulted from its acquisitions made PCS look at where it stood in the industry and evaluate its corporate organization and capability. A five-year plan adopted in 1978 emphasized, "...

it is vital that P.C.S., in the absence of pro-rationing, establish itself as a price and production leader and in effect speak for the Saskatchewan industry."[1] A modest profit level was projected at the outset that could be regarded, on one hand, as good for a large-scale corporation that had just recently been established but, on the other hand, might be claimed as evidence that government should not be in business by those who would denigrate its establishment. One problem was some US customers were still skeptical of a government corporation and would turn first to private companies with whom they had dealt previously.

While the mines churned out potash and loaded railway cars for shipment to markets, PCS turned its attention to a range of other concerns affecting the corporation. A public relations program was developed to provide information for the public about the corporation and about potash as a resource and tool for development. US anti-trust law was given special attention in order to avoid potential problems. The five-year plan was extended into a 10-year plan that visualized PCS having 50% of Saskatchewan producing capacity by the mid-1980s and almost 60% by 1990. Storage capacity was arranged for in Midwest US states. The corporation then began to explore prospects for diversification. It studied manufacturing opportunities including a nitrogen fertilizer plant in Saskatchewan, took part in a phosphate exploration project in northern Saskatchewan, and looked into possibilities of producing potassium sulfate ($K_2SO_4$), a specialty fertilizer used on fruit and tobacco in particular. The project would utilize surface alkaline sulfate deposits east of Saskatoon. A research and development program and participation in an industry mission to the Far East, along with other special studies, contributed to a dynamic environment.

Financial results were positive, with the money staying in Saskatchewan. PCS became recognized as an industry leader and played a noteworthy role in influencing events; for example, it obtained important changes in a federal government potash industry task force report.

Concerns remained about the public view of PCS. Public opinion polls in 1976 and 1977 reported Saskatchewan people were only 20–30% favourable to the new potash policy and whether PCS was good for the province while over 50% were against. This shifted to 63% favourable and 29% against in 1979. PCS continued to monitor public perceptions and opinions. On the question, "Is the Potash Corporation good for Saskatchewan?", the Yes answer grew from 59% in August 1978 to 72.2%

in January 1980, while the No answer dropped from 27.4% to 17.6%. A May 1980 poll was even better. Another question was, "Are the respondents in favour of the government's policy of buying potash mines?" The Yes answer grew from 32.6% in November 1976 to 54.6% in January 1980. The No answer dropped from 49.7% in November 1976 to 36.1% in January 1980. A third question was, "Is the corporation viewed as handling its role in the industry effectively?" The Yes answer grew from 25.4% in November 1977 to 46.6% in January 1980, while the No answer dropped from 20.3% to 15.3%.

A new provincial Potash Resource Payment Agreement, replacing the potash reserve tax, was finalized with implementation scheduled for July 1, 1979. Taxation was reduced significantly. It increased PCS profits for 1978–79 by $4.5 million, plus another $3.646 million rebated for previous years. PCS participated in negotiations on the industry side and approached issues from its own corporate perspective, making proposals that were not always accepted. For example, it wanted to be taxed on its entire operation as one unit rather than on each mine separately. While this approach would have been advantageous to PCS, it was rejected by Mineral Resources.

A program of special activities was prepared for board members. Only one project took place, in late October 1981, with a US tour. I was one of the participants. The Atlanta sales office was visited, followed by a tour of farm operations nearby. It was a thrill to stand in Georgia cotton fields where machinery now did much of the work. I visualized past days when all of the work was done by hand. I recalled some of the songs from that era that my brothers and I learned from our parents. The role of slavery and emancipation, about which I had done considerable reading as my father was born in the United States, flashed through my mind. But, back to the present, I saw the potential for Saskatchewan potash on Georgia fields. Much more than cotton is grown there now.

From Georgia, we went to Illinois where we saw corn, more corn, and still more corn. And all of it needs potash. The Midwest sales staff met us, took part in the tour, and after dinner joined us in a motel room. They took advantage of the opportunity to make a well-prepared presentation on work problems they encountered on the job followed by discussion. One of the salesmen lived nearby and went home for the night. The next morning all of us were eating breakfast when he returned and sat down at my table. After good mornings, he asked, "Well, did you solve all of the problems last night?"

I said, "Yes, we've got it all figured out."
"Oh, what did you come up with?"
"Well, the board are a bunch of dummies, management doesn't know what the hell it is doing, and salesmen are a bunch of bitchers!"

After the laughter subsided, one of the other salesmen commented wryly, "He was doing pretty well until he got to that third one!" We were impressed with the quality of the sales staff in the United States and their commitment to their work. We couldn't have done better.

An interesting difference of view developed between PCS and Crown Investments Corporation (CIC), the successor to Government Finance Office as the umbrella organization for crown corporations. It concerned the amount of dividend that PCS should pay to CIC. At the outset, PCS acknowledged that it recognized that all crown corporations are expected to pay some dividend to CIC out of profits, but it was considered preferable to limit the PCS dividend for 1980 to $25 million rather than the proposed $50 million in order to leave more funds for PCS capital expansion. However, CIC insisted on asking for a $50 million dividend using its legislative authority. PCS had to give in, with some grumbling, and asked for consultations on future dividends well before year-end.

By 1981, the scope of PCS operations was clearly global in nature. The corporate plan identified the goal of becoming a world-scale fertilizer manufacturer, and the corporation had a responsibility to all people in the world as well as to those in Saskatchewan. Looking for reasonable returns rather than pressing for maximum returns would be more effective in securing permanent benefits for the people of Saskatchewan. This had particular implications for sales to developing countries that might not now be able to afford all the potash and other fertilizers they could buy under a maximum return policy. Experience had already demonstrated the merits of this approach.

Marketing strategy was a major concern in PCS relationships with Canpotex. PCS joined Canpotex at the outset, but when its share of marketings increased to more than 60%, there was no change in its status. It was outvoted by other members who had much lower sales but still had one vote. Canpotex pushed prices higher than PCS thought they should be. PCS pressed for major changes in Canpotex including its organization, its ability to allow each shareholder to deal with price and long-term contracts, its right to make key appointments, and several other items. One special issue was moving the Canpotex head office from Toronto to Saskatoon. By August 1980, Canpotex was told PCS was going to opt out if major changes were not made. Enough concessions were made to persuade the board not to opt out. The proposal to move the Canpotex head office, however, was flatly rejected.

An even keel didn't last for long. The fundamentals of the PCS-Canpotex relationship had not changed. The purpose and history of Canpotex conflicted with PCS objectives. Other members were hostile to PCS and, in fact, wanted "to screw it." Pricing policies, in particular, conflicted with PCS objectives. Long-term arrangements were critical for PCS. Secure markets went hand-in-hand with expansion plans. Management pressed the board of directors to get out of Canpotex. Some board members were reluctant, but I was a "hawk" along with several others. I felt we were going to have to leave Canpotex sooner or later because its other members were out to do us in in the long run, so we would be better off to run our own show now. The decision to leave Canpotex was finally made, and on June 30, 1981, notice was given to take effect one year later as required in Canpotex bylaws. By June 30, 1982, the new Conservative government was in power and reversed the decision immediately upon assuming power. If the step had been taken sooner, PCS would have been out of Canpotex by the time the Conservative government came into power.

Aggressive action was required to implement a decision of this magnitude. A new subsidiary, PCS International, was formed to manage all offshore marketing. Top-notch people were recruited for key positions, in contrast with difficulties in obtaining marketing personnel when operations first started. This alarmed competitors and made them realize fully that PCS International would be a formidable adversary. Agronomic teams were dispatched to potential market areas in conjunction with a market research and development group organized to search for new markets. It was clear that an organization was in place that would enable PCS International to function effectively and vigorously from the very outset.

In the five years to the end of 1981, PCS had earned almost $413 million in profits, out of which $100 million was paid to Crown Investments Corporation as dividends. This came from sales of almost $1.25 billion from just over 17.5 million product tonnes of KCl. In addition, taxes and royalties of almost $270 million were paid to the province.

In just over five years, PCS grew from nothing to a major player on the international stage. It went through the normal "growing pains" but ended the five years with a strong management team and an excellent workforce. One board member who was on the board of a national bank and other national companies said it was the best-managed company he had ever seen. It changed Saskatchewan potash from a residual supplier in world markets to one where PCS was becoming the world leader in the industry. The next step was critical.

PCS was preparing to take control of its offshore marketing, which until then had been managed by Canpotex. Price policy was a key element of the new strategy. PCS approved a pricing philosophy that called for moderate pricing designed to obtain profit out of volume rather than price. Long-term contracts were another feature of its strategy. One such contract was approved in October 1980 with CF Industries, an umbrella co-operative for 18 regional co-operatives in the United States. It was a six-year contract with a discount feature that provided for the sale of 751,000 short tons of product in 1980–81 at the outset and growing annually to 1,225,000 tons in 1985–86.

Expansion plans went hand-in-hand with the marketing strategy. One without the other made no sense. Future plans called for total expenditures of $2.5 billion by the end of the decade to triple productive capacity. Factoring in the planned Bredenbury mine would bring capacity to 11.34 million tonnes by 1990. Streamlining transportation called for unit trains, US distribution centres, and enhanced facilities at the Canadian west coast.

The expansion program combined with changes in marketing arrangements were crucial elements in future planning. Both had to run in parallel. One was dependent on the other. Setting up PCS International was designed to develop new markets. Without such markets, the expansion program was not needed. Pricing was the major tool to do the job, and transportation improvements facilitated matters. Integration of marketing and expansion became even more sensitive with a softening market cycle that showed indications of becoming more severe than first thought.

On April 26, 1982, the incumbent government in Saskatchewan was soundly defeated in a general election. It had created and nurtured PCS, supporting it as it grew and developed. The new government was composed of people who had vigorously opposed the creation of PCS and did not sympathize or agree with its philosophical foundations. Now that it was to form the government, a big question was what they were going to do about PCS as well as other government enterprises that had come to be known as "the family of crown corporations." The election result was a surprise. PCS had not considered or prepared for the day when Saskatchewan would be governed by a political party that was not as sympathetic to it as it had experienced until then. The corporation was preoccupied with its development phase and had not as yet matured to the point where it pondered such eventualities.

Things were changing in the world of the early 1980s. The heyday of more interventionist government programs was over. Ronald Reagan was president in the United States. Margaret Thatcher was prime minister of Great Britain. Both were implementing their right-wing agenda, meaning less government, less government interference in the economy, and the introduction of a neo-conservative outlook based on the philosophy of people such as Milton Friedman. Essentially, the market should rule and governments should stay out of the way, he proclaimed.

This was the setting when the Progressive Conservative party won its surprise, resounding victory over the incumbent New Democratic Party in 1982. The extent to which this outcome was a reflection of changes happening elsewhere or how much was due to localized factors of the moment and/or mismanagement of affairs is debatable. The government had continued to expand the scope of its activities, and there were indications of some backlash. There was always a sizable portion of the population fundamentally opposed to the more left-wing outlook of the government. What role the corporate sector played behind the scenes has not been analyzed.

One study of this era summed up the process that occurred.

Step-by-step the neo-conservative program unfolded: the promotion of Christian right moral values, the experiments with supply-side economics, the touting of free enterprise, the reining in of the Crown corporations, the attacks on the civil service, social programs and trade unions, and the massive push towards privatization. The first step toward achieving these goals was the defeat of the NDP government.[2]

A statement by the new premier, Grant Devine, more than eight months after assuming office provided a bizarre analysis of the state of affairs. By this time, he would have had an opportunity to become cognizant of the problems the growing recession was creating: "Saskatchewan has so much going for it that you can afford to mismanage it and still break even."[3]

A new government has a lot to do. But it seems a super-top priority item was the issue of PCS membership in Canpotex along with the activities of PCS International. On May 5, 1982, three days before the new government was sworn into office on May 8, 1982, instructions were sent by it to PCS International "to withdraw immediately from sales and marketing activities in offshore markets."[4] This was followed by instructions to cancel plans to withdraw from Canpotex. This had the immediate, consequential effect of reducing PCS sales. These and some other instructions involving operational matters were made in the form of directives, some verbal and others written.

This caused problems. Management follows instructions given by the legally constituted board of directors. A new board had not been appointed. The first instructions were from people not yet officially in office. The problems created were later addressed at a board of directors meeting on September 2–3, 1982. A board agenda submission discussed the situation and made recommendations. Six incidents were reported, the first two of which (the other four items were on operations) were:

a) On the instructions of Gary Lane for the Transition Committee (Telex of May 5, 1982) a direction to PCS International to withdraw immediately from sales and marketing activities in offshore markets; and,

b) On the instructions of Barrie Hodgson (June 16, 1982) on behalf of Lorne McLaren, a direction to PCS Sales to cancel its previously given Notices of Withdrawal from Canpotex Limited and related entities.[5]

The agenda submission then explained the problem (point 1 has been omitted):

2. Among the first requests to corporate officers from the new Chairman of the Board of Potash Corporation of Saskatchewan, Lorne McLaren, was that "business be carried on as usual."

3. In the opinion of corporate officers, full and complete compliance with all or some of the directives received during the period of transition from representatives of the new government:
   a) were contrary to the policy directives given by the previous lawfully constituted Board of Directors of Potash Corporation of Saskatchewan;
   b) would interfere with the need to protect corporate assets and carry on business as usual; and,
   c) could conceivably put at risk Potash Corporation of Saskatchewan and its subsidiary companies['] operating procedures that result in a minimum exposure of corporate profits to United States income tax.[6]

The submission then asked the board to ratify all acts by management that may have been in conflict with the informal directions given by the new government. Management had not complied in part or in full with the various informal directives given by the incoming government and was now asking for sanctioning of those actions. There does not appear to be a formal record reversing the decision to withdraw from Canpotex, but it is evident from ongoing records that PCS had not done so. The first formal act of the new board was to dismiss the president, David Dombowsky, who had led the organization since its beginnings. He was replaced by Stephen Harapiak as acting president. Harapiak was regarded as the top mining engineer in Canada, had been hired earlier to strengthen the mining division, and at that time was regarded as a potential successor if Dombowsky "stubbed his toe."

The question must be asked, why would the new government move so precipitously, in such haste and in unorthodox if not illegal ways, to stop the PCS withdrawal from Canpotex? The answer is—the private industry got the ear of the new government and persuaded it to act quickly. A news story some months later revealed the picture: "Attorney General Gary Lane, who also sat in on the government's transitional team which made the decision to get back into Canpotex, said some industry representatives had approached the team members 'and convinced us the decision was made in haste and it had to be reconsidered.'"[7] The government listened to the private firms and bought their story. The decision was not made in haste. The private firms knew for some time PCS was thinking of pulling out of Canpotex. PCS told them. It had worked on plans at least since summer 1980. The news story goes on to quote Lane: "we would have practically given away our potash in order to reduce inventory. ... it could have led to the destruction of the rest of the potash industry, including major losses to PCS."[8] Nonsense. They did not even talk to PCS, who would have told them the other side of the story. It was easy to answer that suggestion. Communities adjacent to the other mines would have screamed to the government if the mines were shut down or in trouble because of PCS actions, and the government would have to give PCS a "shareholder direction" to ease off. But PCS still wanted to get its full share of the market and was determined to be industry leader. Saskatchewan would then have some real economic clout. In fact, what the private companies were frightened of is they knew PCS had done a good job of setting up PCS International. They weren't going to "rule the roost" any more.

I had one particularly pleasant and gratifying experience during the summer of 1982. The new government called the Legislature into session as there was outstanding business because the general election had left some legislative business unfinished. One such item was that the crown corporations were required to appear before the Legislative Crown Corporations Committee to review their most recent annual reports. It is somewhat akin to an annual shareholders' meeting. One day the Potash Corporation of Saskatchewan appeared before the committee. By this time, I had been fired by the new government from my post as executive director of the Transportation Agency of Saskatchewan. I was now doing some consulting work for the NDP Opposition members. I came to the meeting as support service for the NDP members on the committee. Curiously, the NDP members were to ask questions about the performance of the corporation for the previous year when the NDP was still in office, and the Conservative minister of finance, Bob Andrew, had to answer the questions.

When PCS management officials including the acting president, Steven Harapiak, spotted me before the meeting started, they immediately clustered around me as we greeted each other jovially and engaged in spirited conversation. All Bob Andrew could do was look on with a sour look on his face. It made me feel good. They looked on me as a colleague and friend who had worked with them for the betterment of PCS in my role on the board of directors.

It was known by this time that the government had directed PCS to reverse its withdrawal from Canpotex, told PCS International to pull in its horns, and fired David Dombowsky. One of the pillars had been knocked out from under the grand strategy for its growth. The question was what they were going to do about the other pillar, the expansion focused on Lanigan. Market conditions continued to deteriorate. PCS had already slowed the pace of the Lanigan project, and options were being considered for delaying start-up. Management now recommended mothballing the project until markets improved, but the board insisted on continuation. It is understood that it was, at the time, the only major development project under way in Saskatchewan and the government was concerned about the potential economic impact of curtailing it. So, PCS was stymied by the new government in its marketing strategy but was left saddled with the other component of its strategy, namely the costs of the development project that went with it. If that wasn't bad enough, management now wanted to undertake an aggressive pricing policy because of market conditions in order to keep market share. The board dragged its feet and deferred decisions to the next meeting, meaning they were going to talk to Cabinet and who knows who else! They had admitted they were talking to the private sector, who would take full advantage of their opportunity, of course, and would be only too happy to see the demise of PCS.

A $50 million dividend was demanded for each of 1982 and 1983 plus a special $12 million dividend in 1984 in spite of losses on operations. In order to deal with its cash flow problems, PCS had to sell mining machinery for $78 million and then lease it back. Later, it was determined by management that completion of the Lanigan expansion prematurely resulted in $125 million in interest added to the capital cost instead of the $29.5 million originally anticipated. In addition, by the end of 1984,

PCS had to settle for a fire-sale price of $135 million (asking price—$220 million; first offer—$125 million) for the Amax potash reserves next to IMC operations. Performance during the 1980s would not have been as buoyant as the period prior to 1982, but by placing financial demands on the corporation, thwarting its marketing strategy, demanding non-commercial activity, delaying government guidance, and creating political interference, the government dragged PCS steadily down to crisis situations where its ongoing viability was in question. By early 1983, management was raising its concerns with the board:

> Saskatchewan has been a residual supplier to the U.S. market gaining the largest share of market growth and losing the greatest amount when the market declines.
>
> Aggressive marketing by PCS Sales could bring additional pressure on the Government of Saskatchewan from other Saskatchewan producers due to lost sales and potentially lower net-backs.[9]

[Note: The wording implies it has already been happening.]

The vice-president, finance, told the board in 1985, "Two non-commercial decisions have added to the Corporation's debt: dividends of $100 million financed by debt and the continuation of Lanigan Phase II after December 1982."[10] His submission stressed that action was essential to overcome financial problems and that the debt–equity ratio was becoming critical.

In mid-1984, I left Canada and spent almost four years in Zambia, where I was team leader on an agricultural planning project sponsored by the Canadian International Development Agency (CIDA) located in the headquarters of the Ministry of Agriculture there. I had virtually no contact with potash affairs during that time except to hear on my annual vacation trip home that PCS was in trouble. I was home again when the privatization battle was on in Saskatchewan. One of the arguments made was that PCS would do so much better under private ownership. No wonder. The Conservative government had completely screwed things up. More recently, when I delved into events after 1982, I was alternately saddened, sickened, and furious about what had happened and how PCS was simply ground down into an emaciated skeleton clinging to the government for life-support, in stark contrast to the economic giant that was emerging only a few short years previously.

Events at the time of the change of government have already been recounted. The order to stay in Canpotex and insistence on continuing the Lanigan project, while not quite a death knell, were the start of a long saga of events. They were both political decisions and were highly detrimental to PCS. After the controversy erupted in early 1983 over what dividend PCS should pay, the board was lectured by Hon. Gary Lane, vice-chairman of the board, who "presented the request of his Cabinet colleagues that PCS recognize the political sensitivity of its activities and that it attempt to avoid getting locked into an inflexible dividend policy."[11] (My! My! He really told them, eh!)

The board of directors maintained its stance, but to no avail. But it did begin to assert itself through a number of actions including a special meeting in Regina where they asked for direction on resource policy and suggested a permanent chairman, a board training seminar, and a clear delineation of board functions. There were other indications the board was taking its job quite seriously. It took steps to organize its activities by setting up committees, pressed for direction on resource policy, endorsed head office proposals, and was interested in corporate diversification.

Political interference continued. For example, at 1984 board meetings, Vice-Chairman Andrew twice raised the question of private sector (travel agents) opportunities to take advantage of PCS's considerable travel requirements. In response, a strong report was submitted demonstrating clearly that existing "in house" arrangements worked the best. The board supported the report but the vice-chairman persisted there would still be cases of travel arrangements routed through the private sector.

Board minutes also record an observation by one member: "Brent Logan ... suggested that decisions were made by the Corporation that were influenced by political considerations to a greater degree than commercial considerations, such as the continuation of Lanigan Phase II."[12]

On June 13, 1985, PCS finally met the government, premier included. While assurances were given that PCS would, in effect, not be allowed to go "down the tubes," steps necessary to place the operation on a sound footing were not forthcoming. The premier was more interested in a nitrogen plant, so PCS reactivated work already done that eventually produced a proposal for an operation associated with the Co-op refinery in Regina.

The board dug in its heels when a $12 million dividend was demanded for 1984, requiring borrowing. Meetings were requested to look at alternatives, and the payment was not made. A standoff lasted for some time, but finally, in 1986, an official request for payment was made and PCS had to cave in. A little later, management reached a deal with IMC for the sale of reserves next to their mine. PCS asked for $220 million while IMC offered $125 million. PCS settled for $135 million because of its desperate need for cash and the political pressure it faced: "Officials of IMC told representatives of the Corporation that if the offer of $135 million were not acceptable to the Corporation, IMC would approach the owner in Regina for a settlement."[3]

You might say "IMC had PCS by the balls." Normally, a good negotiator would respond to IMC pressure with a few well-chosen expletives. That this, apparently, did not occur speaks of the constraints under which PCS management, who were competent people, were functioning. Political interference continued. When approving 1985 strategic plans as well as the 10-year plan, the board took note of a directive from the chairman: "The Honourable Paul Schoenhals stated that the 1986 Corporate Plan must be developed on the basis that all mining divisions will operate."[4] Curiously, a set of draft minutes contained the following words added to the above statement, which were then deleted from the official minutes as approved at the next meeting: "although circumstances could change during the year to alter that plan."[5] Why? The answer is easy! The last general election in Saskatchewan was held in 1982. The year 1986 was four years later, a normal election cycle, and an election could be called at any time. There can be little question Mr. Schoenhals wanted to minimize problems the government might encounter in its re-election bid, and layoffs would not be desirable politically. Later, there was a complaint that directors should have been informed that quarterly reports were not being released. The minutes report: "The Hon. Paul Schoenhals advised that the decision not to release the first Quarterly Report was primarily political in anticipation of a June election but was then reinforced as a result of concerns expressed by corporate management as to the possible antidumping investigation."[6]

The board met on September 22, 1986, and had before it a devastating report on the state of affairs. The Executive Committee could only report:

> Chairman Wright and some members of the Executive Committee had an opportunity to make a brief presentation to the Premier and some of his Cabinet with respect to the concerns related to the debt load of PCS and the restraints that it, as well as other directives, have placed on the operating opportunities for PCS and its subsidiaries to improve their financial performance. The Premier and his Committee accepted the need to direct their attention to the problems of PCS but indicated that no action should be expected within the next couple of months."[17]

While both the board and management had been pleading for help, direction, and/or the removal of restraints since the beginning of the year, it was obvious the government was not going to do anything yet. The reason was obvious. It was the impending election that was finally held on October 20, 1986, and was won by the incumbent government. Losses for the year to the end of August were $67.6 million. There were repeated complaints that the corporation had not been allowed to function as a commercial entity, meaning that layoffs and/or mine shutdowns along with other things were not being allowed because of the political fallout for the government of the day.

The heavy hand of the government continued even after the election was over. For example, on industrial relations, "The Honourable Gary Lane *directed* that PCS Mining not carry out further negotiations at PCS Mining, Cory Division until the review of the overall corporate status has been completed" (emphasis added).[18] Continuing delays in responding to PCS pleas seemed to ignore 1986 losses, now expected to be $110–112 million, and a projected 1987 loss of $143.5 million. With some jiggery-pokery, 1986 losses were reduced to $103.4 million by transferring some interest costs from operating expenses to the capitalized interest cost of the Lanigan expansion. Capitalized interest costs for the Lanigan expansion were finalized at $153.8 million.

Many of the wide range of issues facing PCS in 1985 sprang from decisions made in the previous two and half years, but ongoing events also played a role. A modest profit of $25 million for 1984 did not over-come problems. The debt–equity ratio was not good, and while the dividend demand had been scaled down, it was still more than could be handled. A serious operational problem due to a difficult water flow at the Rocanville mine added to existing problems. The sale of assets was mooted while, at the same time, there was talk of PCS purchasing the remaining 40% of the Allan mine. The president reported that the rest of the industry was at or exceeding 100% of capacity, while PCS lagged at 60–70%.[19] Meanwhile the premier and others in government were criticizing the 1985 strategic plan.

More storm clouds loomed on the horizon. The premier and a num-ber of government officials travelled to England, where they studied the privatization program undertaken by the Conservative government led by Margaret Thatcher. SaskOil was privatized in stages. An American company, Weyerhaueser, bought Prince Albert Pulp Company on generous terms in return for a commitment to add a paper mill to the operation. It was not yet clear, though, how much further the govern-ment was going to go in a privatization program.

PCS faced a growing array of problems. Its share of North American markets continued to drop, and it had slipped back to being a residual supplier in the industry. It was pointed out that unit costs of produc-tion would be reduced by 10–15% if there was full production. Canpo-tex was not doing its best for PCS, leading to thoughts of pulling out again. Asset sales came onto the agenda again, including sale of Amax reserves to IMC, the lowest-cost production division. (Previous nego-tiations were not concluded.) That would increase average unit costs and strengthen IMC's competitive position. The debt burden was now critical, and bankers expressed concern. There were solutions. If the province assumed $300 million of debt in return for equity, it would save $42 million in interest. But there was no action.

Things kept going from bad to worse. First estimates for 1986 were for a $153.4 million loss. The board of directors was alarmed and decided to go to the government with its concerns about the financial future of the corporation and request direction as to its intentions for the corporation. As 1986 unfolded, PCS faced a full-blown crisis. Loss for 1985 was first determined as $60.6 million but ended up at $68.7 million due to adjustments for bad debts, price adjustments, writeoffs, et cetera. Talks were held with Premier Devine, two senior cabinet ministers, and senior officials. Steps proposed to prevent financial collapse included completing the sale to IMC, reducing staff by 400, and closing down at least one operating division. What was the answer they got? Senior officials would study the problem.

It became apparent that a continuation of PCS problems would further downgrade the province's financial rating. Tom Kierans, president of McLeod, Young, Weir, an investment firm, looked at this matter and had more comments about PCS affairs. They included:

- the value of PCS on Heritage Fund books is overstated by $500 million;

- PCS is much overstaffed;

- PCS needs to go into a survival mode;

- doubts PCS is best served by Canpotex; and,

- the specter of a U.S. dumping finding needs special attention.

Efforts continued in search of solutions. Favourable events in 1986 helped to improve the bleak outlook anticipated at the beginning of the year. Other producing companies in Saskatchewan had also experienced losses. An oversupply situation, to which the decision to continue the Lanigan expansion contributed substantially, was at the root of ongoing market difficulties.

Peat Marwick, a consulting firm, studied changes that should be made to PCS. An observation by an official of that firm was recorded: "Regarding decision making, Loboe felt that everything seemed to be deferred or delayed or stopped by the Government policy and U.S. tax concerns."[20] The report contained stinging criticisms of both the government and PCS: "no clear mandate has been conveyed to management by PCS Board of Directors on behalf of the Government of Saskatchewan. Such a statement of fundamental corporate purpose is an essential prerequisite to the development of a strategic plan."[21] Later in the report, it was stated: "The agreed mission should state clearly whether the Corporation is to act commercially or whether its role is also to meet social objectives."[22] The report also contained severe criticisms of the strategic plan prepared by management: "We found that PCS management has not developed a comprehensive strategy for aggressively penetrating the domestic and off-shore markets. Our interviews with domestic marketing personnel revealed serious frustration over the lack of a well-organized and co-ordinated marketing effort."[23] The report contained important recommendations on what should be done, but when the Executive Committee of PCS met with Crown Management Board (the Devine version of Crown Investments Corporations) on June 13, 1986, the item could not be dealt with because of the absence of three key ministers, Premier Devine and ministers Lane and Andrews.

By the next board meeting on August 11, 1986, there was no indication of progress on major outstanding issues. The sharpness and severity of comments in the Peat Marwick report would normally result in major initiatives taken promptly to correct problems identified. Operating loss for the first six months was not as much as expected but all the Executive Committee could say was:

> The Committee concluded that there was a need for an immediate meeting with senior Cabinet representatives, including the Premier, to attempt to gain approval from the Government for PCS to adopt a survival mode that would include restructuring, curtailing of production and reduction of costs—the need to become a low cost producer was evident—and to discuss the need for relief from the current debt load of the Corporation. The Hon. Paul Schoenhals advised the requested meeting would be arranged for early in the week of August 18.[24]

In the meantime, PCS started quietly reducing staff. Management was directed to try and find investors who may be able to take equity in PCS assets and/or production. In spite of ongoing attempts to seek guidance from the government, a stalemate remained, even with the election over, when the board of directors met on November 3, 1986. All they could do was pass another motion:

> The 1987–1996 Strategic Corporate Plan be received by the Board of Directors and that a decision on the Plan be held in abeyance until such time as the Executive Committee of the

Board has had an opportunity, at the earliest possible date, to meet with representatives of the Government of Saskatchewan to attempt to determine the Government's directions for the Potash Corporation of Saskatchewan so that a decision can be made by the Board on the recommendations included in the Corporate Plan. The Committee is to report back to the Board at the earliest possible date.[25]

Something finally began to happen in December. Chairman Cliff Wright resigned from the board and Hon. Gary Lane replaced Hon. Paul Schoenhals as vice-chairman, the latter having been defeated in the general election. Subsequently, he was appointed chairman of PCS. The board was informed on December 18, 1986, the government was now planning to move quickly on PCS affairs, likely in January. In spite of these promises, things dragged on for some months into 1987.

On May 4, 1987, some extraordinary events came to light at an in camera board meeting. The chairman, Paul Schoenhals, revealed that Charles Childers, a former IMC executive, was now CEO. He:

> acknowledged to the Board of Directors that the Hon. Gary Lane, as Minister-in-charge of the Potash Corporation of Sas- katchewan had accepted his recommendation for the appoint- ment of Charles E. Childers as President and Chief Executive Officer of the Potash Corporation ...
>
> The Chairman apologized for the difficulty in providing to the Members of the Board of Directors detailed particulars of the appointments in advance. The Chairman acknowledged that under ordinary circumstances it was the role of the Board of Directors to participate in decisions of this sort and he also acknowledged the importance of communication with the Directors so that they be kept fully informed of activities related to the company.[26]

Thus, the board of directors as a body played no role in changing the chief executive officer of the corporation, the most important function of the board. It appears they had no knowledge that it was about to occur, although there is no record of what might have been said at pre- vious in camera sessions. The above account suggests board members voiced protests to which the chairman had to respond. The thought that comes to my mind is why wouldn't any self-respecting board member resign after having been kicked around this way and PCS having been left dangling for so long.

Appointment of the chief executive officer is not just a formality or a routine matter. For a corporation of the nature of PCS, a long and complex process is generally required. Thus, there were some real sensitivities. In addition, six senior officers whose appointments were also subject to board approval were terminated. Legal requirements were addressed at a June 22, 1987, meeting effectively covering things up. In the final analysis, it would appear board members were prepared to be "pussycats" and accept their fees. A motion was passed ratifying the termination of the six senior officers, ratifying the appointment of the new president, C. E. Childers, and ratifying the action of the chairman and the vice-chairman in dismissing Steven Harapiak, the previous president. The covering agenda item pointed out that the Potash Corporation of Saskatchewan Act provides that business is to be managed by the board of directors, that the appointment of senior executive officers has always been the decision of the board, and that the resolution would "record compliance with the statutory responsibility of the Board of Directors and remove any possible challenge to the legality of the action taken."[27]

PCS affairs were further complicated by an anti-dumping action taken by some US potash producers in early 1987. Saskatchewan producers joined forces to fight this action in US courts. The US investigation was suspended in January 1988 after an agreement was reached between the US Department of Commerce and eight Canadian potash companies. Special legislation passed by the Saskatchewan Legislature helped to resolve matters.

PCS had always followed a low to medium price policy. Now it took the initiative to increase prices sharply, an action that was copied immediately by other Saskatchewan producers. However, in this scenario, PCS produced at only 55% of capacity, while private producers operated at 80–85% of capacity. Another problem was that PCS had to share the costs of a difficult and expensive water leak at the IMC mine under the agreement concerning the mining of PCS ores. On the other hand, potash markets improved during 1987, and PCS showed a modest surplus in some months, bringing total loss for the year much down from original projections.

Hints of privatization or, euphemistically, "public participation" began to surface in 1987. In the meantime, PCS was putting its house in order. Near the end of the year, a massive debt–equity swap took place that at last gave PCS a chance. 1988 operations were much better than previous years. By mid-year, net income was over $61 million, about $20 million higher than budget. The pricing policy change was a major factor, along with the financial changes made at the end of 1987.

The proposition of buying out the remaining portion of the Allan mine surfaced again. This portion, previously called Texasgulf, was now owned by Canada Development Corporation, a federal crown-owned economic development operation, and was managed by a subsidiary, Saskterra. The minutes of a June 14, 1988, board meeting reveal more political interference:

> Saskterra is proceeding with its tender for its potash holdings through the sale of its shares. ... It was the President's view that pursuing the purchase of the Saskterra interests would be a good business decision for PCS. However, after discussion among the Board members, with particular emphasis by the Hon. Gary Lane as to the problems that would be presented if PCS were to buy a new interest in a potash mine at the same time that it was reducing production at Cory and, at the same time, also taking the political position that the province should proceed with privatization of PCS and get out of the potash business, there was consensus that the purchase of Saskterra should not be pursued directly by PCS at this time.[28]

Once again, a decision was based on other than commercial factors. The new president, in accordance with his obligations, pointed the board of directors in the direction of a sound business decision. It was the board that demurred as a result of obvious and forceful pressure from the minister-in-charge of PCS, whose only interest was the government's privatization agenda.

The matter didn't rest there though. At the next meeting, the president brought back another proposal after being approached by a group including the Hill interests in Regina. Business considerations still did not take priority. "It was the President's view that such a proposal would allow PCS to gain absolute control of the Allan mine and would have, as well, a beneficial impact on the market, and therefore should proceed."[29] But that was not to be!

> However, after discussion among the Board members, which discussion centered upon the value of the assets to be exchanged, and upon the relationship of the proposal to the overall privatization process, there was consensus that while a marketing agreement could be pursued at this time with the Hill group, an asset exchange would require the review and approval of Cabinet."[30]

External control over decisions was extended to other things such as salary increases, which were made subject to "Ministerial and other governmental approval."[31]

By the end of 1988, corporation affairs were much improved. Year-end profit was over $106 million, much higher than the $60.7 million budgeted. A dividend was paid to CIC and $42.7 million of equity was repaid. The removal of the debt burden together with improved markets made all the difference. Record sales, production, safety, and productivity made for a profitable year. The record production feature of 1988 performance was achieved by tackling storage and layoff issues that management had been prevented from acting on previously. 1988 production was about 5.1 million compared to 8.6 million tonnes capacity. Reduced production was achieved through severe cuts at the PCS Cory mine.

The glowing picture of future prospects painted by the president and chief executive officer, C. E. Childers, in comments contained in the 1988 *Annual Report* is puzzling in the light of events that were to occur very shortly after. Childers, after all, was the appointee of the incumbent government: "We look forward to the future, eager to take advantage of market growth as more and more countries provide better diets for a growing world population. PCS, through its nearly four million tonnes of excess capacity, is well positioned to respond to this anticipated increase in world demand for potash."[32]

The first board meeting of 1989 learned of developments pointing to a fundamental change. PCS was next on the list of crown corporations planned for privatization:

The President reported that shortly after the December 1988 Board meeting, Minister Lane requested that PCS develop proposals for privatization. As a result of that request, four investment houses were asked to provide their assessments of privatization options for PCS. Those assessments were unanimous in suggesting that PCS privatize by way of a public share offering, with a first issue in the Spring of 1989, if possible. [Isn't that something like the practice, past and current, where people about to be executed must dig their own graves?]

As a result, PCS management is recommending such an offering to take place in June 1989 with special consideration given to the Saskatchewan market, and with provision for employee share purchase and executive share option plans.

The President advised as well that accounting and legal firms have been retained (Deloitte Haskins and Sells and Robertson Stromberg) to provide necessary professional advice.[33]

Privatization had been rumoured and talked about for some time. Prior to the 1986 election, some steps had been taken, but there was no indication that much more would happen soon. Any suggestions to that effect were denied during the 1986 election. Indications after the election were that it was still not a priority. It was only in November 1987 that the government made a public commitment to a full-scale privatization program, including PCS. There is evidence that planning for the process had been well under way for some time and certainly at the time when the PCS board of directors was pleading for help. A number of crown corporations were disposed of before they turned their attention to PCS.[34]

The board of directors discussed privatization again on March 23, 1989. Corporate resources were being utilized in managing the process:

The President reported on the progress of the privatization initiative and the work being done on corporate re-organization, tax and valuation issues and legislative matters. Legislation is anticipated for the week of March 27, 1989 but no firm legislative agenda has yet been determined. The proposed legislation will contain provisions regarding maximum shareholdings for any one person, provisions on foreign shareholdings and restrictions on head office location. ... Gary Lane then provided the Board with a review of certain matters related to the privatization process including the underwriter selection, timing of the privatization and selection of a new Board.[35]

On April 11, 1989, the board reviewed a draft prospectus on the privatization, and a resolution was passed authorizing its completion for presentation in draft form to regulatory authorities. NDP members in the Saskatchewan Legislature then blocked the legislation for some time in the famous "bell-ringing" incident where they prevented a vote by not coming into the legislative chamber. While the bell-ringing was under way, NDP Opposition members fanned out across the province, holding rallies explaining their stance and raising public ire against the government's actions. The government wanted to privatize the natural gas utility, SaskEnergy, at the same time. The Opposition created quite a storm. I attended one of those rallies. But in the final analysis, the government backed down on SaskEnergy and pushed through the PCS legislation. They had accomplished their goal. Eric Berntsen, deputy premier for the nine years of the Devine Conservative government, told some NDP members informally, "When you guys get back into power, we have things so tied up that you won't be able to do anything for 10 years."

In spite of a lengthy delay, preparations went ahead for privatization. In a telephone conference call on June 20, 1989, the board approved the payment of a dividend of $106,120,000 to Crown Investments Corporation. This was the net income for 1988. The net income of $49,363,000 for the first five months of 1989 was left in PCS. At the same time, a new entity, PCS Inc., was established as a vehicle for the privatization process and PCS lent it $40 million without interest. In this way, PCS helped create and fund the instrument that would be used to buy it out.

The board of directors dealt with ongoing business on July 13, 1989. The only item out of the ordinary was that the chairman, Paul Schoenhals, announced he was tendering his resignation as chairman effective August 1, 1989, but he would stay on as a member of the board. When the next and final meeting of the board of directors was held on October 30, 1989, the last item of business was a motion to approve severance compensation for Mr. Schoenhals. It is not often that a corporation rewards its chairman for having taken an active role in its demise.

The major item of business at the final meeting of the corporation was approval of a raft of resolutions necessary to effect the transfer of substantially all assets and affairs to the privatized entity, PCS Inc. The legislation had passed by this time after lengthy debate and the prolonged "bell-ringing" affair in the Saskatchewan Legislature. PCS had all 35 million shares in PCS Inc. initially. PCS then sold 12,860,000 of its common shares for $231 million plus underwriting fees, commissions, and issue costs totalling $23 million.[36] Among the resolutions passed were three that sold shares to Merrill Lynch Capital Markets; Merrill Lynch; Pierce, Fenner & Smith Incorporated; the First Boston Corporation; Goldman Sachs & Co.; Credit Suisse First Boston Limited; Wood Gundy Inc.; BNF Capital Market Limited; Deutsche Bank Capital Markets Limited; Nomura International plc; RBC Dominion Securities International Limited; N. M. Rothschild & Sons Limited; UBS Phillips & Drew Securities Limited; RBC Dominion Securities Inc.; Nesbitt Thomson Deacon Inc.; Scotia McLeod Inc.; Richardson Greenshields of Canada Limited; and Gordon Capital Corporation. I see very few Canadian names on that list. I see no Saskatchewan names. However, I should acknowledge that out of the 12,860,000 shares, there were 88,300 shares sold to employees at a discounted price, that is, less than one percent of the total.

While PCS retained 10,951,700 shares as an investment in PCS Inc., another 11,100,000 common shares were placed in trust with a trustee in order to reserve them for a Potash Ownership Bond program. The Province of Saskatchewan issued $192 million of these bonds for sale to Saskatchewan residents. These bonds could be exchanged for shares to Saskatchewan residents. These bonds could be exchanged for shares after December 1, 1990. The exchange rights terminated with the maturity of the bonds on December 1, 1992.

The 1989 *Annual Report* of PCS reported a loss on its investment in PCS Inc. of $441.5 million, which was derived from the difference between the book value of PCS Inc. shares and their market value on November 9, 1989. Other costs were $22.5 million. The recorded cost to Saskatchewan taxpayers was only a book value. It did not assess the real or commercial loss to the province. A complicated set of transactions enabled the government to arrange for the sale of its remaining interests in the potash operation to the public.

With little fanfare and a lengthy ream of legal documents dealt with and approved in a matter of minutes, Potash Corporation of Saskatchewan passed into history. The denuded corporation changed its name to CIC Mineral Interests Corporation on January 10, 1990, in order to house the remains of an entity that had the potential to help make Saskatchewan a much greater province than it is now or likely ever will be.

# CHAPTER 12
## The Privately Owned Industry, 1989 to Now

Saskatchewan's potash industry has been completely privately owned since 1989. "None of this public ownership nonsense" would be some views. A block of PCS Inc. shares were still publicly owned after privatization, but that didn't last long. A seismic shift in the industry had taken place, and things were designed so it would last for a long time. PCS Inc. started out as the largest operator in Saskatchewan, and it soon became the dominant player. This discussion starts out with an outline of PCS Inc. settling into its new status and then how it strengthened its position. This is followed with a review of activities in the remainder of the industry.

On the first day of business for PCS Inc., you might almost think nothing had changed. The president was in his office, all the other senior executives were at their posts, the same comely, smartly dressed personal secretary to the president was there to greet callers with a friendly smile. The miners went down into the mines with the same kind of camaraderie as before. There was only one big difference. The primary goal of the previous crown corporation was to maximize benefits from Saskatchewan's potash production for the people of the province. The primary purpose of the new privatized corporation, Potash Corporation of Saskatchewan Inc. (PCS Inc.), was to maximize profits for its shareholders. Not that the province did not receive benefits from potash activity—it did, of course. The issue was, what was the primary goal of its activity? Who came first?

Changes in personnel came in time. One change of interest was a move from government to PCS Inc. Wayne Brownlee was the Budget Bureau analyst in the Department of Finance whose assignments included the Department of Tourism and Renewable Resources when I was associate deputy minister there. He was a competent and pleasant person with distinctive, heavy, black eyebrows. In time, he became associate deputy minister of finance. In 1989, he coordinated the privatization of PCS from a crown corporation to a private company or, as it is otherwise described, "a publicly traded company." In his new role, he headed expansion and development programs in the 1990s to the tune of $4 billion while serving as a senior executive. More recently, he has been "Executive Vice-President, Treasurer and Chief Financial Officer." In a 2006 interview I had with him, Brownlee outlined his perception of the atmosphere surrounding changes that took place in the potash industry over time:

> ... I think it was a combination of political ideology, opportunism and just a sign of the times. ... you could go back in history and argue that the company actually became a crown corporation and nationalized in the '70s and the Saskatchewan government wasn't significantly out of step with what was going on in the rest of Canada and in fact around the world, that there was a lot of government ownership of industries that was happening as a way for governments to try and take control of their own destiny. Saskatchewan really wasn't any different than that and maybe took it to a greater extent than some governments did, but that was certainly in vogue with the politics of the day in the '70s and I would argue that in the same way that privatization subsequently, in 1989, was in vogue with the political sensitivities of the day as well. It fell on the heels of the privatization in Britain, it fell on the heels of some privatization activities in Ottawa or in fact it may have led on some of those. ... you see governments trying to take ownership and then governments trying to get out of ownership. And I'm not sure that it was much different than that.[1]

Privatization did make some matters easier to manage. Investments outside the province that are beneficial for its operations could be pursued more easily because crown corporations have to be more sensitive about such initiatives. The particular interests of the province, however, may not necessarily take the same priority in making decisions. Private corporations have two sensitive points of interaction with shareholders. One is the annual meeting. The other is the interaction between the company and shareholders through investment houses who "put their feet to the fire" about company performance. Crown corporations appear before the Crown Corporations Committee of the Legislature, which serves much the same function as an annual meeting, but the nature of questioning can be different because purposes and interests may be different. Wayne Brownlee discussed this issue from the viewpoint of a private corporation in my interview:

> I would actually argue that in a publicly traded sector, we're actually more accountable than you are in the public sector, period. I mean we meet with investors on an ongoing basis. We go through our total shareholder base easily twice a year with one-on-one situations and we do numerous presentations. I mean the annual report or the annual meeting of shareholders, you know, from time to time it's got some important issues, but it's the ongoing public accountability that you have with your shareholders. And when you watch your share price, it's a discipline in and of itself, because if it's going one way, it sends you a message and if it's going the other way, it sends you a message. ... if you look at the current internal control environment that we have to deal with as a publicly traded company, where we're subject to both US and Canadian requirements, the internal control here is significantly higher than anything I had ever experienced in the public service. ... So it forces good management.[2]

The early 1990s were difficult for the potash industry. Economic and political uncertainty plagued many of the industry's major players. The reunification of Germany, the collapse of the Iron Curtain in Eastern Europe, and the move toward free-market-based economies throughout much of the former Communist world destabilized potash markets. Both the former USSR and East Germany were major producers of potash, which for the most part was sold internally, although some did go to western Europe. Political and economic instability in the former Eastern bloc led to much lower fertilizer consumption in the region. Combined with lower consumption in India and China due to the removal of government subsidies for fertilizer and decreased demand in the United States, worldwide potash demand dropped 30% between 1988 and 1993.[3]

The brunt of the downturn was borne by producers in Germany and the former Soviet Union. Their costs were higher than Saskatchewan mines. Six of 10 mines in former East Germany were closed in 1991, followed by a series of mergers and amalgamations of the industry in Germany. 1994 German production was less than 50% of 1988 levels.[4] The Carlsbad Horizon mine in the United States also closed. Global potash demand still fell faster than capacity reduction in Germany and East Europe. Surplus Russian and German potash was sold in Asia and Latin America, which cut into Saskatchewan markets. The need for hard foreign currency motivated them to drop prices.

In spite of these factors, PCS Inc. did surprisingly well. Saskatchewan was no longer the shareholder. The new shareholders looked for profits and were not particularly concerned about other effects. Profits dropped to $25.4 million in 1990 from $83.3 million the year before but recovered to $63.1 million in 1993. The NDP Government of Saskatchewan, beset by large budget deficits inherited from the previous Conservative regime, took advantage of a rise in stock price to divest most of the 30% that it still owned in the company and reduced its ownership to only 1.2% of the company. The Opposition Conservatives didn't say much about that because they were responsible for the deficit situation, but when the stock price unexpectedly rose much higher after the sale, they had lots to say, and the NDP government had to be very apologetic.

Remaining profitable in the poor potash market was possible because of the high grade of Saskatchewan potash and the cost-effectiveness of its mining and refining. The PCS Inc. bottom line was further helped by an existing strong transportation system of rail and ships that allowed it to deliver potash to international markets more predictably than Eastern European mines. The sound efforts by PCS, the crown corporation, materially benefited the privatized PCS Inc. However, the market situation led the company to operate much below capacity by limiting shifts at some mines and routinely closing down its mines for four weeks each summer.

After privatization, PCS Inc. owned four mines located at Allan
(60%), Cory, Lanigan, and Rocanville, plus its reserves mined by IMC
under contract at Esterhazy. Even with weak potash markets, PCS Inc.
did what Gary Lane would not let PCS do. It expanded by purchasing the remaining 40% of the Allan mine for $47 million plus working
capital. A small mine at Moab, Utah, came with the purchase, but it
was sold later with PCS Inc. retaining the marketing function.[5] Next,
the company made its first venture beyond mining and refining and
acquired Florida Favorite Fertilizers, a company that blended and sold
fertilizers in Florida, Georgia, and Alabama.

In October 1993, PCS Inc. made the biggest purchase to date, buying the potash assets of Potash Corporation of America. It acquired the
Patience Lake mine near Saskatoon and a potash mine at Sussex, New
Brunswick, along with potash storage and port facilities at St. John, NB.
The latter mine differed from Saskatchewan mines because the potash
bed was steeply inclined, making it more expensive to mine. This factor
was offset by the advantage of nearby port facilities that also provided
better access to European markets. PCS Inc. was now the only potash
company with shipping facilities on the Atlantic as well as the Pacific
and the Gulf of Mexico (through Canpotex). PCS Inc. also made an
agreement with all but one of the New Mexico potash mines to act as
broker for their international potash sales. This, along with the New
Brunswick mine, allowed the company to sidestep Canpotex and sell
potash directly to international markets.

While PCS Inc. now accounted for 13% of worldwide production,
it had 20% of worldwide capacity. The company thus had 40% of the
world's excess capacity, which would not benefit the company until
markets improved, which they finally did in 1994. Consumption grew
for the first time since 1988, revenue rose by almost 60%, and earnings
per share nearly doubled. Why? Eastern European and Russian mines
stopped undercutting the international price.[6] Higher prices, coupled
with increased consumption in nearly every market, particularly China,
drove growth. PCS Inc. retired nearly all of its debt and doubled stock
dividends.

Markets continued to grow in 1995. Production and sales records
were broken again, and potash sales remained strong until late in the
decade. Market strength together with absence of debt allowed PCS
Inc. to diversify and become a full fertilizer company selling all major

nutrients. This was foreseen by PCS, the crown corporation, as a long-term goal. PCS Inc. made a forceful move into the phosphate industry, purchasing two major North American companies, North Carolina based Texasgulf and Florida-based White Springs Ag Chemical in 1995, for over $1.1 billion, financed mostly through debt and share offerings.[7] Both companies had high-quality phosphoric mines and processing facilities that allowed rock to be refined into phosphoric acid, which was then converted into liquid and solid fertilizers, feed supplements for livestock, and raw chemicals for industrial users.

The two phosphate mines acquired accounted for about 8% of the world industry. Seven feed phosphate plants were also acquired that produced 50% of the American supply of feed phosphate, widely used as a supplement in the beef, pork, and poultry industries. In 1999, PCS Inc. added to its strength in the feed phosphate industry by purchasing a plant in Brazil that provided products for the growing ranching industry in South America.

The next year, PCS Inc. expanded further by entering the nitrogen fertilizer industry. It purchased Arcadian Corporation, the largest producer of nitrogen in the western hemisphere through its seven nitrogen plants in the United States and a large facility in Trinidad. These plants used natural gas and steam to form hydrogen and then converted it to ammonia. The latter is used to create a number of nitrogen-based fertilizers as well as a number of other industrial products. Unlike phosphates and potash, nitrogen was a highly regional business with little export beyond the producing area. Nearly all of the nitrogen produced by PCS Inc. was consumed in the United States.

With its substantial potash holdings and major acquisitions in the phosphate and nitrogen industries, PCS Inc. was now one of the largest players in the worldwide fertilizer industry and the largest company that sold all three basic fertilizer products. In 1997, a flooded mine with a potash mill in New Brunswick was purchased, adding another facility owned in that province. The mill was used to process excess production from Saskatchewan and provided more product to sell to Europe and eastern North America.

PCS Inc. also attempted to expand its potash business beyond North American shores but had limited success. Its first move was to attempt to buy a controlling interest in the major German potash company, Kali und Salz AG, in 1996. This was the company that emerged from the consolidation of the German potash industry after the unification of East and West Germany. It accounted for 15% of world potash production.[8] The move was blocked in early 1997 when the German government stopped the sale. Undeterred, PCS Inc. turned its sights on one of the largest potash producers in the Middle East, Israel Chemicals Ltd. Again, it tried to purchase a controlling interest but was blocked by the Israeli government, which limited PCS Inc. to 9% of the company[9] at first and to 11% by 2009. PCS Inc. did add to its Middle East potash position by purchasing 26% of the Arab Potash Corporation of Jordan between 2003 and 2005.

PCS Inc. then gave attention to increasing its presence in South America. In 1999, it purchased a new potash mine nearing completion at Yumbes, Chile. The mine came into operation within a year and mined potassium nitrate and sodium nitrate for specialty fertilizer markets. In 2001 and 2002, PCS Inc. also invested in Chile's main potash producer, Sociedad Quimica y Minera de Chile (SQM), buying 20% of the company and increasing its holdings to 32% later. However, success at the Yumbes mine proved difficult. High start-up costs associated with the new mine and slumping potash prices at the time prevented the property reaching the profitability PCS Inc. had expected, and the mine was sold back to SQM in 2003.

After its 10 years of operation as a private company, aggressive acquisitions had increased company assets by four times while sales multiplied 11 times.[10] The nitrogen division encountered difficulties, and in 1998 and 1999, three plants were closed. Nitrogen markets were more competitive than potash and phosphates, and pricing was more sensitive. As more Russian nitrogen fertilizer came on the market and prices dropped, PCS Inc. cut back its production. However, it was partially insulated from the price softening as 30% of its nitrogen was sold to industrial consumers at a higher price. The potash and phosphate divisions experienced variable markets influenced by factors such as grain volumes, inventory levels, the Canadian dollar, shipping costs, and international productive capacity. Even in market downturns, PCS Inc. was the only major North American fertilizer company to remain profitable. A high price policy paid off for private shareholders.

Nitrogen continued to cause PCS Inc. problems. New capacity in the developing world came on stream, increasing competition. Rising natural gas prices hurt profits still more. Decreased demand for nitrogen in the United States depressed prices further in 2000.[11] While the collapse of the market hurt PCS Inc., it was well positioned because it supplied a large number of industrial users outside the fertilizer industry and hedged natural gas prices, locking in lower costs especially at its large Trinidad plant. Nevertheless, PCS Inc. was forced to suspend production at two more plants in 2003.

2003 was the bottom of the fertilizer slump. PCS Inc. lost over $126 million that year, partly due to the costs of plant closures. The downturn was short lived as the world economy strengthened. Increased demand for fertilizer led to an era of spectacular growth. Company revenues rose in 2004 and PCS Inc. made just under $100 million. Profits increased to $543 million in 2005 and $632 million the following year. The strong market continued as the company made over a billion dollars for the first time, a $1.1 billion profit. In 2007, profit more than tripled to $3.49 billion. Record potash production of 9.2 million tonnes accounted for most of the increase.[12] Prices increased by 169% in 2008 alone as the company took full advantage of market conditions.[13]

While potash was the major factor in the company's performance, all products contributed. Both nitrogen and phosphate divisions achieved record profitability in 2008. This led to an expansion in capacity at the Trinidad plant and reopening of a previously closed nitrogen facility. High potash prices also triggered plans for major expansions for all its mines, with the aim of adding over 10 million tonnes of capacity by 2012 at a cost of $7 billion dollars.[14] The first round of these expansions was completed in 2008 at the Allan, Rocanville, and Lanigan mines.[15]

The increased revenue allowed PCS Inc. to expand its international investments by adding to its holdings in SQM, Israel Chemicals Ltd. and the Arab Potash Company. The company also turned to Chinese acquisitions, purchasing 20% of Sinofert, a vertically integrated fertilizer company, in 2005. Another 2% was added in 2008. The purchase was designed to invest in the Chinese fertilizer market, where a large percentage of PCS raw potash was shipped.[16]

Increased profitability enabled the company to repurchase 9% of its shares in 2005 and another 7% in 2008. These purchases and growing profitability caused stock value to rise 368% between 2002 and 2006[17] but by mid-2008 it peaked. At $241 per share, it was almost five times higher than 2006. But that didn't last. The price fell sharply as the mortgage crisis and the collapse of several major financial institutions in the United

States caused global markets to fall sharply. Prices fell back to the 2006 level. The 2008 *Annual Report* of PCS Inc. described the state of affairs:

> We are the world's largest fertilizer enterprise, producing the three primary plant nutrients: potash, phosphate and nitrogen. Among these, potash—the main focus of our business—delivers the highest quality earnings. With large low cost operations, plans to expand capacity significantly and strategic global investments, we have an unmatched ability to meet the needs of North America and growing offshore markets.

Total assets in 2008 were over $10.2 billion, double the number in 2004. Potash gross margin in 2008 was $3.1 billion, which was attributed to higher prices that helped to offset a lower sales volume. While acknowledging the impact of the economic downturn in late 2008, the company was still optimistic. The president, in his report, pointed out that, "The long term need to increase food production remains a critical issue." He then emphasized that to meet future needs, the company was investing $7 billion to raise potash capacity to 18 million tonnes by 2012.

In Note 1 to its 2008 financial statement the following producing assets were listed:

| | |
|---|---|
| **POTASH** | five mines and mills and mining rights to potash reserves at a sixth location, all in the province of Saskatchewan |
| | one mine and mill in New Brunswick |
| **PHOSPHATE** | a mine and processing plants in the state of North Carolina |
| | a mine and two processing plants in the state of Florida |
| | a processing plant in the state of Louisiana |
| | phosphate feed plants in five states |
| | an industrial phosphoric acid plant in the state of Ohio |
| **NITROGEN** | three plants in the states of Georgia, Louisiana and Ohio |
| | large scale operations in Trinidad |

PCS Inc. is a very successful company. Shareholders will be quite happy. Some time ago, it was identified in *Fortune* magazine as a number one attraction for investment. After having reached the top of the roller coaster in 2008, it experienced severe cutbacks in its production, profits, and share price. It was well placed to weather the storm and had a solid standing as an attractive investment. It seemed to be well established as a top-notch firm in the industrial world. But, as described later, it attracted the attention of a huge Anglo-Australian mining firm as a desirable takeover. This added another potential dimension to the role of potash that remains to be played out.

\* \* \*

The other firms in Saskatchewan's potash industry avoided becoming targets in the midst of the dramatic events surrounding the 1975 legislation. The most important firm was International Minerals and Chemical Corporation (IMC). It was the largest Saskatchewan operation at the time. Aided by a measure of good fortune, it manoeuvred affairs so that it never became an active target for purchase or expropriation. Potash was a key component of its operations, so the company was anxious to protect its assets. Targeting IMC was considered by PCS at one time in order to reach the government's objective of 50% public ownership in the industry, but it was not pursued after other acquisitions were made. By not acquiring IMC, PCS knew that it would be its major competitor. Later, IMC added to its strength by acquiring Kalium Mines at Belle Plaine, a solution mine producing a more refined product.

In 2004, IMC combined with Cargill Crop Nutrition to form the Mosaic Company, a full-service global fertilizer company. Both IMC and Cargill already operated on a global scale, and the merger created an even stronger operation marketing all major plant nutrients. IMC, with over 5,000 employees, was dwarfed by Cargill with over 100,000. Cargill assumed 64% ownership making it the dominant partner. It was not surprising that the new chief executive officer was a former Cargill executive. The new company did not have to consider itself in second place in marketing now.

Next, Mosaic purchased the former Noranda mine at Colonsay. The industry was now effectively rationalized. There were now three firms, the third being Agrium, managing the entire Saskatchewan potash industry compared to the 12 firms that operated 10 mines in the original configuration. While PCS Inc. was still the largest operator, Mosaic was a formidable adversary, able to compete effectively. It had four mines, one of which produced white potash, a superior product. The three firms, Mosaic, Agrium, and PCS Inc. jointly own Canpotex, the offshore marketing agency.

In January 2011, Cargill made a surprise announcement that it intended to dispose of its shares in Mosaic.[18] This occurred because of internal corporate problems. A major shareholder in Cargill, a privately owned firm, died leaving virtually all of her estate to her favourite charity. Cash was needed to settle affairs, and Cargill decided to sell its holdings in Mosaic in order to get the funds needed. Control of Mosaic as a result of these events concerned the company. Recently, they bought back some of the shares that had been sold.

Currently (2012), Mosaic's production capability is 10.4 million tonnes annually, making it the third largest in the world; $5.5 billion is being invested now at the Belle Plaine solution mine. More than $2 billion is also being invested in a third mine at Esterhazy, plus another $1 billion at Colonsay.[19]

Agrium, the third company producing potash in Saskatchewan, is a diversified fertilizer producer and retailer with widespread holdings including its potash mine at Vanscoy, southwest of Saskatoon. It was known as Cominco Fertilizers Ltd. until 1995. The company maintained its independent position on the potash scene over time and resisted all overtures and efforts to buy it out.

Earlier, it was known as the Cominco mine, its origins being with Consolidated Mining and Smelting Company, at one time majority owned by the Canadian Pacific Railway, and had a major smelting and refining operation at Trail, British Columbia. In time, it changed its name to Agrium. While its potash operations have been smaller in scale than both PCS Inc. and Mosaic, the company's total presence is significant, and it is currently attempting to expand the scale of its operations. It has been endeavouring to establish a greater fertilizer presence in the United States by attempting to purchase a major US company. The Agrium potash mine at Vanscoy is being expanded at a cost of $1.5 billion, and the company is actively considering the development of a new $2.5 billion potash mine near Yorkton. It is also engaged in other exploratory work in Saskatchewan.

A small potassium sulphate operation must also be noted. It is Big Quill Resources located near Wynyard and produces up to 40,000 tons per year of this specialized product. It has upgraded its facility recently.

From the early 1990s until more recent years, a period of relative calm and stability existed in the industry. Companies were recovering from the difficult markets existing as the decade rolled in. The NDP government was wrestling with the mammoth deficit and debt inherited from the previous Conservative government. Revenue from the potash industry might be considered reasonable. A host of other issues occupied its attention. Thoughts of potash ownership were far down on its agenda.

That set the stage for a fundamental change. The consequence was that the government, by its actions or inaction, accepted the new state of affairs involving a tolerance of the role of the private sector managing the potash industry and the withdrawal of the government as a participant in the industry. Busy as it was with a host of other demanding issues and hampered by insufficient resources to get involved, the government in effect succumbed to the general shift to neo-liberalism in the western world. The Blakeney era, and much that it achieved, was gone!

It was only a matter of time until the Romanow and Calvert governments, left wing in name, took steps that would normally be viewed as the approach of a right-wing government. First, a block of shares in PCS Inc. still held by the government was sold, and then the "golden share" was removed, followed by the requirements for a specified number of Saskatchewan and Canadian directors on the board of directors.

Between 1998 and 2005, a number of substantial changes were made to regulations that reduced government revenue from potash considerably. A critical amendment designed to promote mine expansions as well as new mines was a provision to write off such expenditures against royalties. The private companies held out until they got the concessions they wanted. The government had to give away some of the revenue that was theirs.

Other things were changing at the same time. The continuing growth in world population means more food is needed, which brings on an inexorable increase in the demand for potash. Much of that potash has to come from Saskatchewan. For some time, the question has been should that demand be filled by new mines or the expansion of existing mines. Expansions are much more economic than new mines but, eventually, new mines will be needed. Existing producers have a built-in advantage.

All three producing companies in Saskatchewan are now actively involved in expansion programs. PCS Inc. completed a $7 billion expansion program in 2012. Mosaic spent $3.15 billion to increase its capacity by 50% to 17 million tonnes per year by 2010, mostly in Saskatchewan. Along with the Agrium plans, these projects will make Saskatchewan an even larger player on the world potash scene. A Saskatchewan Potash Producers Association advertisement in the *Leader-Post*, September 10, 2011, stated, "Producers have unveiled plans to invest nearly $12 billion in expansions by 2020."

The consequences are astonishing. Natural Resources Canada reports Saskatchewan was Canada's second leading mineral producer in 2011 with sales of $9.2 billion. Ontario was the number one provincial producer with sales of $10.7 billion, and British Columbia was third with $8.2 billion. Potash led the way to put Saskatchewan in a position that would have been unbelievable not too many years ago.

The potash tax system, a complicated structure, played a central role in the unfolding series of events. While the basic crown royalty has been in place since 1960, new features were added in subsequent years. A potash production system was put in place in 1990, and a profits tax plan is also in effect. Major changes were made in 1998, 2003, 2005, and 2010. Changes made involved tax credits, tax holidays of up to 10 years for new entrants, raised tax brackets, tax incentives, writeoffs, corporate allowances, and depreciation. Changes made in 2003 and 2005, in particular, were designed to encourage potash exploration and development by the private sector. More changes were made in 2010. These changes are bound to come under scrutiny in the future. One example has already occurred. A candidate for an NDP political leadership contest recently announced his intentions in this area:

> I would allow potash companies to immediately write off every dollar they actually invest in Saskatchewan, but stop giveaways that are not linked to new investment. ... end the indefinite holiday that exempts all tonnage above the average sold in 2001 and 2002 from profit tax, scale back the inflated 120% investment write-off to 100% of the amount actually invested, stop the subtraction of Crown royalties from Potash Production

Tax, and remove the Saskatchewan Resource Credit. ... $475 million ...[20]

Wayne Brownlee, in my 2006 interview with him, commented on the impact of changes made to that time: "pricing in potash will not justify new mine construction with the current tax rate. It makes doing debottleneck activity feasible, and that's what's being done, but it's still too high to encourage new mines."[21] He then went on to point out that a 10-year royalty holiday wasn't really 10 years. In the first place, it takes some two years to get the expansion done before it is ready to produce. When the expansion is finished, market conditions may have changed such that the added capacity will not be used for some time, even though it will be required eventually.

The results produced by these enticements are evident. Saskatchewan Energy and Resources reported in 2011, "There are currently more than a dozen potash projects underway and they range from the early exploration to feasibility stages."[22] BHP Billiton, the Anglo-Australian mining giant, has the highest profile. It began acquiring exploration rights in 2006 and now has projects under way in five locations. The most prominent is the Jansen Lake project where $1.2 billion in spending was previously approved, and shaft sinking is well under way for a huge mine. Production was expected to start in 2015 and would eventually reach eight million tonnes. A transportation option had already been chosen, but after delaying a final decision for some time, it was announced that a decision to finalize the mine had been postponed at least until 2013. Another $2.6 billion in spending was committed in 2013, but there was still no firm commitment on going into production. A BHP official said, "We think very long term."

At the same time, BHP Billiton is actively pursuing four other projects in the province, at Burr, Young, Boulder (near Watrous), and Melville. A company official has indicated "that Young or Melville would likely be the company's next targeted mine area, with production from one of those areas expected by 2017."[23] BHP Billiton in 2010 aggressively pursued an unsuccessful attempt to acquire PCS Inc. (See Chapter 13). The company has made it obvious that it plans to get into the potash business in a big way. It is apparent that its intention is not just to be another operator but to play a major role in the industry. Given the size and strength of the company, this has significant implications for the future of the potash industry. A negative comment came out on October 23, 2012, when news reports revealed that two analysts with BMO Capital Markets released a study in which they say, "We believe that the best decision for BHP is not [to] build or buy its way into the potash industry. ... the economics of Jansen are not attractive."[24] Their view is that present and planned capacity will be adequate for market requirements for some time.

In the meantime, K+S Legacy beat BHP Billiton to the draw by announcing the first new mine in 40 years. It broke ground June 19, 2012, for a new $3.25 billion dollar (now $4 billion) solution mine near Bethune, north of Moose Jaw. K+S Legacy is the subsidiary of a German company, Kali und Salz. This company owns six potash mines and was formed with the consolidation of German potash mines after East and West Germany were reunited in the early 1990s. Some German mines had been closed over a period of years. Marketing difficulties, high costs, and questionable reserves contributed to their demise. They decided to look elsewhere for potash. They bought out a junior company in the Saskatchewan mining industry, Potash One. Kali und Salz is also the world's biggest producer of salt and has several mines in Canada.[25]

Another international mining giant, from Brazil, Vale (pronounced val-lee) is also exploring for potash southeast of Regina, with attention centred on the community of Kronau. The company is considering a 2.9 million tonne per annum solution mine that would cost $3 billion. Decisions were expected in 2013[26] but recently the company announced an indefinite hold on its plans. Vale already has potash operations in Brazil and Argentina.

Other projects cited by Saskatchewan Energy and Resources in its publication *Saskatchewan Exploration and Development Highlights 2011* include:

1.  Western Potash Corporation at Milestone;

2.  Karnalyte Resource Inc. at Wynyard (potash-magnesium);

3.  Encanto Potash Corporation at Muskowekwan First Nation (near Lestock);

4. M&J Potash Corporation, subsidiary of Zhongchuan International Mining Holding Ltd. at Hanley;

5. Rio Tinto and a Russian subsidiary—nine exploration permit areas; and,

6. Yancoal Canada Resources Co. Ltd. (China)—19 potash permits.

When we look at the list of everyone investing in potash, it includes the largest mining companies in the world, as well as China and Russia. Their own self-interest is their primary concern. These interests have also purchased or traded Saskatchewan potash rights between each other. That makes Saskatchewan potash a pawn in the hands of international mining giants and companies owned by foreign nations. And—all of that is done with "our potash."

Much has changed for Saskatchewan over the past 100 plus years. Markets for and the price of wheat were what mattered most to the province for many years. They were the overwhelming determinant of well-being. Two examples come to mind. Canada signed a five year agreement in 1945 to sell wheat at a moderate price to England, which was exhausted at the end of the war. A loosely worded "have regard to" clause would compensate for inflation. After five years, England had to pay nothing, and prairie farmers carried the burden for Canada's contribution to English recovery. This caused a political storm that had a major impact, federally and provincially. The second example is in 1968 when I was elected a Member of Parliament. At an all candidates meeting in Fort Qu'Appelle, one of my opponents was a former minister of agriculture, Alvin Hamilton. I opened my closing statement: "A great deal of discussion tonight has centred on the price of wheat." Demolishing the positions of my two opponents played a significant role in my victory.

Change has continued since. A *Leader-Post* special feature on potash, September 28, 2013, carried the headline, "... Potash mines $14 billion investment in Saskatchewan." Now, potash is regarded as a major factor affecting the province's well-being. Not that wheat is no longer important; it is, of course. Agriculture has become more diversified as well. For example, in 2012, acreage of canola seeded on the prairies was very near the acreage of wheat.

For more than a century, Saskatchewan has been famous for its high-quality wheat. It still is. But now, the value of potash sales has exceeded the value of wheat and durum wheat sales in every year but one since 2000.[27] This is what makes careful management of potash affairs so important. It is a major determinant of the well-being of Saskatchewan and its people.

# CHAPTER 13
## BHP Billiton Blows the Big Buyout

I n recent years, PCS Inc. has emerged as one of the "big boys" in the corporate world. Its performance has made it a number one choice for investors. The bulk of its shares are now in the hands of a limited number of large investment firms and foreign investors, mainly American, who own more than one half of the shares. It is the world's largest producer of fertilizers including the "big three"—potash, phosphates, and nitrogen—that constitute the bulk of demand. With a market capitalization of over $45 billion, it operates in seven countries, and in Canada produces potash from six mines in Saskatchewan and one in New Brunswick. It had 5,136 employees at the end of 2009 and is expected to exceed 17 million tonnes capacity by 2015.[1]

Not too long ago, large firms, where one or a limited number of shareholders held a sizable portion of the shareholdings, were considered relatively immune to takeover attempts. But, in recent years, there has been an increasing number of successful attempts, often audacious, to target large firms. Canada has had more than its share recently. Stelco was taken over by US Steel; Inco by Vale, one of the largest miners in the world; Alcan by Rio Tinto, another giant; Falconbridge by Xstrata; and others have been taken over, including Algoma Steel, Dofasco, Hudson's Bay Company, and Cognos. In Saskatchewan, Viterra, the successor to Saskatchewan Wheat Pool, expanded first by acquiring a larger competitor and then by merging with two Australian firms in the field of agricultural marketing and supplies. Now it has been acquired by an international firm, Glencore International.

On August 17, 2010, BHP Billiton, an Anglo-Australian mining giant, made a move that shook the potash world as well as the Saskatchewan scene and the financial world. Prior to that there were probably some financial gurus who weren't quite sure where Saskatchewan was on the map. They sure knew after that. BHP Billiton announced that it was making a bid to buy Potash Corporation of Saskatchewan Inc. shares for $130 per share at a cost of US $38.6 billion for the entire company. It was a hostile buyout because the day before the announcement PCS Inc. had rejected the offer privately on the basis that the price seriously undervalued the company.

It was known for some time that BHP Billiton was interested in adding potash to its diversified mining operations. The company, with total assets of almost $100 billion, is either one of the top world producers or a major producer of a wide range of products including aluminum, copper, silver, lead, uranium, iron ore, zinc, and manganese. It also has major positions in other commodities including coal, oil, natural gas, and diamonds. The company has had potash holdings in Saskatchewan since 2006 and has concentrated much of its efforts on a project known as the Jansen or Jansen Lake mine. It announced in late 2010 that it was embarking on a feasibility study, an advanced stage of the Jansen Lake mine project. A final decision on construction was anticipated by summer 2011, but for some unclear reason it had not been announced by mid-year 2012. By mid-year 2011, it had already invested close to a billion dollars in its potash activities,[2] and in 2012, it increased authorized spending to $1.2 billion and had commenced shaft sinking at Jansen. In spite of that, in mid-August, BHP Billiton announced that it was delaying final approval of the project until at least 2013, at which time it delayed final approval again but still put in more money.

BHP followed up its announcement concerning PCS Inc. with major initiatives that made it clear the company had prepared a carefully planned strategy. It indicated that it wanted to do its own marketing offshore rather than allow the cartel, Canpotex, to do the job. This intention caused concern in a number of circles immediately, including the Saskatchewan government. The government announced that it would undertake a study of the merits of the proposed acquisition. Premier Brad Wall elaborated:

> ... I've asked the minister of environment and resources to retain independent counsel, experts in the industry, so we can make sure, as we evaluate all of this, that we are keeping Saskatchewan's interests at the top of our priority list. ...
>
> We're concerned about the future of Canpotex ... It is a strength of Saskatchewan that these companies work together to market the potash and we want to find out what the implications of all this are for Canpotex. ...[3]

Soon, the premier made more comments that made apparent the issue was being taken seriously:

> The Saskatchewan Party government is exploring potential options to bind any buyer of Potash Corporation of Saskatchewan Inc. to potash marketing agency, Canpotex ... the government is looking at all the tools it has at its disposal when it comes to ensuring any deal is in the best interest of Saskatchewan residents on issues such as royalties and the location of the company's head office ...[4]

Still more comments were made, indicating the conditions on a licence and the role of Investment Canada were being examined in studying the situation. A key requirement for the success of the bold BHP venture was to obtain approval from the federal government under the terms of the Investment Canada Act that regulates foreign interests attempting to take stakes in Canadian companies. Early on in the process, it was thought that this requirement would not cause much difficulty as only one acquisition had ever been denied out of over 1,600 applications made under the legislation.

PCS Inc. fought off the BHP action vigorously. One key step taken was the introduction of what is known as a "poison pill" that authorized the creation of new shares that, if implemented, would prevent the potential buyer from gaining control of the company. The board of directors recommended that shareholders not accept the BHP offer. The company engaged in an intensive public relations program designed to illustrate to both shareholders and the public the merits of the status quo, the inadequacy of the offer price, and the value of numerous community projects supported by the company. However some embarrassments also came to light when the company came under greater public scrutiny. It was revealed that most of the company executives were now located in Illinois rather than Saskatchewan, along with about 200 head office employees, about the same number located in Saskatoon. This was a clear violation of 1994 legislation that imposed head office conditions in return for allowing the sale of more shares outside Canada.

BHP took advantage of this weakness by saying it would ensure a full head office operation in Saskatoon, which would create many more jobs in that city. It also came to light that the president and chairman of the PCS Inc. board, William Doyle, could benefit to the extent of some $445 million or more if the sale went through. At the same time, it was not totally clear whether PCS Inc. was really resisting the acquisition because it wanted to preserve its existing identity or whether it was simply trying to get a higher price than had so far been offered. Company spokesmen talked openly about the prospect of other bidders and allowed them access to confidential information. President Doyle was quoted as saying, "I am not saying that we are opposed to a sale, but what I am saying is we are opposed to a steal of the company."[5]

The role of Canpotex quickly became a central issue. This organization was formed in 1970 as a marketing consortium for offshore sales (that is all sales outside United States and Canada) and has been in operation since 1972. All of Saskatchewan's producers at that time joined with the blessing of the Saskatchewan government. Offshore sales of Saskatchewan potash since that time have been managed by Canpotex. PCS, the crown corporation, also joined Canpotex when it went into operation. As it became fully knowledgeable of Canpotex's inner workings, PCS concluded that Canpotex was keeping prices too high and that this policy conflicted with PCS goals and objectives. The private companies insisted on keeping existing policies and outvoted PCS even after it contributed well over half of the product. PCS still had only one vote and pressed for changes. It got some minimal changes when it threatened to leave the consortium. Eventually, PCS did withdraw from Canpotex so it could sell its own potash and was within two months of completing the change in 1982 when a new government ordered it to stop the process. Canpotex has remained in place since that time and manages offshore sales of Saskatchewan potash. It has operated as a duopoly along with the Russian potash cartel. The two organizations controlled 70% of world potash sales outside of Canada and the United States. Recent events, however, place the future of the Russian cartel in doubt.

BHP Billiton's stated intention to withdraw from Canpotex, if it acquired PCS Inc., created concern in Saskatchewan beyond the government. The expressed reason for the concern was that a drop in selling prices would reduce resource payments to the province. It is questionable, however, why royalty and resource payments could not simply be adjusted as necessary. Saskatchewan had become accustomed to what it considered to be the benefits of the cartel in existence. The future of Canpotex became the focus of much of the resistance to the takeover that then developed. Canpotex, now headquartered in Saskatoon, was somehow regarded as a Saskatchewan institution. As a result of the reaction to its expressed intentions concerning Canpotex, BHP clarified and softened its stance by pointing out that it would honour existing arrangements and that changes made would be done slowly. But close study of its comments makes it clear that its long-run intentions are to do its own marketing rather than market through Canpotex.

There was another fundamental issue involved in the debate, that is, the impact of a cartel on consumer nations, Third World nations in particular. This was spelled out in a letter to the *Financial Times* from Frederic Jenny, professor of economics, ESSEC Business School, Paris, France, and former chairman, WTO working group on trade and competition. It is useful as it illustrates how the rest of the world viewed the issues at stake:

> ... Potash, an important nutrient, particularly for cereals, is exported to 150 countries, most of them developing countries. For more than 40 years the Canadian potash export cartel, which represents more than 30 per cent of world exports of potash, has striven to maintain artificially high world prices by restricting competition among suppliers and by restricting output when demand was weak. In recent years this policy has led to a decrease in the use of fertilizers in developing countries, contributing to the food crisis. Yet, aware of the fact that this cartel agreement is exempt from Canadian competition

law and that foreign investors are required to show that their transactions bring net benefit to Canada, the local authorities in Saskatchewan have sided with the cartel members for fear of a price war that would lower the profitability of potash producers and the revenues of the province.

One can only hope that the Canadian regulator will not fall for this "beggar thy neighbor" approach to international trade and will not consider that what is an unjustified monopolistic rent imposed on masses of poor farmers and consumers in developing countries should be counted as a benefit for the Canadians of Saskatchewan.

It is not acceptable to see developed countries tolerate export cartels while preaching the virtues of competition. This issue was raised repeatedly by developing countries in the WTO working group on trade and competition, and the failure to address it contributed to the abandonment of discussions on competition during the Doha Round. Let us take this opportunity to argue in favour of a ban on export cartels.[6]

It has to be concluded that BHP wanted to break the pricing structure that had dominated the industry for a long time and replace it with a market-based price structure designed to serve the company's long-term interest. That was consistent with the company's policy in dealing with other commodities it produces. The general trend in commodity pricing was toward shorter-term pricing. One essential difference in its approach from that of PCS, the crown corporation, when it wanted to leave Canpotex in 1982 was that PCS wanted to place more stress on longer-term contracts, which it considered would have been more beneficial to all concerned at that time.

While there was an expectation in many circles that the BHP deal would be completed, there were some significant commentaries other than the expected ones suggesting that the purchase should not be allowed. Resistance came from some financial circles, and arguments were raised from a broader Canadian perspective. For example, Dick Haskayne, a former chief executive officer and past chairman of several large resource companies, wrote an article in the *Calgary Herald* that was reprinted in the *Leader-Post* of Regina on September 27, 2010. He stated he was, "absolutely opposed to this takeover bid with the

prospect of losing another one of our Canadian corporate champions."
He then went on to declare that, "this potential acquisition by a foreign company becomes critical particularly because of the 'hollowing
out' of the mining industry experienced in the past few years through
foreign takeovers of several Canadian mining champions." After
quoting several senior executives who also questioned the broader
implications of the offer, he stated, "This news would send a message
that Canada is prepared to sell any of its prized resource companies."
After spelling out further particulars of his viewpoint, he stated in his
conclusion: "Ultimately, however, this is about being good stewards of
this country's natural resources for the benefit of future generations.
... I believe in the long-term value of the company, and would rather
benefit by continuing to hold the shares rather than sell out to the
highest bidder."[7]

Former premier Allan Blakeney, once a strong supporter of Canpotex, wasn't sure either: "In an era of freer trade and tougher international trade rules, that will only open Canada up to attack."[8]

After the announcement, PCS Inc. shares rose from just over $100
per share to a high of $157 before settling back to just over $145. All
of this was in the expectation by speculators that BHP would have to
raise its offer, and they would consequently reap a handsome profit. A
point of concern for Saskatchewan was that if a buyer such as BHP pays
too much there will be pressure on it as the new owner to resist wage
increases and press for lower resource payments, both of which would
not be in the province's interest. BHP did make it clear, however, that
its approach would be disciplined and inferred that there was a limit
to how much it was prepared to pay for PCS Inc. Its plan would be
one of running mines at full capacity, which would push prices down
in the short run, resulting in the elimination of marginal higher-cost
competitors or the deferral of new higher-cost production, leading to
greater market strength for them in the long term.

In the meantime, the premier of Saskatchewan, Brad Wall, continued to make strong statements expressing doubts about what benefits there were for Saskatchewan in the proposed transaction. Polling
already showed that a majority of respondents opposed the deal, and
he was probably testing public reaction to his stand. It became increasingly evident that the pivotal moment would be the decision the federal government made in determining whether the transaction was in

Canada's best interest based on the criteria spelled out in the Investment Canada Act.

The Conference Board of Canada (CBC) was commissioned by the Government of Saskatchewan to study the proposed acquisition. Its report was submitted on October 1, 2010. The report examined the state of the potash industry and the consequences of the BHP bid. Among other observations, CBC noted that 51% of the PCS Inc. shares were held outside Canada (38% US; 13% other) while 49% were held by Canadians of which only a small fraction were in Saskatchewan. The board of directors consisted of eight Canadians (two from Saskatchewan), three US citizens, and one other foreign citizen. It also noted there were two major headquarters, one in Saskatoon and a subordinate office in Chicago, each with about 200 employees. The executive management team consisted of nine Americans and six Canadians, and it was noted the president/CEO was an American who spent much of his time in Chicago. One-third of the operations are located in Saskatchewan but those generate most of the profit. The BHP operation produces nine commodities, and it pursues a long-term strategy rather than a short-term one. The report concluded after extensive economic analysis that there was a "minimal risk" in a BHP acquisition and said Saskatchewan should not oppose it. It also advised not taking sides on Canpotex one way or the other.

Debate on the BHP bid continued through the month of October. BHP maintained its position and carried on an extensive public relations program with both investors and the public. PCS Inc. also engaged in its own public relations program while hoping for a second bidder. The efforts of both, for example, included numerous full-page advertisements in the *Leader-Post* and the *StarPhoenix*, the two major daily newspapers in Saskatchewan, no doubt delighting the papers' managers and owners. Despite hinting, coaxing, and holding the door open, PCS Inc. never got a second bidder. The most likely possibility of a second bidder was from a group that would include a significant Chinese presence. This would have caused Saskatchewan a problem as China is now a major importer of potash. Obviously, China's interest would be to keep potash prices down.

During October, Saskatchewan government spokespersons, led by Premier Wall, increased their negative comments, questioning whether any benefits would be gained from the acquisition. Polling indicated a majority of people in the province were still opposed to the prospect, and an increasing number of prominent people expressed the same view. Premier Wall and a number of cabinet ministers repeatedly emphasized the absence of net benefits from the transaction and thus rejected the position recommended by the Conference Board of Canada. Government of Saskatchewan spokesmen emphasized that the province would lose $2 billion in revenue over a 10-year period because depreciation from the Jansen mine would offset profits from ongoing PCS operations. It was also argued that the BHP position on Canpotex would hurt Saskatchewan due to reduced sales.

On October 21, 2010, the premier announced the government had concluded that the proposed takeover "does not provide a 'net benefit' to the people of Saskatchewan and Canada."[9] He went on to state that Saskatchewan could not support the BHP Billiton bid. Reasons given were that the net benefit test was not met in three areas: jobs and investment; Canadian control of an important Canadian resource; and provincial revenues. He underlined that the proposed takeover would put a strategic natural resource at risk.[10] He further questioned whether there was a desire to put PCS Inc. under "foreign control."[11]

The premier then went on an extensive speaking tour, both in province and out of province, in support of his position. He presented his position to the federal government in Ottawa. He gained the support of several other provincial premiers for his position. While his viewpoint was supported by some noteworthy leaders in the financial community, the bulk of the financial and investment community still favoured the deal and fully expected that the federal government would approve the takeover bid. On the morning of the federal government announcement, it was still generally expected that the bid would be approved.

Thus, it was a stunning announcement when Industry Minister Tony Clement announced in the House of Commons late on November 3, 2010, after financial markets were closed, that the BHP bid had not been approved. This surprised virtually everyone. Reports are that when Premier Wall spoke to the media after the announcement, he had to use handwritten notes rather than the usual prepared news release because he had expected the opposite.

Federal Minister Clement explained his decision by saying that BHP Billiton did not meet the net benefit test under the Investment Canada Act. All reports indicate that the ministry had recommended approval of the bid to Mr. Clement. In addition to the pressure brought on the federal government by Saskatchewan's premier as well as several other provincial premiers, indications are that Prime Minister Harper intervened due to his concern about possibly losing a number of Saskatchewan constituencies in the House of Commons in an election, anticipated shortly, where he wanted to gain a majority government.

Speaking of "politics"! Politics and potash have always been intertwined in Saskatchewan because potash has, from the beginning, been recognized by the major political parties as the potential answer to the problems that each has wrestled with when in power. More recent events have contributed to the mix. The current Saskatchewan Party government has been in office since November 2007. Legislation was enacted decreeing that the next general election would be in November 2011. The Leader of the Opposition and leader of the New Democratic Party was Dwain Lingenfelter, a seasoned politician who wanted to put the NDP back in power. An ambitious program was developed for implementation if he became premier. Increased potash levies were proposed to help finance the program, making potash an important issue in the forthcoming election. The BHP attempt to acquire PCS Inc. made potash an even hotter issue. If Premier Wall had not taken the stand he did, it would have given Lingenfelter a ready-made issue that could very well have won him the election rather than the crushing defeat he incurred. Wall and his colleagues no doubt had real and legitimate concerns from their perspective. But they also knew that Lingenfelter was breathing down their necks, and he could very well have reversed the 49–9 Saskatchewan Party win.

Lingenfelter, however, had his own "baggage" in dealing with the political situation. Energy and Resources Minister Bill Boyd responded to criticisms made by Lingenfelter by saying:

> ... Lingenfelter dealt away Saskatchewan's "golden share" in PotashCorp. [Now he was trying to have this veto power reinstated.]
>
> In 1994, under the NDP government, Boyd said Lingenfelter oversaw the removal of a number of ownership restrictions including that Canadian residents had to own at least 55 per cent of PotashCorp's voting shares and the majority of the company's directors were required to be Canadian residents, with at least three from Saskatchewan.[12]

BHP was given 30 days to present a revised proposal. However, within two weeks, the company announced it was withdrawing its bid for PCS Inc., stating the three issues on which Industry Canada required improvement would have conflicted with the company's corporate strategy. A BHP spokeswoman, Bronwyn Wilkinson, explained:

> We understood that, amongst other things, we would have been required to make firm commitments on executing Jansen and also remaining in Canpotex, and those would have run counter to our position as a responsible investor that [is] intent on creating shareholder value. ...
>
> While we were prepared as a condition of the Minister's approval to remain in Canpotex for considerable time, we believe that extending that undertaking would have run counter to our stated preference of marketing our commodities directly and also raise potential scrutiny from regulators in customer countries.[13]

The third issue concerned capital expenditure commitments. Again, this would have locked in BHP in a way that was contrary to its culture. After all, when you get big enough, you don't like being told what to do.

In February 2011, BHP Billiton reported its financial results for the second half of 2010. They reported profits for the half year were $10.686 billion. They also reported that expenditures in its attempt to acquire PCS Inc. during that period were net $176 million. All was expensed during the second half of 2010. If these expenditures had not been incurred, profit for the half year would have been $10.862 billion rather than $10.686 billion. Their attempt to buy PCS Inc. reduced profit by just over one and a half percent. Later, it was revealed that BHP spent $314 million in total while PCS Inc. spent $75 million. When the elephants dance, the chickens get hurt—"Saskatchewan chickens."

We haven't heard the last of this episode. There has been more than one suggestion that Canpotex won't be around for the long term. While Canpotex does not sell into the United States, an anti-trust action was launched in mid-2012 by the United States on pricing issues against the three Saskatchewan producers who happen to constitute the membership of Canpotex. BHP Billiton, as previously noted, takes a long-term approach on issues. The company announced it would delay final approval of the Jansen Lake project until at least 2013. Since then it has committed another $268 million. While it has not made a final commitment on Jansen, even a company of its size would not commit almost $1.5 billion in expenditures to see it wasted. An eventual capacity of eight million tonnes and possibly more with other projects in the future will give it market clout. BHP Billiton made a basic decision that it was going to add potash to the list of commodities it produces. Doing so would provide it some strategic advantages, contributing to its comprehensive corporate strategy. A little setback like not buying out PCS Inc. won't stop it. Its response to the events of 2010 may well be, "Don't get mad! Get even!"

BHP Billiton may have another opportunity. There may be an opportunity to acquire the majority of Mosaic shares because Cargill decided to sell its holdings in Mosaic.

There is one final item. During the debate on the acquisition, Premier Wall said more than once, "Resources belong to the people." Now that there is universal recognition of this principle, it will play a significant role in future events in Saskatchewan regardless of the political persuasion of the party in power. It is up to citizens to make sure all parties are held to that principle.

# CHAPTER 14

## What Can We Learn?
### *What is Best for Saskatchewan?*

S ales of Saskatchewan potash since production commenced in
1962 have now surpassed the $70 billion mark. Provincial revenue
from these sales has been almost 10 per cent of the total but with
a wide range of percentages from year to year. Some of this variation can be attributed to industry performance and market conditions.
A significant portion, however, is due to changes in government policies and programs. A review of the past 60 years leads to the conclusion
that an assessment of the future direction of polices would be timely.

Saskatchewan's potash industry has now been totally privately
owned for almost 25 years. For some years now, there have been only
three private operators in Saskatchewan, and they own and control all
of the mines as well as jointly owning Canpotex, the offshore marketing
agency. All three are now actively engaged in expansion programs. Current exploration and/or development activities by other companies are
outlined in Chapter 12. One new company, K+S, has started construct-
ing a solution mine, while another, BHP Billiton, has started development and spent a lot of money but still has not committed itself to going
into production. Existing mines have a clear advantage over new mines
because of much lower capital costs to expand. The difficulties facing

new producers are generally known. For example, Agrium spokesman Richard Downey was quoted in the press as saying: "the cost of building a new mine from scratch is too high to make economic sense for most fertilizer firms these days."[1]

It remains to be seen how many new mines will come into being as a result of current activities. Lessons from the past may not be remembered in planning. It takes time to bring new production into place, and when it does, it comes on stream in big chunks. The lessons of the late 1960s should be stark reminders. Seven new mines increased total capacity dramatically over a very short time frame, and supply soon vastly outstripped demand growth. Demand does not grow in the same way. This concern was raised recently by Rabobank, a European bank, with respect to current activities: "Global supplies of potash could outstrip demand by between 59 and 100 per cent by the end of the decade, a research report from Rabobank warns. ... 'From a pure economics angle, many of these investments might render losses if prices come under pressure due to oversupply.'"[2] It should also be borne in mind that there is potash activity in other parts of the world, and this could add even more to world supply if development takes place.

Public ownership has not been talked about much over the last quarter century, but recently it did receive minimal attention. The industry learned from the past, and while it might grumble, it realizes that the province will get a significant return for the resource as it is produced. Negotiations take place between the industry and government before agreement is reached, with some give and take on both sides. The end result is that whatever the outcome, the province will likely get a significant amount of revenue. The question of whether the province is getting as much as it should (or could) remains outstanding and, as a result of recent events, it is once again entering the arena for debate.

Changes in the resource payments system were made in 1998, 2003, 2005, and 2010 on the basis that further development would be done by the private sector. The 2005 changes in particular provided for a 10-year tax holiday from a large block of the payment system, and more amendments were made in 2010. These concessions were necessary in order to entice new exploration and development activity. When the province as owner and manager of a large portion of the resource depends on the private sector for exploration and development, it has no choice but to accept private industry yardsticks for the development desired.

My 2006 interview with Wayne Brownlee, executive vice-president of PCS Inc., previously reported, confirms this picture. He pointed out the 2003 and 2005 changes in payment provisions were sufficient to induce expansion activities but were not yet adequate for new mine commitments.

In both quantity and quality, Saskatchewan has the best potash reserves in the world. This gives the province the potential for significant market strength. Fundamental questions such as price must be addressed. Over 30 years ago, the publicly owned corporation deliberately adopted a moderate pricing policy as part of its strategy in order to develop new markets, particularly in Asia and South America. That policy was continued through the mid-1980s, even when the corporation was in financial trouble. PCS switched to a high price policy in 1988, followed immediately by other Saskatchewan producers. That policy has been maintained since. Company profits improved sharply, but Saskatchewan again became a residual supplier. Through the late 1970s and the early 1980s, Saskatchewan, led by PCS, had become an industry leader. That had significant implications for the province. Under both scenarios, Saskatchewan has much more economic strength than in the past. That strength, however, has to be managed with prudence. The temptation to submit to the human folly of greed is real and has to be resisted in the best long-term interests of the province and, indeed, Canada.

The economic strength that now flows from the exploitation of the potash resource is shared between Saskatchewan, through its government, and the private industry in its capacity as the entrepreneur. The province does have added strength, as was demonstrated during the BHP Billiton versus PCS Inc. affair in 2010. But much of the remaining potential strength is dissipated within the separate private operations in place.

Saskatchewan's experience with both public and private ownership is unique. The experiences with both approaches have taught the province some lessons. The fundamental question to be addressed in assessing the options is whose interests are paramount. In the case of a private corporate owner, its first responsibility is to its shareholders who, for the most part, reside far away from Saskatchewan and do not have any particular attachment to or association with the province. The shareholders are primarily interested in financial returns either in the form of dividends or increased share value. In the case of the publicly owned enterprise, the corporation is also responsible to the shareholder, the people of the province, through their duly elected government. Their interest may involve more than direct financial returns. It can also include other elements such as the spinoff resulting from development and related activity. As recounted earlier, there are potential problems associated with both ways of doing things. For the most part, the pattern in Canada has been heavy reliance on private ownership of economic development. Saskatchewan has had some noteworthy experience with public ownership and had good results in utilities and mineral operations but mixed results in some industrial operations.

We have the best supply of potash in the world, one that is mostly exported and is an essential nutrient in providing food for a growing world population. Saskatchewan has an important role in managing world potash markets. Without the potash Saskatchewan is now exporting, it would be much more difficult to produce enough food in parts of the world to supply the needs of the population. Certainly, it would be significantly more costly to do so, and in some cases, it could well be prohibitive. Saskatchewan producers can either take a narrow corporate view or they can adopt a broader strategy that addresses the situation more effectively. In the first years of its operations, Potash Corporation of Saskatchewan deliberately adopted a moderate pricing policy that was designed to open markets for countries with limited resources. In that way, it would also help pave the way for longer-term markets. In the long run, this would benefit both Saskatchewan and potash buyers. It was a key element of the strategy that made Saskatchewan and PCS in particular an industry leader.

Saskatchewan producers have also had considerable experience in pursuing a high price policy. When the new high price policy was first introduced in 1988, PCS profit returned to a more satisfactory level than when operations were burdened with the requirements and/or restraints imposed by the Devine government. Higher profitability was achieved in succeeding years despite some difficult periods, but production remained much below capacity. Prices and profits started to soar in 2004 and 2005 and reached a peak in 2008. This was done by testing the market to the limit. This would be much to the glee of shareholders but, predictably, a market crash followed as farmers and other buyers said "enough" and stopped buying potash. Mines were shut down and personnel laid off. This sort of turbulence on both the producer and consumer side is unhealthy and does not contribute to the long-term well-being of all concerned. Farmers' fields do not get fertilized and workers in mines get laid off. It can even be speculated that there might be marginal producers who would not now be in operation if the high price policy had not been maintained. The high cost of building a mine means that once it is opened it stays in operation as long as variable costs are met. Evidence to date is that moderate pricing helps build more stable market conditions and is in Saskatchewan's best long-term interest.

It was previously pointed out that there are advantages and disadvantages associated with both forms of ownership used in Saskatchewan. A number of eclectic factors may lead to a decision to utilize one form or the other. The ideological outlook of those who are making decisions can also be the underlying determinant. One form that has not been used is joint public-private ownership, although it was the basic format in the original Blakeney government proposals in the early 1970s. This approach was used successfully by Saskatchewan Mining Development Corporation (SMDC) in developing minerals in northern Saskatchewan. The standard pattern of operation was a 50–50 sharing with private companies. These entrepreneurs were only too happy to enter into joint ventures with SMDC. In time, this operation was also privatized by the Devine government and now constitutes the core of Cameco, a world-leading uranium producer, also with a Saskatoon headquarters.

In making rational decisions, it needs to be recognized that regardless of the ownership structure, there are basic elements that do not change. One is that most of the resource is publicly owned and the public is entitled to an adequate return for its exploitation. The second is that there are costs as well as risks in undertaking development. Third is that huge amounts of capital are required. Finally, skills are required and intensive efforts made in organizing and managing the enterprise as well as recognizing there are real risks in undertaking development. Private enterprise expects a return for all of these factors. The expectations of a publicly owned project may be the same but may be approached differently.

A privately owned potash operation in Saskatchewan acquires most of its holdings through mineral leases or dispositions, which are crown owned. Where the resource is crown owned, royalties and other payments to the province associated with production can be considered rent in an economic sense. Payments to the province not related to production must be considered a tax. Where the resource is privately owned, royalties and all other payments to the private owner are considered economic rent. While this constitutes a smaller portion of total mineral rights, it is still a noteworthy fraction of the total. Payments to the province for production from privately held property are a tax. Crown-owned mineral rights constitute public ownership of the resource, and development by a private party constitutes a buyer-seller transaction with whatever financial requirements being the price.

The distinction between crown-owned mineral rights and privately owned rights is noted because a significant portion of mineral rights in Saskatchewan are still privately owned. That means all minerals—oil, gas, coal, potash, et cetera. The great bulk of private rights including Indian Reserves, Hudson's Bay Company lands, Canadian Pacific Railway award land, and the initial portion of homestead land patents have historic origins. The 1930 Natural Resources Agreement transferred crown mineral rights from Canada to Saskatchewan (as well as Alberta). Some privately owned mineral rights have been retrieved by the province since. From 1930 on, the province owned and managed its crown mineral rights.

Conceptually, profit constitutes the return for entrepreneurship. But the profit shown on a financial statement also includes the interest value on internally generated capital. If the mandate and purpose of a publicly owned entity is to ensure maximum financial returns to the province, the economic rent portion of the operation as well as the entrepreneurial profit portion both accrue to the province. The province, as owner of the resource, may have legitimate reasons for foregoing a portion of its total potential returns, but it does need to recognize that it is paying a price in doing so. For example, when potash development was first undertaken in Saskatchewan, the province had neither the financial nor the technical resources to undertake such a venture.

Another element that has received attention in more recent years is the disposition of "windfall" profits. Such unexpected surges in profits are often the result of inflation or changes in the supply–demand balance of the product causing a sharp change in prices. Where a private operator is exploiting a publicly owned resource under mutual agreement, what should happen when the price goes up sharply and unexpectedly?

Does the private entrepreneur get all of the benefits? It has been argued by governments of varying political stripes that the public, as owner of the resource, is also entitled to a share of the unexpected profit.

The resource companies that undertake most private development are powerful economic entities and have considerable political strength and influence. Governments often do not have the strength and/or will to stand up to them in negotiations. The outcome of negotiations between governments and resource companies over time has often seen private companies securing generous concessions so they received not only the profit portion of the economic pie but also a share of the rent component. Private companies have often pushed government to concede lower royalties and have also pressed governments to commit themselves to the provision of associated infrastructure as the price for securing development. Highly visible contributions by the companies to community or charitable projects can camouflage the reality of such arrangements.

The recent episode involving the BHP Billiton attempt to acquire PCS Inc. provides a good example of concerns about relative strength in the government-industry interface. This company is so huge that it would have an inordinate amount of strength in dealing with the Saskatchewan government. *Fortune* magazine, July 23, 2012, reported 2011 BHP Billiton revenues as $71.7 billion. If it only develops the Jansen project now, it will already have a significant presence in the industry. If that were combined with PCS Inc. operations, it would have had a towering position in both the industry and in its relations with government.

It is evident now that companies the size of PCS Inc. are not immune to corporate takeovers. One assault was resisted, but more can come that may be more difficult to ward off. Even so, PCS Inc. indicated by its actions a major concern was one of price. In 2010, Cargill decided to dispose of its holdings in Mosaic, making future control of that company uncertain. Adding in the horse-trading other operatives have engaged in leads to the conclusion that "our potash," as it is now generally recognized, is being manipulated like a pawn in the hands of international mining giants and financial investors who are interested primarily in their own financial gains and do not have any vested interest in Saskatchewan or the well-being of its people.

Governments of whatever political persuasion have to contend with the realities they encounter. There are some notable examples in the history of potash development. In each case, it would be reasonable to conclude that the government in question would likely have preferred to take a different course of action than it did:

1. The original decision by a social democratic government in 1950 that private enterprise was the only way to get a potash industry;

2. The decision by a private enterprise government that government intervention was the only way to address the oversupply crisis in 1969;

3. The decision by the Blakeney government in 1972 that it had to break its promise to do away with the pro-rationing program;

4. The continuation of PCS as an operating entity for seven years after the election of the Conservative government in 1982; and,

5. The decision by the Romanow NDP government in 1992 that it could not reverse the privatization program implemented by the previous government.

On the other hand, there are two notable examples of governments acting in accord with their philosophical outlook. The first was the action of the Blakeney New Democratic Party government in 1975 to acquire potash facilities by expropriation if necessary. The second example was the action of the Devine Conservative government in 1989 to privatize the publicly owned potash company, thus reversing the program introduced by the Blakeney government.

Potash development, even with its volatile and turbulent history, has brought with it much change to the Saskatchewan economy. A relative era of calm existed for some 20 years after PCS was privatized, a sharp contrast to previous history. The industry has matured and, as a consequence of events over time, has since been rationalized. While government revenues are significant, they are still much less than they might be. Saskatchewan plays an important role on the world potash scene, but it

171

is still not playing the full leadership role it might. Due to market growth and incentives introduced in recent years, the industry is now engaged in a massive expansion program. The question is, how are the benefits going to be shared? It is doubtful Saskatchewan will get the share it should as the owner of the resource. The province wanted more development and, being dependent on the private sector for that development, the private sector extracted its "pound of flesh" from the province. The province is the prisoner of the private sector in trying to achieve its goals. The excitement about current events hides that basic fact.

If that is not enough, now Premier Wall is talking about changing the royalty/resource payment system from a price base to a volume base. If that happens, the government will be throwing out the principle put in place by Allan Blakeney. If the price goes up, then the share that goes to the province should go up. That was a widely accepted principle when it was introduced and has remained in place for nearly 40 years. If that principle is abandoned, the province will be abandoning its responsibilities for management and stewardship of resources.

The potash industry was known as a cartel when Saskatchewan first contemplated potash development. A small number of producers dominated the industry and effectively controlled the business. Looking at the situation now, not too much has changed! Saskatchewan's entry into the potash business was followed shortly by the formation of Canpotex, in 1970, which was designed to manage all overseas sales from Saskatchewan. The cartel was effectively continued, and today the industry is a duopoly of Canpotex along with the Russian market agency. Recent events have created nervousness about future prospects. Historically, two-thirds of Saskatchewan shipments went to the United States (57–58% now) where producers, mostly American owned, also had to contend with US anti-trust legislation and other measures designed to maintain competition. The United States is a stable market with a modest rate of growth. The areas with the greatest potential for market growth are South Asia, East Asia, and Brazil. Many of these countries, however, have limits on their capability to buy potash. Pricing policies play a key role in a strategy for developing new markets or expanding existing ones.

If the objective is to get the best long-run benefit for Saskatchewan from potash, this can only be accomplished through public ownership and operation of a substantial portion of the industry. Economic analysis, as previously outlined, supports this conclusion. The province had to give away a portion of the benefits from development when it had to turn to the private sector for development at the outset. The private industry had both financing and the technical know-how required, and they wanted their reward. The province now has the potential capability to mobilize and organize the requirements to play a full role. Leadership on the international market scene would be more effectively exercised by a publicly owned organization based in Saskatchewan. The private industry, on the other hand, made up of a number of corporate firms each with its own corporate objectives and responsible first of all to its own shareholders is less likely to place Saskatchewan and international interests at the top of its priorities.

There are offsetting factors to public ownership that must be acknowledged. For example, the damaging impact of crass political interference during the Conservative government era in the 1980s as earlier described must be recognized. The only way to overcome this problem is with a more mature society where political leaders do not exercise their power irresponsibly and the public does not tolerate such activities. Another offsetting factor concerns the initiatives of PCS Inc., which strengthened its market position by undertaking the marketing of some US production and also by making overseas investments in other potash operations. It is open to question whether a publicly owned PCS could have done all of those things. In addition, the political leaders, to whom a public enterprise is still answerable, might possibly "lose their nerve," either with far-flung initiatives that are vulnerable to political criticism and where benefits are not immediately clear or because other governmental priorities demand available resources. On the other hand, private industry leaders are also capable of "losing their nerve" or finding themselves subject to external pressures.

In summary, the options for the future are:

- the status quo, i.e. private ownership of the potash industry.

- complete public ownership through means to be determined. Very difficult to achieve.

- substantial public ownership, again, through means to be determined. This would also be difficult to achieve.

Complete ownership is not necessary to meet goals. Some private ownership remained during the last episode. Joint venture public-private operations are also an option.

- Joint venture public-private operations. May only meet purposes partially.

In my view, there is a strong case for a major role for public ownership! In summary:

1. It is important that the owner of the resource gets a full return. As spelled out previously, under private ownership they get more than their fair share of returns. Experience has been that in economic terms private owners get not only the profit portion of returns as entrepreneurs, but they also manage to receive a portion of the rent component of returns, which are properly due to the owner ( in this case, the province). The only way of ensuring the province gets its full share of returns is through ownership.

2. The private sector has the upper hand in dealing with the province prior to development. The province may want to see further industry growth, but the private sector can hold out until it gets the deal it wants.

3. Past experience has demonstrated that stability is the best way to secure long-term benefit. Paced expansion in line with market growth is the best course. Under private ownership, each owner wants to gain advantage. The oversupply crisis in the late 1960s and recent events featuring skyrocketing prices, followed by a market crash and now frenetic activity by numerous firms, illustrate the point. Concerns have been expressed recently that supply is going to overtake demand again, with negative consequences for producers.

4. The role of potash in increasing food production for a growing world population gives it a global dimension that is best managed by the public sector. In this way, objectives

that are broader than financial gain can be best managed. It has already been demonstrated that concerns about food production in the future are high priority among international issues.

5. Potash development contains the potential for economic strength that can be of great benefit to Saskatchewan. That strength can be best mustered through public ownership. It is essential that once mustered, it must be managed responsibly and in the public interest.

6. The economics of operations point toward a rationalized industry rather than the widely dispersed operations originally established. The public interest is then best served when a major portion of the industry is in the public domain.

7. The large initial investment required before production commences and the consequent result of a high ratio of fixed costs to variable costs make it preferable for mines to operate at a high level of capacity, which lowers average costs. This can be best accomplished under a managed system rather than a free-market system.

There is no easy course of action for building a publicly owned potash industry again. It is not the purpose of this study to explore the means for accomplishing that goal. The existing industry is well ensconced and takes a more careful approach in its dealings with public authorities. Government is getting a noteworthy amount of revenue from the exploitation of the resource. A stake in the industry now would likely be very expensive. Reconstructing a public industry with the strength to play the role I have suggested is a formidable challenge. Otherwise, other than taking the plunge by participating in new developments, Saskatchewan may have to be content to learn lessons from the past and satisfy itself by making the best of the status quo.

Recent events illustrate the state of affairs. PCS Inc. has announced large-scale layoffs including 440 Saskatchewan employees, as well as the shutdown of some operations because of current market conditions.

Premier Wall appealed to the company to change its position. That is like Don Quixote tilting at windmills. The Premier was a part of operations when the Devine government sold off the company in 1989. The province is no longer in charge. The company is managing affairs in the best interest of *its* shareholders and the president made that clear in his response.

Potash could have done so much more for Saskatchewan. We let it slip out of our hands. Saskatchewan may have better days now than in the past, but it is not comparable to the strength it might have had. There is so much more that might have been accomplished.

But, there still are other resources to be considered. Uranium, gold, diamonds, for example, are in the picture now. Others will come. Potash, on the other hand, will be around for a long time. There is a proverb, "It is a long road that has no turns!"

There really was a pot of gold at the end of the rainbow for Saskatchewan. It was in the form of potash. Unless some new path is found in the future, the province will have to settle for much less than the full pot of gold that was there. Did we have to let it happen?

Are we going to let it happen again?

# APPENDIX A

## Potassium

*The following are excerpts from a pamphlet,* Potassium—The Regulator, *published by the Potash & Phosphate Institute, Atlanta and Saskatoon, and the Foundation for Agronomic Research, Atlanta (undated):*

... It is a nutrient essential for all plant, animal and human life. Potassium (identified by the letter K, its chemical symbol) is found in every cell. It is the third most abundant mineral in our bodies, surpassed only by calcium (Ca) and phosphorus (P). More than 85 percent of the body's K is found in major tissues and organs such as muscles, skin, blood, the digestive tract and the liver.

### IS POTASSIUM NUTRITION DIFFERENT IN PLANTS?

Potassium's role in plant growth is quite similar to that for humans. ... Under severe deficiency, plants will often develop visible symptoms. In general, the edges of older leaves will turn brown while yield and quality decline. ... orange trees will drop their fruit; strawberries do not fully develop their sweet taste; corn stalks will break, sending ears to the ground; tomatoes will be small and contain too much white tissue. Each plant is an individual food production factory. ... Potassium is one of the key raw materials. The following illustrates the K content of certain crops: (A one acre yield showing K uptake in pounds) 200 bushel corn–220; 60 bushel soybean–120; 80 bushel wheat–135; 8 ton alfalfa–400; 30 ton tomatoes–280.

### POTASSIUM IS A NATURALLY OCCURRING PLANT FOOD ELEMENT

Fertilizer K is often referred to as "potash." Early American settlers coined that name. They produced potassium carbonate needed for making soap by evaporating water filtered through wood ashes. The ash-like residue remaining in the large iron pots was called "pot ash." ... Canada now supplies about three-fourths of the potash used in U.S.

crop production. ... Nearly 95 percent of the commercially produced K is used in agriculture. The remaining 5 percent is used for industrial purposes and for products common in the home.

## HOW POTASSIUM WORKS TO INCREASE YIELDS.

1. Helps retard crop diseases.
2. Maintains turgor; reduces water loss and wilting.
3. Increases protein content of plants.
4. Produces grain rich in start.
5. Helps translocation of sugars and starch.
6. Aids in photosynthesis and food formation.
7. Reduces respiration, preventing energy losses.
8. Assists many enzyme functions.
9. Builds cellulose and reduces "lodging" caused by weak stalks.
10. Increases root growth and improves drought resistance.

## POTASSIUM HELPS TO PROTECT THE ENVIRONMENT.

Nitrogen use efficiency by a plant is highest when K is readily available. Why? Because K regulates N uptake and helps to build plant proteins. ... Potassium helps plants reach optimum productivity ...

## POTASSIUM HELPS IMPROVE USE EFFICIENCY OF OTHER NUTRIENTS

Potassium is known to interact with almost all of the other essential plant food nutrients. It helps P produce higher grain yields and improves seed quality. In some cases the improved market value of the grain alone pays the fertilizer K bill. The yield improvement due to K is an added bonus. Potassium helps most crops to better use available water. ...

## SUMMARY

Potassium is often described as the "regulator" in crop production. It has earned this distinction due to its influence upon protein and starch formation, its regulation of over 60 enzyme systems controlling the development of crop quality, and its positive interaction with N, P and other essential crop production inputs.

*Excerpts of an article published by Postmedia Saskatchewan in the* Leader-Post, *September 28, 2012, as "A Special Feature" on the occasion of Mosaic's "Esterhazy 50" anniversary:*

## WHAT IS POTASH?

Potash is a naturally occurring mineral created during the evaporation of ancient sea beds. Some of these ancient seas evaporated long before dinosaurs roamed the earth and are buried thousands of metres below the surface. Most economically recoverable potash reserves were formed as sea water evaporated and K salts crystallized to become the beds of potash ore being mined today. These deposits are a mixture of crystals of potassium chloride (KCl) and sodium chloride (NaCl) or common table salt.

Potash is the most widely used potassium fertilizer. Potassium is one of the three primary crop nutrients required for plant growth. Mosaic potash products vary in color from red to white and are available in several sizes, providing choices for most application options.

## WHY CROPS NEED POTASH

Potash, or potassium, is known as the "regulator" of crop nutrients and provides the following benefits to growing plants:

- Protects plants from extreme temperatures and helps them to fight stress and disease.
- Leads to the formation of a larger, deeper and stronger root system.
- Stops wilting.
- Assists in transferring food.
- Helps plants use water efficiently.

## Saskatchewan Potash Mines, 1970

| MINE | LOCATION | OWNERSHIP | HEAD OFFICE | INCORPORATION | ORIGINAL COST $MILLION | FIRST PRODUCTION | CAPACITY TONS K2O | 1972 PRODUCTION TONS K2O | 1972 SALES TONS K2O | REMARKS |
|---|---|---|---|---|---|---|---|---|---|---|
| Allan | Allan | Swift Canadian – 20%; Texas Gulf – 40%; U.S. Borax – 40% | Swift: Etobicoke; Texas Gulf: New York; Borax: Los Angeles | Swift: Canada; Texas Gulf: Texas; U.S. Borax: Nevada | 80.0 | May 1968 | 912,700 | 523,479 | 493,103 | Jointly Owned. Swift: Uses all of its production. Texas Gulf: Mine at Moab, Utah. U.S. Borax: Sold Carlsbad Mine. |
| Alwinsal | Lanigan | French-German Potash | Toronto | Canada | 60.0 | Dec. 1968 | 600,000 | 297,565 | 314,678 | Mines in France and Germany |
| Central Canada | Colonsay | Noranda – 51%; CF Ind. – 49% | Toronto | Ontario | 90.0 | Sept. 1969 | 900,000 | 648,687 | 592,651 | Sales contract with CF Ind. |
| Cominco | Vanscoy | CP Invest – 53% | Vancouver | Canada | 65.0 (77.0 Cominco) | Mar. 1969 | 720,000 | 50,751 | 31,354 | |
| Duval | Vade | Duval Corp. (Pennzoil Co.) | Houston | Texas | 69.0 (77.0 other sources) | May 1968 | 732,000 | 434,578 | 391,647 | Mine at Carlsbad. |
| IMC(C) | Esterhazy | IMC (Illinois) | Toronto | Canada | K-1 65.0 | June 1962 | 1,280,000 | 776,205 | 1,142,223 | Mine at Carlsbad. |
| IMC(C) | Esterhazy | | | | K-2 60.0 | Apr. 1967 | 1,050,000 | 398,785 | | Mine at Carlsbad. |
| Amax | near IMC | American Metal Climax | New York | Delaware | | — | — | 167,277 | 140,286 | Mined by IMC. Mine at Carlsbad. |
| Kalium | Belle Plaine | PPG Ind. | Regina | Canada | 60.0 | Oct. 1964 | 937,500 | 470,437 | 413,061 | Solution mine. Secret process. |
| P.C.A. | Patience | Ideal Basic Ind. | Denver | Colorado | 68.5 | Dec 1958 (May 1965) | 460,000 | 252,027 | 233,603 | Mine at Carlsbad. |
| Sylvite | Rocanville | Div. Of HBM&S (About 28% owned by So. African interests) | Toronto | Canada | 70.0 (66.0 HBM&S) | Sept. 1970 | 732,000 | 309,701 | 300,945 | Sells considerably to Terra Chem, Iowa in which HBM&S has 15% equity. |
| TOTAL | | | | | $683.5 – 707.5 | | 8,334,200 | 4,329,492 | 4,053,551 | |

Copied from *A Potash Policy for Saskatchewan*, Saskatchewan Archives, R-900, XV-37a.

# APPENDIX C
## Pro-rationing Regulations

*November 17, 1969.*
*Saskatchewan Regulation 287/69*

*Under the Mineral Resources Act*
*(O.C. 1733/69)*

*Published in* The Saskatchewan Gazette, *Friday November 21, 1969;*
*Volume 65, No. 47; pps. 568 & 569.*

*(Filed November 17, 1969)*

Regina, November 17, 1969. Approved and Ordered. Lieutenant Governor. The Executive Council has had under consideration a report from the Minister of Mineral Resources, dated October 31, 1969, stating:

1.  that section 3 of The Mineral Resources Act reads in part as follows:
    "3. The purposes of this Act are:
    (a)  to promote and encourage the discovery, development, management, utilization and conservation of the mineral resources of Saskatchewan;
    (b)  to regulate the disposition of Crown mineral lands;
    (c)  to protect the correlative rights of the owners of surface rights and of mineral rights;"

2.  that section 9 of the Act reads in part as follows:
    "9. The minister may do such things as he deems necessary
        to discover, develop, manage, utilize and conserve the
        mineral resources of Saskatchewan......................";

3.  3. that section 10 of the Act reads in part as follows:
    "10. — (1) the Lieutenant Governor in Council may make
        such regulations and orders not inconsistent with
        this Act as he may deem necessary for the purpose of
        carrying out its provisions according to their obvious
        intent or to meet cases that may arise and for which
        no provision is made therein......................";

4.  4. that it is deemed advisable and in the public interest to
    pass "The Potash Conservation Regulations, 1969" as here-
    inafter set forth in the attached schedule.

Upon consideration of the foregoing report and on the recommendation of the Minister of Mineral Resources, the Executive Council
advises that His Honour's Order do issue under The Mineral Resources
Act, effective on and after the date hereof, making The Potash Conservation Regulations, 1969 as set forth in the attached schedule.

M. A. DE ROSENROLL
Clerk of the Executive Council.

* * *

## REGULATIONS UNDER THE MINERAL RESOURCES ACT

Short Title 1. These regulations may be cited as "The Potash Conservation Regulations, 1969."

Production of potash without licence prohibited

2. (1) On and after January 1, 1970, the production of potash is prohibited unless a producing licence authorizing the production is granted by the minister which licence shall be in such form and subject to such conditions as the minister may determine.

(2) The minister may issue a producing licence to produce potash in compliance with these regulations in such form as the minister may determine and subject to such conditions as may be stated in the licence, or he may refuse to grant a producing licence.

Disposal of potash without licence prohibited

3. (1) On and after January 1, 1970, the disposal of potash is prohibited unless a licence authorizing the disposal is granted by the minister.

(2) The minister may issue a licence to dispose of potash in compliance with these regulations and subject to such conditions as may be stated in the licence, or he may refuse to grant a disposal licence.

Inquiry 4. (1) For the proper utilization and conservation of potash and for the protection of correlative rights of the owners of mineral rights the minister may, if he deems it advisable, order that a public inquiry be held at such time and at such place as he may designate for the purpose of determining any or all of the following;

Inquiry
(continued)

(a) a fair and reasonable price to the producer of potash, free on board at the potash plant gate in Saskatchewan, for all potash produced in the province;

(b) the productive capacity of each potash mining property;

(c) a proportionate share of production, if any, that may be allocated to each potash mining property required to meet the market demand for potash;

(d) the demand for potash or potash products for reasonable current requirements and current consumption or use within and outside the province, together with such amounts as are reasonably necessary for building up or maintaining reasonable storage reserves and working stocks of potash and potash products;

(e) any other matter that the minister deems advisable.

(2) Notice of an inquiry shall be published in one issue of the Gazette at least ten days prior to the date set for the inquiry.

(3) Notice of an inquiry shall be given by registered mail at least ten days prior to the date set for the inquiry to every owner of a mine that produces potash or is, within the next six months from the date set for the inquiry, likely to produce potash.

(4) The inquiry shall be held by a board consisting of at least three members.

(5) The Lieutenant Governor in Council shall appoint the members of the board and shall designate one member as chairman.

Inquiry
(continued)

(6) The members of the board shall hold office for such term as may be determined by the Lieutenant Governor in Council.

(7) Every member of the board, including the chairman thereof, has all of the powers of a commissioner under the Public Inquiries Act.

(8) The members of the board shall receive such remuneration as may be fixed by the Lieutenant Governor in Council.

(9) The board may exercise the powers and shall perform the duties conferred or imposed by these regulations, and shall inquire into the matters referred to it by the minister under these regulations and make a report to the minister thereon.

Allocation of
production

5. (1) Where the minister decides that it is advisable to limit the total amount of potash that may be produced in the province he shall allocate the allowable production among the potash mining properties in production in the province and may, in determining such an allocation, consider the following factors:
   (a) basic allowables;
   (b) definite and bona fide requirements for disposal;
   (c) inventory requirements;
   (d) any other matter that the minister deems advisable.

(2) The minister may amend, revise or vary the allowable production allocated to any or all potash mining properties in production, with or without an inquiry as he deems advisable, to meet changing conditions or circumstances.

Statements to be submitted by potash producers

6. a(1) Every owner of a mine that produces potash during any month shall, on forms obtained from the department or approved by the minister, file with the department not later than the twentieth day of the immediately following month a statement showing potash ore and all grades of potash products produced.

(2) Every owner of a mine that disposes of potash during any month shall, on forms obtained from the department or approved by the minister, file with the department not later than the twentieth day of the immediately following month a complete and detailed report of the disposition of such potash.

(3) Every person who intends to dispose of potash produced in Saskatchewan shall, on forms obtained from the department or approved by the minister, file with the department not later than the twentieth day of the middle month of the quarter a statement showing in detail;

   (a) definite and bona fide requirements for disposal of potash for the immediately following quarter;

   (b) a forecast of the requirements for disposal of potash for the first and second quarters following the quarter mentioned in clause (a); and for the purpose of this subsection "quarter" means a period of three calendar months in each year commencing the first day of January, April, July and October of such year.

Statements to
be submitted by
potash producers
(continued)

(4) Every owner of a mine that produces potash shall submit any other information that the minister deems necessary for carrying out the provisions of these regulations.

Provision for tests    7.    The minister may order an owner of a mine that produces potash to carry out tests to determine the productive capacity of the mine and for such determination the minister or any person authorized by him may collect data , make inspections, investigations, examine properties, plans, specifications, books and records concerning the mine or its operations.

# APPENDIX D

Potash Deposits and Mines in Saskatchewan.

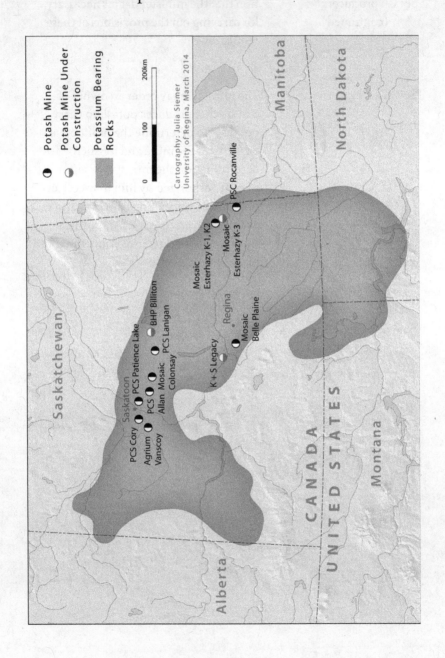

# APPENDIX E

## Capital Outlay in Saskatchewan Potash Mines Relative to Plant Capacity

| MINE | CAPACITY (TONS K2O/YEAR) | CAPITAL OUTLAY ($MILLION) | CAPITAL COST PER TON OF CAPACITY ($) |
|------|--------------------------|---------------------------|--------------------------------------|
| IMC (two) | 2,330,000 | 125 | 53.65 |
| Kalium | 937,500 | 60 | 64.00 |
| Allan | 912,700 | 80 | 87.65 |
| Cominco | 720.000 | 65 (77?) | 90.28 (106.94?) |
| Duval | 732,000 | 69 (77?) | 94.26 (105.19?) |
| Sylvite (HBMS) | 732.000 | 70 (66?) | 95.63 (90.16?) |
| Awinsal | 600,000 | 60 | 100.00 |
| Central Canada | 900,000 | 90 | 100.00 |
| PCA | 460,000 | 68.5 | 148.91 |
| Total | 8,324,200 | 683 – 707.5 | 82.11 – 84.99 |

Sources: Data on "Capacity" and "Capital Outlay" is from Saskatchewan Archives, R-900, XV-37a, "A Potash Policy for Saskatchewan" prepared by Department of Mineral Resources and John S. Burton, Planning and Research, February 1974. "Capital Cost per Ton of Capacity" was prepared by the writer.

## NOTES:

1 IMC had the advantage of being allowed one shaft at each mine as they are connected underground while the other mines needed two shafts except for the Kalium solution mine.

2 Inflation would account for some increased costs for mines constructed later.

3 IMC facilities were relatively complete while some other mines were not completely developed at that time.

4 Kalium, as a solution mine, had lower capital costs than most mines but higher operating costs.

5 PCA capital costs were higher due to expensive rehabilitation of the mine.

6 Data applicable to 1969-1975 period.

# APPENDIX F
## Analysis of IMC Data on Potash Reserve Tax, February 1975

| Price/ton K2O $ | Sales $mm‡ | Operating Profit $mm‡ | RESERVE TAX FULLY DEDUCTIBLE | | | | R.T. PT. DED.† | RESERVE TAX NOT DEDUCTIBLE | | | |
|---|---|---|---|---|---|---|---|---|---|---|---|
| | | | Total Taxes $mm‡ | Includes Reserve Tax* $mm‡ | Net Earnings $mm‡ | ROI** % | ROI** % | Total Taxes $mm‡ | Includes Reserve Tax $mm‡ | Net Earnings $mm‡ | ROI** % |
| 50.00 | 50.0 | 33.6 | 20.5 | (9.9) | 13.1 | 16.8 | 12.7 | 25.2 | (9.9) | 8.4 | 10.7 |
| 60.00 | 60.0 | 43.6 | 30.0 | (18.9) | 13.6 | 17.3 | 10.4 | 38.1 | (18.9) | 5.5 | 7.0 |
| 70.00 | 70.0 | 53.6 | 39.8 | (28.4) | 13.8 | 17.7 | 7.4 | 51.6 | (28.4) | 2.0 | 2.6 |
| 80.00 | 80.0 | 63.6 | 49.7 | (38.0) | 13.9 | 17.8 | 4.5 | 65.1 | (38.0) | (1.5) | Loss |
| 90.00 | 90.0 | 73.6 | 59.8 | (47.8) | 13.8 | 17.7 | 1.2 | 78.9 | (47.8) | (5.3) | Loss |

\* Amount is included in "Total Taxes."

\*\* Return on Investment (Percentage of Net Earnings to $78 million).

† Reserve Tax Partially Deductible.

‡ million.

## NOTES:

1  Data compiled from tables supplied by R. A. Lenon, then CEO of IMC. Calculation of ROI done by the writer.

2  Return on Investment (ROI) when the "Reserve Tax is Partially Deductible" is taken from a table supplied by R. A. Lenon which is structured in the same way as the tables dealing with "Reserve Tax Fully Deductible" and "Reserve Tax Not Deductible," but the other particulars have not been included above.

3  The references to "Deductible" address the issue of the extent to which provincial royalties, taxes, and other payments can be deducted from taxable income.

4  The data in this table applies to the tax after it was amended and implemented. It shows the impact on the industry clearly. The impact of the original proposals revealed on April 29, 1974, would have been more severe applied to the above price levels but would have been less severe at the then prevailing prices which were under $50.00 per ton.

# APPENDIX G
## Potash Sales and Royalty/Tax Revenues to the Government of Saskatchewan

| YEAR | VALUE OF SALES [1] ($ 000) | GOVERNMENT REVENUES [1] ($ MILLION) | PERCENT REVENUES/ SALES [2] % |
|---|---|---|---|
| 1962 | 3,000 | n/a | – |
| 1963 | 22,500 | n/a | – |
| 1964 | 31,162 | n/a | – |
| 1965 | 55,971 | 1.1 | 1.96 |
| 1966 | 62,665 | 1.9 | 3.03 |
| 1967 | 67,395 | 2.2 | 3.26 |
| 1968 | 65,121 | 2.1 | 3.22 |
| 1969 [3] | 69,383 | 2.9 | 4.17 |
| 1970 | 108,695 | 2.7 | 2.48 |
| 1971 [4] | 145,966 | 2.8 | 1.91 |
| 1972 [5] | 146,014 | 5.6 | 3.83 |
| 1973 [6] | 195,025 | 8.3 | 4.25 |
| 1974 [7] | 311,621 | 34.6 | 11.10 |
| 1975 [8] | 348,494 | 80.7 | 23.15 |
| 1976 | 358,399 | 96.1 | 26.81 |
| 1977 | 389,694 | 109.8 | 28.17 |
| 1978 [9] | 492,473 | 125.3 | 25.44 |
| 1979 | 730,636 | 152.1 | 20.81 |
| 1980 | 1,007,418 | 228.3 | 22.66 |
| 1981 | 989,940 | 264.7 | 26.90 |
| 1982 [10] | 632,480 | 80.6 | 12.74 |
| 1983 | 674,367 | 41.2 | 6.10 |
| 1984 | 802,342 | 64.8 | 8.07 |
| 1985 | 599,199 | 45.3 | 7.56 |
| 1986 | 542,728 | 34.0 | 6.26 |
| 1987 | 649,162 | 36.5 | 5.62 |
| 1988 | 932,496 | 83.4 | 8.94 |
| 1989 | 848,313 | 69.0 | 8.13 |
| 1990 | 784,258 | 30.9 | 3.94 |
| 1991 [11] | 765,000 | 48.5 | 6.33 |

# POTASH SALES AND ROYALTY/TAX REVENUES

| YEAR | VALUE OF SALES [1] ($ 000) | GOVERNMENT REVENUES [1] ($ MILLION) | PERCENT REVENUES/ SALES [2] % |
|---|---|---|---|
| 1992 | 812,000 | 53.8 | 6.62 |
| 1993 | 800,000 | 55.6 | 6.95 |
| 1994 | 1,109,000 | 71.1 | 6.41 |
| 1995 | 1,217,000 | 96.9 | 7.97 |
| 1996 | 1,116,000 | 109.0 | 9.77 |
| 1997 | 1,505,000 | 126.2 | 8.38 |
| 1998 | 1,624,000 | 215.8 | 13.29 |
| 1999 | 1,682,000 | 199.3 | 11.85 |
| 2000 | 1,744,000 | 166.1 | 9.52 |
| 2001 | 1,622,000 | 165.7 | 10.22 |
| 2002 | 1,718,000 | 187.0 | 10.88 |
| 2003 [12] | 1,632,000 | 144.8 | 8.87 |
| 2004 | 2,168,000 | 192.5 | 8.88 |
| 2005 [13] | 2,697,000 | 350.8 | 13.01 |
| 2006 | 2,210,000 | 134.7 | 6.09 |
| 2007 | 3,056,000 | 269.9 | 8.83 |
| 2008 | 7,386,000 | 1,183.2 | 16.02 |
| 2009 | 3,067,000 | 133.9 | 4.37 |
| 2010 | 5,366,000 | 237.1 | 4.42 |
| 2011 | 6,714,000 | 350.7 | 350.7 |
| 2012 | 5,972,000 | 398.6 | 6.67 |

Source: Government of Saskatchewan, Ministry of Economy

## KEY:

1. Calendar year.
2. Some payments to government are made in the year following and adjustments are also made at a later date so they are not completely comparable. Nevertheless, the numbers presented do provide a general picture of the government's share of the potash dollar.
3. Pro-rationing introduced.
4. Blakeney government elected.
5. Pro-rationing fee introduced.
6. Pro-rationing fee increased.
7. Potash Reserve Tax introduced late in the year.
8. Expropriation legislation introduced Nov. 12, 1975.
9. New revenue sharing agreement reached.
10. Market downturn; Devine government elected.
11. Romanow government elected.
12. Incentives introduced reducing government revenues.
13. Further incentives introduced to encourage new mines.

# APPENDIX H
## Canpotex Limited

*Excerpted from Industry Canada website description of the company based on information provided by it.*

Canpotex, the world's premier potash exporter, is an international marketing and logistics company wholly-owned by the Saskatchewan potash producers Agrium Inc., the Mosaic Company through its wholly-owned subsidiary, Mosaic Canada Crop Nutrition, LP, and Potash Corporation of Saskatchewan Inc. As a competitive world supplier, Canpotex markets and distributes Saskatchewan potash to customers offshore—principally to countries in Asia, Latin America, and Oceania. Operating since 1972, Canpotex has corporate offices in Saskatoon, Singapore, Vancouver, Tokyo, and Shanghai. Canpotex's potash sales average approximately 8-9 million metric tonnes per year. Canpotex has sold nearly 200 million tonnes of potash to approximately 60 countries since its inception. Its major international markets include Australia, Brazil, China, India, Indonesia, Japan, Korea, and Malaysia. Canpotex's marketing team maintains direct contact with buyers around the world and brings vast industry experience to the task of meeting customer requirements for potash used in both agricultural and industrial applications. A cohesive operations group maintains daily communications with its shareholders, mine sites, railways, and terminals to ensure cargo availability and the timely loading of vessels at port. With an extensive vessel chartering and brokerage network, and in-house expertise in ocean transportation, Canpotex offers comprehensive ocean freight services to its customers.

SERVICE NAME: Marketing and logistics company that exports Saskatchewan potash to markets outside Canada and the United States.

# NOTES

## CHAPTER 1: INTRODUCTION

1. See Appendix A for further information on the nature and uses of potash and potassium.
2. Source: *Sask Trends Monitor*.
3. When I was elected our children were quite small and we moved to Ottawa. We spent 10 months of the year there and the other two months at a cottage in Saskatchewan.
4. D. J. Hall, "Clifford Sifton: Immigration and Settlement Policy 1896-1905," in *The Settlement of the West*, ed. Howard Palmer (Calgary: University of Calgary, 1977), 77, quoted in Dale Eisler, *False Expectations: Politics and the Pursuit of the Saskatchewan Myth* (Regina: Canadian Plains Research Center, 2006), 21.

## CHAPTER 2: BEGINNINGS AND DEVELOPMENT

1. Saskatchewan Department of Natural Resources, *Annual Report, 1946-47*, and subsequent annual reports.
2. Jim F. C. Wright, *Saskatchewan, the History of a Province* (Toronto: McClelland and Stewart, 1955); John H. Archer, *Saskatchewan: A History* (Saskatoon: Western Producer Prairie Books, 1980); Bill Waiser, *Saskatchewan: A New History* (Calgary: Fifth House Ltd., 2005).
3. Saskatchewan Department of Natural Resources, *Annual Report, 1946-47*, and subsequent annual reports. I also had conversations with J. T. Cawley, a former deputy minister of mineral resources who managed these activities. He made arrangements for potash exploration in conjunction with oil drilling. Some arrangements would not be on record.
4. John Richards and Larry Pratt, *Prairie Capitalism: Power and Influence in the New West* (Toronto: McClelland and Stewart, 1979); J. L. Phelps Papers, GS-14, Saskatchewan Archives.
5. It is not connected to Western Potash Corporation, currently engaged in potash exploration in Saskatchewan.
6. Joseph W. Burton, MLA 1938–43; MP 1943–49; MLA and provincial secretary 1952–56.
7. John Stratford Burton, "Public Ownership in Saskatchewan Potash: An Analysis of Factors Leading to the Saskatchewan Government's Decision" (master's thesis, University of Regina, 2004), 20–21.
8. *J. H. Brockelbank Papers*, GR-85, Saskatchewan Archives; Richards and Pratt, *Prairie Capitalism*.
9. Saskatchewan Department of Mineral Resources, *Potash: Challenge for Development*, (Regina: Queen's Printer, 1976).
10. "A Memorable Date," Editorial, *Leader-Post*, 19 September 1962.

## CHAPTER 3: OVERSUPPLY CRISIS AND GOVERNMENT INTERVENTION

1. Dale Eisler, *Rumours of Glory: Saskatchewan and the Thatcher Years* (Edmonton: Hurtig Publishers, 1987).
2. Richard A. Lenon, personal interview, 22 September 2003.
3. Eisler, *Rumours of Glory*.

4. Ibid. This price is quoted per ton of KCl, the product, based on 60% K2O (potassium oxide) content, an industry measure of potassium availability. The Saskatchewan Mineral Resources publication, *Potash: Challenge for Development*, quotes prices based on 100% K2O equivalent. It states prices dropped from an average of $37.53 a ton in 1965 to an average of $19.87 in 1969.

5. Ibid.

6. Richard A. Lenon (retired chairman and president of International Minerals and Chemical Corporation), personal interview, 22 September 2003; Dr. Ralph L. Cheesman, personal interview, 29 September 2003. Cheesman is former chief geologist with the Department of Mineral Resources; in 1971, he became a consulting geologist; and soon was consultant-manager of the Saskatchewan Mining Association. Described more fully in Eisler, *Rumours of Glory*.

7. International Minerals and Chemical Corporation (Canada) Limited, *The Canadian Potash Industry: A Study in Government Co-operation* (Printed in Canada, 1972). There was a guilty finding on the anti-dumping charges.

8. Eisler, *Rumours of Glory*, gives an account of his actions.

9. John Burton, Memorandum to File, reporting on a telephone conversation with Cliff Kelly, 11 November 2002.

10. John Burton, photograph of the framed picture transmitted by email, sent by Ryan Willett, son of Boyd Willett, 27 January 2003.

11. Richard A. Lenon, personal interview, 22 September 2003.

12. International Minerals and Chemical Corporation, *Annual Report for the year ending June 30, 1969*.

13. News Release, New Potash Regulations, November 1969, *Darrel Heald Papers:* R-49,428, Saskatchewan Archives.

14. Memos, Warren to Pepin 3 September 1969 and General Director, Office of Area Relations to J. H. Warren, 27 August 1969, John Burton Papers, R-900, XIV-18y, Saskatchewan Archives.

15. Memorandum, Roy S. Meldrum to Hon. D. V. Heald, Attorney General, on "Potash Regulations," 21 November 1969, Darrel Heald Papers, R-49, 428, Saskatchewan Archives. Mr. Meldrum incorrectly named the federal Department of Industry and Commerce.

16. Memorandum, Roy S. Meldrum to J. Cawley, Deputy Minister of Mineral Resources, "The Potash Conservation Regulations, 1969," 25 November 1969, Darrel Heald Papers, R-49, 428, Saskatchewan Archives.

17. Letter, Roy Meldrum to D. S. Maxwell, copy to D. V. Heald, 2 December 1969, Darrel Heald Papers, R-49, 428, Saskatchewan Archives.

18. Memorandum, Hon. Darrel V. Heald to Premier W. Ross Thatcher, 14 January 1970, Darrel Heald Papers, R-49, 428, Saskatchewan Archives.

19. Letter, Hon. Darrel V. Heald to Hon. Jean Luc Pepin, 4 February 1970, Darrel Heald Papers, R-49, 428, Saskatchewan Archives.

20. Memorandum, Heald to Meldrum, 4 March 1970, Darrel Heald Papers, R-49, 428, Saskatchewan Archives.

21. Letter, E. R. Olson to R. S. Meldrum, 10 March 1970, John Burton Papers, R-900, XIII-8, Saskatchewan Archives.

22. Included with a paper, "Excerpts from Noranda Submission to Potash Conservation Board," December 8, 1969, Allan Blakeney Papers, R-800, I-52, Saskatchewan Archives.

23. Ralph L. Cheesman, personal interview, 29 September 2003.

## CHAPTER 4: THE DYNAMICS OF POTASH POLITICS

1. New Democratic Party of Saskatchewan, *New Deal for People*, (Regina: Service Printing, 1971).
2. Ibid.
3. Ibid.
4. Ibid.
5. Richard A. Lenon, personal interview, 22 September 2003.
6. John Burton, *House of Commons Debates* (Ottawa: Queen's Printer, June 5, 1972), 2865, 2869.
7. Allan Blakeney, personal interview, 10 July 2002.
8. *"NOTES ON POTASH SITUATION,"* A. E. Blakeney, MLA, December 1969, Allan Blakeney Papers, R-800, I-52, Saskatchewan Archives.
9. Ibid.
10. Richard A. Lenon, personal interview, 22 September 2003.
11. Ibid.
12. Richard A. Lenon, letter to John Burton, 22 January 2004.
13. Letter, Allan Blakeney to Dan Anderson, Plunkett, Saskatchewan, 25 February 1971, Allan Blakeney Papers, R-800, I-52, Saskatchewan Archives.
14. Richard A. Lenon, personal interview, 22 September 2003.
15. Ibid.

## CHAPTER 5: NEW REALITIES

1. Allan Blakeney, personal interview, 10 July 2002.
2. Ralph L. Cheesman, personal interview, 29 September 2003.
3. Richard A. Lenon, personal interview, 22 September 2003.
4. Memo, Allan Blakeney to Honourable Ted Bowerman, Minister of Mineral Resources, 22 July 1971, Allan Blakeney Papers, R-565, III-508, Saskatchewan Archives.
5. Memo Bowerman to Blakeney, 27 July 1971, Allan Blakeney Papers, R-565, III-508, Saskatchewan Archives.
6. Letter G.R. (Ted) Bowerman to All Producers of Potash in Saskatchewan, 12 October 1971, Allan Blakeney Papers, R-565, III-508, Saskatchewan Archives.
7. Garry Beatty (Deputy Minister of Finance, 1972-76), personal interview, 24 September 2002.
8. Memo Blakeney to Bowerman, 8 November 1971, Allan Blakeney Papers, R-565, III-510, Saskatchewan Archives.
9. Memo Blakeney to Bowerman, 24 November 1971, Allan Blakeney Papers, R-565, III-508a, Saskatchewan Archives.
10. "Saskatchewan pro-rationing." Phosphorus and Potassium No. 62, November/December 1972, *John Burton Papers*, R-900, XIV-18d, Saskatchewan Archives. Most of the response by the premier was drafted by the Department of Mineral Resources. See Memo, J. G. Wotherspoon, Deputy Minister to Brian Coulter, Special Assistant to the Premier, Allan Blakeney Papers, 28 June 1972, R-565, III-510, Saskatchewan Archives.
11. Bowerman became full time Minister of Northern Saskatchewan.
12. Kim Thorson, personal interview, 21 November 2002.
13. George Cadbury was a British industrialist and Labour Party activist who came to Saskatchewan in 1945 as a key economic adviser, later headed a United Nations

program, and was involved in a variety of international activities. At one time, he worked closely with Allan Blakeney and continued to keep in touch with Saskatchewan activities.

14. Letter, Pepin to Thorson, 11 May 1972, Allan Blakeney Papers, R-565, III-508, Saskatchewan Archives.
15. Letter, Thorson to Pepin, 16 June 1972, Allan Blakeney Papers, R-565, III-508, Saskatchewan Archives.
16. Ibid.
17. History of Relationship With Industry, October 1975, John Burton Papers, R-900, XVI-77, Saskatchewan Archives.
18. J. G. Wotherspoon to D. E. G. Schmitt, President, Central Canada Potash Co. Ltd., 20 September 1972, Allan Blakeney Papers, R-565, III-510, Saskatchewan Archives.
19. Allan Blakeney, personal interview, 10 July 2002.
20. International Minerals & Chemical Corporation (Canada) Limited, *The Canadian Potash Industry: A Study in Government Co-operation* (Esterhazy, SK, Summer, 1972).
21. Richard A. Lenon, personal interview, 22 September 2003.

## CHAPTER 6: DEFINING GOALS AND FINDING NEW DIRECTIONS

1. Statement quoted in "A Potash Policy for Saskatchewan," Prepared by Department of Mineral Resources and John Burton, Planning and Research, February 1974, John Burton Papers, R-900, XV-37a 7/7, Saskatchewan Archives.
2. Garry Beatty, personal interview, 24 September 2002.
3. Allan Blakeney, personal interview, 10 July 2002.
4. Kim Thorson, personal interview, 21 November 2002.
5. Memo Blakeney to Thorson, 24 January 1973, Allan Blakeney Papers, R-565, III-511, Saskatchewan Archives.
6. John Burton, Memo to File, 11 November 2002.
7. "IMC Says Gov't Action Saved Potash Industry," *Leader-Post*, 22 June 1972.
8. Report to Cabinet on Government Participation in the Potash Industry, Prepared in Response to Cabinet Minute #4160, Department of Mineral Resources and John Burton of the Department of Finance, June 1973, Allan Blakeney Papers, R-565, III-511a, Saskatchewan Archives. Also found in John Burton Papers, SA R-900, XV-37e.
9. R. L. Cheesman, personal interview, 29 September 2003.
10. Ryan Willett and John Burton, telephone conversation, 17 January 2003.
11. Memo Burton to Blakeney, Potash Strategy, 29 June 1973, Allan Blakeney Papers, R-565, III-508c, Saskatchewan Archives. Also found in John Burton Papers, R-900, XIV-181.
12. Ibid.
13. Letter, Kelly to Thorson with brief, 13 August 1973, Allan Blakeney Papers, R-565, III-508c, Saskatchewan Archives.
14. Correspondence from companies to Hon. Kim Thorson or J. G. Wotherspoon, 31 August 1973 to September 14 1973, John Burton Papers, R-900, XV-44(2/2), Saskatchewan Archives.
15. Memo, Burton to Blakeney, "Potash," 26 September 1973, Allan Blakeney Papers, R-565, III-511, Saskatchewan Archives.
16. "Potash Policy" submitted to Planning Committee to the Cabinet, 11 October 1973, *Allan Blakeney Papers*, R-565, III-511, Saskatchewan Archives.

17. Minutes, Planning Committee to the Cabinet, 11 October 1973, Allan Blakeney Papers, R-565, III-511, Saskatchewan Archives.
18. *Leader-Post*, "Government Considering New Potash Policies," 27 October 1973.
19. Allan Blakeney, personal interview, 10 July 2002.
20. "A potash Policy for Saskatchewan" Prepared by Department of Mineral Resources and John S. Burton, Planning & Research, February 1974, John Burton Papers, R-900, XV-37a 7/7, Saskatchewan Archives.
21. Allan Blakeney, personal interview, 10 July 2002.
22. Statement by Hon. Elwood Cowley, May 1974, John Burton Papers, R-900, XIV-3a, Saskatchewan Archives.

## CHAPTER 7: THE POTASH RESERVE TAX

1. Allan Blakeney, personal interview, 10 July 2002.
2. Letter, Randolph to Blakeney, 8 May 1974, John Burton Papers, R-900, XVI-77, Saskatchewan Archives.
3. Ibid.
4. Allan Blakeney, personal interview, 10 July 2002.
5. "Saskatchewan Potash Policy," Statement by Hon. Elwood Cowley, Minister of Mineral Resources, 23 October, 1974, John Burton Papers, R-900, XIV-15a, Saskatchewan Archives.
6. Canadian Centre for Policy Alternatives, *The CCPA Monitor: Most corporations pay little or no tax*, June 2002: Vol.9, Issue 2: 26.
7. Attachment to "Saskatchewan Potash Policy," 23 October 1974, John Burton Papers, R-900, XIV-18a, Saskatchewan Archives.
8. News Release, Canadian Potash Producers Association, 24 October 1974, Allan Blakeney Papers, R-565, III-509, Saskatchewan Archives.
9. Allan Blakeney, personal interview, 10 July 2002.
10. David L. Anderson, *The Role of Mineral Taxation in Industry/Government Conflict*, (Kingston, ON: Centre for Resource Studies, Queen's University, 1981).
11. Ibid.

## CHAPTER 8: A CRISIS LOOMS

1. Richard A. Lenon, personal interview, 22 September 2003.
2. Ralph L. Cheesman, personal interview, 29 September 2003.
3. Richard A. Lenon, personal interview, 22 September 2003.
4. Ralph L. Cheesman, personal interview, 22 September 2003.
5. "History of Relationship with Industry." October 1975, John Burton Papers, R-900, XVI-77, Saskatchewan Archives.
6. "Investigations started into potash industry," *Globe and Mail*, 25 January 1975.
7. Memo, John S. Burton to Hon. A. E. Blakeney and Hon. Elwood Cowley with attached letter dated February 21, 1975 from ·Canadian Embassy, Washington to Burton, 28 February 1975, Allan Blakeney Papers, R-565, III-508d, Saskatchewan Archives.
8. "Potash Policy – History of Developments," 30 September 1975, John Burton Papers, R-900, XVI-77, Saskatchewan Archives.
9. Ibid.
10. "Summary – Potash Reserve Tax Situation", 24 February 1976, John Burton Papers, R-900, XVI-77, Saskatchewan Archives.

11. "Summary of First Meeting – May2/75 Potash Industry—Government of Saskatch-ewan Working Committee on Potash Taxation," John Burton Papers, R-900, XIII-8, Saskatchewan Archives.
12. Allan Blakeney, personal interview, 10 July 2002.
13. Cliff Kelly, unrecorded telephone conversation with author, 11 November 2002. See John S. Burton, Memorandum to File, 11 November 2002.
14. History of Events, 6 February, 1976, John Burton Papers, R-900, XVI-77, Saskatch-ewan Archives.
15. Allan Blakeney, personal interview, 10 July 2002.
16. Richard A. Lenon, personal interview, 22 September 2003
17. Allan Blakeney, personal interview, 10 July 2002.
18. Richard A. Lenon, personal interview, 22 September 2003.
19. John Soganich, "Tax relief hint cheers potash," *Financial Post*, 10 July 1975.

## CHAPTER 9: THE DECISION—PUBLIC OWNERSHIP

1. Allan Blakeney personal interview, 10 July 2002.
2. John S. Burton, "Summary – Government Assistance to the Potash Industry," 24 February 1976, John Burton Papers, R-900, XVI-77, Saskatchewan Archives.
3. Saskatchewan NDP, *New Deal '75* (Regina: Service Printing, April 1975).
4. Allan Blakeney, personal interview, 10 July 2002.
5. Ibid.
6. Ibid.
7. Roy Romanow, Elwood Cowley, Walter Smishek, Gordon MacMurchy, and Gordon Snyder.
8. Gordon MacMurchy, personal interview, 20 July 2004.
9. Roy Romanow, personal interview, 26 August 2004.
10. Allan Blakeney to John S. Burton, correspondence, 23 June 2004.
11. Allan Blakeney, personal interview, 21 July 2004.
12. Roy Romanow, personal interview, 26 August 2004.
13. Elwood Cowley, personal interview, 10 September 2002.
14. Donald Tansley, informal conversation with the author, 30 April 2004.
15. "History of Events—Saskatchewan Potash," 30 September 1975, John Burton Papers, R-900, XVI-77, Saskatchewan Archives.
16. This episode is also described by Dennis Gruending in *Promises to Keep, A Political Biography of Allan Blakeney* (Saskatoon: Western Producer Prairie Books, 1990) based on an interview with me.
17. Garry Beatty, personal interview, 24 September 2002.
18. Cliff Kelly, unrecorded telephone conversation with John Burton, 11 November 2002.
19. Ralph L. Cheesman, personal interview, 29 September 2003. Peter Jack was General Manager of Potash Company of America at Patience Lake.
20. Richard A. Lenon, personal interview, 22 September 2003.
21. Saskatchewan Department of Mineral Resources, *Potash: Challenge for Development*, (Regina: Queen's Printer, 1976).
22. Ibid.

## CHAPTER 10: GETTING STARTED

1. "AmEmbassy Ottawa to SecState WashDC, September 1976 signed Enders," telex. Transcript obtained by a request for information made to the US government under their Freedom of Information Act.
2. All immigrants through the Port of New York are quarantined for a week at Ellis Island before being released.
3. Justice and Legal Affairs Committee, House of Commons of Canada, December 3, 1984.

## CHAPTER 11: SASKATCHEWAN'S GOLDEN OPPORTUNITY

1. Minutes, Potash Corporation of Saskatchewan, Board of Directors, June 29-30, 1978.
2. James M. Pitsula and Kenneth A. Rasmussen, *Privatizing a Province, The New Right in Saskatchewan* (Vancouver, New Star Books, 1990).
3. *Leader-Post*, 19 January 1983. Also quoted in Pitsula and Rasmussen, *Privatizing a Province.*
4. Agenda Item 3, Board of Directors meeting, Potash Corporation of Saskatchewan, September 2-3, 1982.
5. Ibid.
6. Ibid.
7. "Pullout seen ruining potash industry," *Star-Phoenix,* 16 December, 1982.
8. Ibid.
9. Agenda Item 3, Board of Directors meeting, Potash Corporation of Saskatchewan, January 10, 1983.
10. Agenda Item 5, Board of Directors meeting, Potash Corporation of Saskatchewan, May 14, 1985.
11. Minutes, Potash Corporation of Saskatchewan, Board of Directors, April 11, 1983.
12. Minutes, Potash Corporation of Saskatchewan, Board of Directors, May 14, 1985.
13. Agenda Item 5, Board of Directors meeting, Potash Corporation of Saskatchewan, November 5, 1985.
14. Minutes, Potash Corporation of Saskatchewan, Board of Directors, November 5, 1985.
15. Draft minutes, Potash Corporation of Saskatchewan, Board of Directors, November 5, 1985.
16. Minutes, Potash Corporation of Saskatchewan, Board of Directors, August 11, 1986.
17. Minutes, Potash Corporation of Saskatchewan, Board of Directors, September 22, 1986.
18. Minutes, Potash Corporation of Saskatchewan, Board of Directors, December 18, 1986.
19. Minutes, Potash Corporation of Saskatchewan, Board of Directors, March 12, 1985.
20. Meeting Notes, Potash Corporation of Saskatchewan, Executive Committee, May 12, 1986.
21. Agenda Item 7(a)(i), Board of Directors meeting, Potash Corporation of Saskatchewan, June 17, 1986. Taken from an Executive Summary of the Peat Marwick report. It is marked "Draft for Discussion Purposes Only" but was nevertheless the document on which Board discussions were based.
22. Ibid.
23. Executive Summary Peat Marwick Report.
24. Minutes, Potash Corporation of Saskatchewan, Board of Directors, August 11, 1986.

25. Minutes, Potash Corporation of Saskatchewan, Board of Directors, November 3, 1986.
26. Minutes, Potash Corporation of Saskatchewan, Board of Directors, May 4, 1987.
27. Agenda Item 6, Board of Directors meeting, Potash Corporation of Saskatchewan, June 22, 1987.
28. Minutes, Potash Corporation of Saskatchewan, Board of Directors, June 14, 1988.
29. Minutes, Potash Corporation of Saskatchewan, Board of Directors, August 17, 1988.
30. Ibid.
31. Minutes, Potash Corporation of Saskatchewan, Board of Directors, October 20, 1988.
32. Potash Corporation of Saskatchewan, 1988 Annual Report.
33. Minutes, Potash Corporation of Saskatchewan, Board of Directors, January 26, 1989.
34. See Pitsula and Rasmussen, *Privatizing a Province*, Chapter 9 in particular.
35. Minutes, Potash Corporation of Saskatchewan, Board of Directors, March 23, 1989.
36. Potash Corporation of Saskatchewan, 1989 Annual Report.

## CHAPTER 12: THE PRIVATELY OWNED INDUSTRY, 1989 TO NOW

1. Wayne Brownlee, personal interview, 31 October 2006.
2. Ibid.
3. 1993 Annual Report, Potash Corporation of Saskatchewan Inc., p.5.
4. Ibid, p. 24.
5. 1990 Annual Report, Potash Corporation of Saskatchewan Inc., p. 3.
6. 1994 Annual Report, Potash Corporation of Saskatchewan Inc., p. 3.
7. 1995 Annual Report, Potash Corporation of Saskatchewan Inc., p.5.
8. 1996 Annual Report, Potash Corporation of Saskatchewan Inc., p.3.
9. 1998 Annual Report, Potash Corporation of Saskatchewan Inc., p.4.
10. 1999 Annual Report, Potash Corporation of Saskatchewan Inc., p.3.
11. 2001 Annual Report, Potash Corporation of Saskatchewan Inc., p.41.
12. 2007 Annual Report, Potash Corporation of Saskatchewan Inc., p.6.
13. 2008 Annual Report, Potash Corporation of Saskatchewan Inc., p.6.
14. Ibid.
15. 2008 Financial Review Annual Report, Potash Corporation of Saskatchewan Inc., p. 16.
16. 2008 Annual Report, Potash Corporation of Saskatchewan Inc., p.3.
17. 2006 Annual Report, Potash Corporation of Saskatchewan Inc., p.4.
18. News Release, *The Associated Press*, 18 January, 2011.
19. Advertising Feature, *Leader-Post*, 19 May 2012, p. AA6.
20. Weir, Erin, *Closing Tax Loopholes*, 22 October, 2012.
21. Wayne Brownlee, personal interview, 31 October 2006.
22. Saskatchewan Ministry of Energy and Resources, *Saskatchewan Exploration and Development Highlights 2011*.
23. Ibid.
24. "BHP should not build Jansen potash mine: BMO," *Financial Post*, 23 October, 2012.
25. Advertising Feature, *Leader-Post*, 19 May, 2012, p. BB8.
26. Advertising Feature, 19 May, 2012, p. AA2, and Saskatchewan Ministry of Energy and Resources, *Saskatchewan Exploration and Development Highlights 2011*.
27. *Sask Trends Monitor*.

## CHAPTER 13: BHP BILLITON BLOWS THE BIG BUYOUT

1. Postmedia News; reported in the *Leader-Post*, 18 August 2010; Website: bhpbilliton. com.
2. Ibid.
3. *Leader-Post*, 20 August, 2010.
4. *Leader-Post*, 27 August, 2010.
5. *Leader-Post*, 20 August, 2010.
6. *Financial Times*, 31 August, 2010.
7. *Leader-Post*, 27 September, 2010.
8. Paul Waldie, "Canpotex and potash: The monopoly behind the mineral," *Globe and Mail*, 29 October, 2010.
9. News Release, Government of Saskatchewan, 21 October 2010.
10. Concern was expressed by some that if BHP was successful, potash would just become a bargaining chip in its overall dealings with China where its sales of iron and coal are huge. It is also of interest that during the debate on the proposed acquisition, there was little mention of the problems created for Saskatchewan in facing a company with over $10 billion in profits for a half year which is on a par with Saskatchewan's budget level for a full year.
11. It is puzzling why the Premier would make such a statement when it would be reasonable to expect he was aware of the company's existing ownership structure where 51 per cent of the shares are owned by non-Canadians.
12. *Leader-Post*, 9 September 2010.
13. *Leader-Post*, 16 November 2010.

## CHAPTER 14: WHAT CAN WE LEARN?

1. Lauren Krugel, the Canadian Press, *Leader-Post*, 27 June 2012.
2. Ibid.

# REFERENCES

Anderson, David L. *The Role of Mineral Taxation in Industry/Government Conflict.* Kingston, Ontario: Centre for Resource Studies, Queen's University, 1981.

Archer, John H. *Saskatchewan: A History,* Saskatoon: Western Producer Prairie Books, 1980.

Blakeney, Allan and Sandford Borins. *Political Management in Canada: Conversations on Statecraft,* second edition. Toronto: University of Toronto Press, 1998.

Brooks, Stephen and Andrew Stritch. *Business and Government in Canada.* Scarborough: Prentice-Hall Canada, 1991.

Burton, John S. "Resource Rent and Taxation - Application of New Principles and Approaches in Saskatchewan." In *Policy Innovation in the Saskatchewan Public Sector, 1971-82,* ed. E. Glor. North York: Captus Press, 1997.

Burton, John S. *Setting the Stage for Potash Development.* Paper prepared for Administration 824 class, University of Regina, 15 December 2001.

Canada. *House of Commons Debates,* pp. 585-6, 6 November 1969. Ottawa: Queen's Printer, 1970.

Canada. *House of Commons Debates,* pp. 1590-1, 4 December 1969. Ottawa: Queen's Printer, 1970.

Canadian Centre for Policy Alternatives. *The CCPA Monitor,* June 2002, 9-2.

Dyck, Rand. *Canadian Politics - Critical Approaches.* Scarborough: Nelson Canada, 1996.

Eisler, Dale. *Rumours of Glory.* Edmonton: Hurtig Publishers, 1987.

Fact Book. *Speaker's Notes.* Office of the Leader of the Opposition, 13 May 1971.

Federal Government Operations. *Case Study: Potash in Saskatchewan.* Prepared under direction of Donald H. Thain, University of Western Ontario, 1976.

*Globe and Mail.* "Potash producers defer expansions worth $200 million," 11 January 1975.

*Globe and Mail.* "Investigation started into potash industry," 25 January 1975.

Grescoe, Paul. "A Sharp Turn to the Left." *The Canadian*, 13 March 1976.

Gruending, Dennis. *Promises to Keep, A Political Biography of Allan Blakeney*. Saskatoon: Western Producer Prairie Books, 1990.

Guy, James John. *People. Politics and Government: A Canadian Perspective*, fifth edition. Toronto: Pearson Education Canada Inc., Printed in U.S.A., 2001.

International Minerals and Chemical Corporation. *Annual Report for the Year Ending June 30, 1969*.

International Minerals and Chemical Corporation (Canada) Limited. *The Canadian Potash Industry: A Study in Government Cooperation*. Printed in Canada, 1972.

International Minerals and Chemical Corporation (Canada) Limited. *Potash from IMC-Canada*. Printed in Canada, undated [it is 1980 or later].

Johnson, A. W., *Dream No Little Dreams*. Toronto: University of Toronto Press, 2004.

*Leader-Post*, "IMC says gov't action saved potash industry," 22 June 1972.

*Leader-Post*, "Government considering new potash policies," 27 October 1973.

Legislative Assembly of Saskatchewan. *Debates and Proceedings. 1st Session of the 18th Legislature*. Regina: Queen's Printer, 1975-76.

New Democratic Party of Saskatchewan. *New Deal for People*. Regina: Service Printing, 1971.

New Democratic Party of Saskatchewan. *New Deal '75*. Regina: Service Printing, 1975.

Potash Corporation of Saskatchewan Inc. *Annual Reports*, 1989 to 2012.

Richards, John and Larry Pratt. *Prairie Capitalism: Power and Influence in the New West*. Toronto: McClelland and Stewart, 1979.

Saskatchewan Department of Mineral Resources. *Potash: Challenge for Development*. Regina: Queen's Printer, 1976.

Saskatchewan Department of Natural Resources. *Annual Reports*, 1946-47 to 1952-53. Regina: Queen's Printer.

Smith, David E. *Prairie Liberalism - The Liberal Party in Saskatchewan 1905-71*. Toronto and Buffalo: University of Toronto Press, 1975.

Soganich, John. "Tax relief hint cheers potash." *Financial Post*, 10 July 1975.

Stevenson. Garth. *Unfulfilled Union: Canadian Federalism and National Unity*, fourth edition. Montreal and Kingston: McGill-Queen's University Press, 2004.

Waiser, Bill. *Saskatchewan: A New History.* Calgary: Fifth House 2005.

Wright, Jim F.C. *Saskatchewan. The History of a Province,* Toronto: McClelland and Stewart, 1955.

## ABOUT THE AUTHOR

John Burton grew up on a Saskatchewan farm and later operated his own farm. His studies at the University of Saskatchewan, the University of Regina, and the London School of Economics earned him bachelor degrees in arts and agriculture and later a master's degree. After a period of time in government service, he was a Member of Parliament. Returning to government service, Burton played a major role in Saskatchewan's 1975 decision to acquire potash-producing facilities, and from 1975 to 1982 he was a member of the board of directors of the crown-owned Potash Corporation of Saskatchewan. From 1984 to 1988, he was a team leader on an agricultural planning project in Zambia. Maintaining his interest in potash affairs, he has written papers and articles on the subject.